MW00352542

TABLE OF CONTENTS

Top 20 Test Taking Tips

1. Carefully follow all the test registration procedures
2. Know the test directions, duration, topics, question types, how many questions
3. Setup a flexible study schedule at least 3-4 weeks before test day
4. Study during the time of day you are most alert, relaxed, and stress free
5. Maximize your learning style; visual learner use visual study aids, auditory learner use auditory study aids
6. Focus on your weakest knowledge base
7. Find a study partner to review with and help clarify questions
8. Practice, practice, practice
9. Get a good night's sleep; don't try to cram the night before the test
10. Eat a well balanced meal
11. Know the exact physical location of the testing site; drive the route to the site prior to test day
12. Bring a set of ear plugs; the testing center could be noisy
13. Wear comfortable, loose fitting, layered clothing to the testing center; prepare for it to be either cold or hot during the test
14. Bring at least 2 current forms of ID to the testing center
15. Arrive to the test early; be prepared to wait and be patient
16. Eliminate the obviously wrong answer choices, then guess the first remaining choice
17. Pace yourself; don't rush, but keep working and move on if you get stuck
18. Maintain a positive attitude even if the test is going poorly
19. Keep your first answer unless you are positive it is wrong
20. Check your work, don't make a careless mistake

Introduction to the TExES Series

Why am I required to take this TExES Assessment?

Your state requires you to take this TExES Assessment in order to test the breadth and depth of your knowledge in a specified subject matter. Texas has adopted the TExES series in order to ensure that you have mastered the subject matter you are planning to teach before they issue your teaching license.

Because the issuance of your license ensures competence in the subject area it is important that you take studying seriously and make sure you study thoroughly and completely.

Two Kinds of TExES Assessments

The TExES Series consist of two different kinds of assessments multiple choice questions and constructed response test.

The multiple choice test consists of questions followed by several answer choices. From these answer choices you select the answer that you think best corresponds with the given question. These questions can survey a wider range because they can ask more questions in a limited time period.

Constructed response questions consist of a given question for which you write an original response. These tests have fewer questions, but the questions require you to demonstrate the depth of you own personal knowledge in the subject area.

Understanding Students

Human Development

Cognitive Development

Stages

<u>Infancy, toddlerhood, early and middle school age:</u> Infancy is typically considered to extend from birth until the age of 2. During this period, the individual develops social attachments, basic motor skills, and an idea of cause and effect. Toddlerhood is though to extend from age 2 until age 4, and is marked by the development of language, the exploration of life through fantasy and play, and an improvement in self-control. Between the ages of 5 and 12, sometimes called early and middle school age, the individual learns the value of cooperation, basic morals, gender roles, and some basic skills. This is also the period in which individuals typically are able to begin honestly appraising themselves and considering their place in the world.

<u>Adolescence and early adulthood:</u> Adolescence is generally thought to extend between the ages of 13 and 22. During this period, individuals undergo a rapid physical maturation. They will typically begin to have sexual relationships, will seek to develop a personal identity, and may emphasize a peer group more than the family. During this period, individuals should begin to consider possible careers, and should be establishing an internal set of moral values. Early

- 5 -

adulthood is thought to extend from age 23 to 30, and to involve a movement towards marriage or longer-lasting romantic relationships. Early adulthood often is focused on the establishment of a career, though individuals will often have children of their own during this period.

Middle and later adulthood: Middle adulthood is generally though to extend from about the age 31 until the age of 50. During this period, individuals are usually occupied with the maintenance of their household, and the rearing of children. Many individuals will also devote a great deal of their middle adulthood to advancing their professional interests. Later adulthood begins at 51 and last until death. It is inaccurate to suggest that all personal growth has been accomplished by this point. On the contrary, most individuals in later adulthood will gradually accept the events of their life, will develop a healthy perspective on life and death, and will begin to redirect their personal energies to new roles and responsibilities.

Jean Piaget: Jean Piaget noted four stages of cognitive development in children. Sensorimotor stage is the period from birth until approximately age 2, during which the infant develops his or her sense organs and learns that objects still exist even when they are out of the visual field. The preoperational stage typically lasts from age 2 to age 7, and is marked by the child's increasing ability to imagine the mental lives of others; in other words, to develop sympathy. The concrete operational stage generally lasts from age 7 until age 12, as the child develops a number of cognitive structures, including the rule of conservation (the understanding that an object's volume does not decrease if its shape is changed). The final stage is known as the formal operational stage and takes place after age 12. In this stage, which not every human goes through, the capacity for abstract thought (the ability to theorize rather than to rely on direct observation for knowledge) is developed.

Physiological needs: In order to reach your highest potential, you have to satisfy a number of basic needs. To illustrate this, health professionals have set up a pyramid of psychological health, so that individuals can see what conditions must be met before they can excel. Before anything else is accomplished, your physiological needs for food, water, shelter, and sleep must be met. Then, if these needs are satisfied, you can work on achieving safety for yourself and your loved ones. When this is accomplished, you are free to develop loving relationships and fit into a society. These relationships are a necessary foundation for self-esteem and a healthy respect for other people. The person who has satisfied all of these needs is said to be ready for self-actualization, the fulfillment of his or her potential.

Early childhood

Theories of Piaget: According to Piaget, students in early childhood Ð the years between 2 and 6 spanning preschool to kindergarten Ð generally are incapable of grasping abstract concepts such as those dealing with time and space. They are developing motor skills, usually through play, as well as language skills and the ability to imitate events. These skills will grow and develop during these years, which will be reflected in their use of language, increased motor skills, and the appearance of more concreteness in their drawings. During this time, they are egocentric, however they are also developing social skills relating to their peers as well as the ability to regulate some of their own emotional responses. Counselors will be well served to use a child's imaginative skills in the session, as well as some of the theoretical concepts of childhood experts such as Piaget.

Erik Erikson stages: In this theoretical paradigm, these key years of development are defined by a series of crises, resulting in positive or maladaptive behaviors. Each developmental stage is preceded by a crisis that ideally is resolved through positive development of skills and behaviors. For instance, ego development may be prompted by the crisis of self-promotion being perceived as counter to obligation to others, i.e. the drive to grow and develop being possibly tempered by a sense of guilt. Refining the balance between these two directives, incorporating self-worth, imagination and sometimes gender, contributes to the child's self-discovery. Counselors should encourage students to explore positive behaviors or actions that may be out of the student's normal realm, toward development of new skills. Further, increase in language and motor skills tends to encourage this action toward self-promotion and self-discovery. Opportunities for developing these skills are beneficial in the counseling setting.

Using a play-time setting: For the child between the years of 2 and 6, play is an integral part of their development. Children often express emotions, describe events, and project their desires in a play setting. In the counseling session, a good strategy is for the counselor to interact with the child in play setting, using such manipulatives as dolls, other toys, puppets, art projects, or other favorites. The play-time setting can be a wonderful opportunity for children to explore not only their environment, but also their own capabilities and skills. The counseling session will be best served if the child is allowed sufficient and reasonable latitude for exploring the boundaries of self-discovery, self-confidence and emotional self-regulation. The play setting provides an environmental medium for developing and regulating skills and behaviors. Counselors can provide such media as dolls, animals, art supplies and animals through which children can express and explore their self-discovery.

Middle childhood

Developmental stages
Middle childhood, generally associated with the ages between 7 and 11, is most easily distinguished by the ability to think logically, increased literacy skills, and the ability to mentally reverse actions. While they are still unable to grasp many abstract ideas, students in this age group are nonetheless increasingly able to manipulate concrete information. They are able to generalize about their actions or their environment based on this information. The development of logical thinking allows children in this age group to interact more cooperatively, partly because they are more able to recognize intentionality and are becoming less egocentric. Counselors working with this age group can use such strategies as exploration, manipulation of information, and action. Sessions are best served if the counselor remains aware that students in this age group are generally able to reason logically, based on concrete information, often called the concrete operational stage.

Impact of positive feedback: Middle childhood is distinguished by a developing, and often fragile sense of competency. This sense of competency is particularly dependent on external feedback, from friends, family and authority figures. A sense of competency is also encouraged by the student's own success in accomplishing increasingly challenging tasks, or conversely discouraged by failure. Counselors working with this age group need to be sensitive to this fragility, and respond by providing tasks that are manageable and more likely to be successful for the student. Positive, encouraging feedback is also very valuable to students in this age group. Both positive feedback and opportunities for success provide valuable buffers against the development of feelings of inadequacy in students in middle childhood, including self-fulfilling behaviors that validate a sense of incompetence and failure.

Encouraging peer relationships: During this time of competency development, peer interaction is particularly important for the student in middle childhood, for a number of reasons. Not only is peer feedback important, but also peer interaction provides an opportunity for students to observe the same fragility and balance of successes and failures that they experience, thus validating and endorsing their own vicissitudes of self-confidence. Likewise, students in this age group develop a sense of understanding and tolerance for differing appearances and behaviors through healthy peer interaction. A counselor can provide opportunities for peer interaction by holding group counseling sessions, as well as encouraging healthy friendships for students in this age group. Often, friendships are formed that become significant, such as that of a best friend. These friendships can be pivotal to the development of a student's sense of self-competency and significance among their peers.

Adolescents

Counseling approaches and intervention strategies need to all be determined and assessed within the context of developmental theory. In other words, counselors should be trained in and cognizant of the different stages of development in adolescents, including the appropriate behaviors for a particular age group. Counselors may dismiss behaviors that would be unacceptable for an adult, but perfectly normal for a child in a particular age group. Conversely, if a child is exhibiting behavior that is not typical of his/her age group, this may be a symptom or behavior that needs to be addressed in the counseling session. Further, counselors developing intervention strategies should be mindful of the range of reasonable expectations within an age group. It is important that counselors enter each session with an understanding of the age group of the student, referring to outside resources for that information if necessary.

Distinguishing characteristics : Adolescence is a time of breakthrough transition between childhood and adulthood, and is generally divided into three sub-stages. Although the stages are very individualized, the years between the ages of 11 and 14 usually frame adolescence, between 15 and 18 middle adolescence, and 18 and above late adolescence. The accomplishments realized during these three stages affect physical appearance, social interaction, and thinking processes. Physical changes are those defined as puberty, resulting in physical maturation. Students in this age group develop a more comprehensive understanding of social roles and relationships. Further, thinking processes evolve from concrete to formal, resulting in an increased ability for abstract thinking. Counselors working with this age group need to be mindful of both the stage at which a student is operating and also the next phase of development, and provide opportunities for that development.

Therapeutic strategies: Adolescent students are increasingly able to apply abstract thinking to possible solutions and scenarios of situations. Counselors working with this age group can take advantage of this abstract thinking by soliciting the student's collaboration in generating and implementing solutions to dilemmas or problems. The beginning of this process can be asking a student to view a situation differently, allowing for a larger spectrum of options for its solution. These students are able also to participate in reflective thinking, allowing for ownership and responsibility for actions. Students in this age period are also increasingly egocentric, and less dependent on external feedback, sometimes resulting in reckless behavior. They are also more self-conscious, particularly with students of their age group. Counselors are best served by facilitating the student's ability to balance these feelings with increased social awareness and abstract thinking skills. Counselors can also provide students in this age group with opportunities for development and implementation of alternate approaches to problem solution.

Effect of puberty: The onset and evolvement of puberty complements and often perpetuates role confusion for the adolescent student. Adolescence is a pivotal time in which students refine self-concepts of worth, value in the larger society, and life goals. This self-definition is often validated by peer interaction. The counselor should work with students in this age group by encouraging them to develop goals and values of their own, not necessarily those of their peer group. Counselors can assist students in developing their own sense of identity and worth, separate from social cliques or idolized hero symbols. Students in this age group begin to understand that their actions and beliefs form an integral part of their role and their value system. Counselors can positively facilitate this connection when working with adolescents. It is important that counselors endorse the idea of worth and significance of every individual.

Intricacies of peer relationships: Adolescent students are simultaneously developing a sense of self-worth and self-identity, while at the same time developing close ties with peer groups. It is important for the counselor to assist the student in balancing the significance of peer relationships with the evolvement of his or her own self-definition. Students in this age group often develop a sense of ethnic identity before that of self-identity. While the role of a peer group can bolster and validate a student's ethnic or cultural identity, it is also important to develop personal and individual goals. Counselors can work with adolescent students to help them identify personal goals as well as changing ideas and perceptions. The effect of commonality of beliefs and behaviors can sometimes deter development of individuality. Nonetheless, because peer relationships are very important to this age group, counselors should also encourage and endorse healthy peer relationships.

Psychosocial development

Individual values

Every individual has a set of values, criteria by which they understand and judge the world. Sometimes, though, individuals may claim to have a certain set of values even though they appear to act on another. In order to clarify your values, it is a good idea to consider carefully the consequences of your choices and ensure that they are moral and positive. Health professionals define individual values as being either instrumental or terminal: instrumental values are ways

- 9 -

of thinking that a person holds important, for instance being loyal or loving; terminal values are goals or ideals that a person works towards, for instance happiness. The values of an individual and even of a society are constantly changing, so you have to be sensitive to the values that you are promoting with your choices.

Self-esteem

Self-esteem is the way that you think about yourself. Every person wants to feel as if they are important and valued in society, and as if they are living up to their potential. Having healthy self-esteem is not only derived from these feelings, but it makes it possible for you to do the things necessary to make yourself happy and content. Most health professionals agree that an individual's self-esteem is largely determined during childhood. Low self-esteem often haunts those who have been abused in the past, and can unfortunately lead people to seek out relationships in which they are treated poorly. One technique that many health professionals recommend for boosting self-esteem is positive thinking and talking. Even if it feels forced, studies have shown that encouraging the mind to take an optimistic viewpoint can eventually make good self-esteem a habit.

Areas of emotional intelligence

In recent years, health professionals have determined that what is known as emotional intelligence may be just as important as an individual's IQ. According to the psychologist Daniel Goleman, there are five areas of emotional intelligence: self-awareness, altruism, personal motivation, empathy, and the ability to love and be loved. Studies have shown that individuals with a high level of emotional intelligence will succeed at work and in developing positive personal relationships. An individual's emotional intelligence is not the same throughout his or her life, and many businesses have begun taking active steps to develop the emotional intelligence of their employees. Essentially, developing one's emotional intelligence requires listening to one's feelings and respecting them.

Managing moods

Moods are emotional states lasting for a few hours or days. Though every individual will have bad moods from time to time, some are better at managing their moods than others. Researchers have demonstrated that the most effective ways to solve a problem, and hence emerge from a bad mood, are to take immediate action, think about other successes, resolve to try harder, or reward oneself. Individuals who try to distract themselves, perhaps through socializing, will find that this only partly improves their mood. The worst things to do when you are in a bad mood are to vent at another person, isolate yourself, or give up. Using alcohol or drugs to escape a bad mood is also an ineffective way to feel better.

Relationships

Dating

Though the word dating has come to assume a romantic connotation in American society, dating is really any time that is set aside to spend exclusively with another person. Friends are dating if they make a point to see one another. Unfortunately, the tendency to confuse dating with casual sex and drinking has led to a decrease in the amount of casual dating in the United States. Many people assume that dating is strictly for finding a mate, whereas dating has a host of other benefits, from teaching one to make good conversation to introducing them to various kinds of people and ways of life. Dating, in its ideal form, is a great way to explore oneself by getting to know a wide variety of people.

Sex and gender

Many people confuse sex and gender. Whereas a person's sex is strictly dependent on his or her sex chromosomes, hormone balance, and genital anatomy, gender refers to the psychological and social parts of being a male or female. Every individual has a sexual identity that is out of his or her control. To a certain degree, gender is also out of the individual's control, as it is a result of the way the individual is raised and how society treats that individual. Still, many people make conscious decisions to alter their gender identity. Some people simply feel more comfortable a gender other than the one they have been raised in, and they may alter their dress, appearance, and behavior to suit their new gender identity.

There are only a few basic physiological differences between males and females. Males have the ability to make sperm and to contribute the y-chromosome that enables a female to give birth to a male. Only females are born with sex cells, menstruate, give birth, and are capable of breast-feeding. In the embryonic stage, males and females have similar sex organs. After a few weeks of development, though, the gonads differentiate into either testes or ovaries. This differentiation depends on the genetic instructions given by the sex chromosomes. If a y-chromosome is present in the embryo, it will develop into a male; if there is no y-chromosome, the embryo will develop as a female. All future differentiation will be motivated by the gonads, not the chromosomes.

Hormones

Hormones are the chemicals that motivate the body to do certain things. They are produced in the organs that make up the endocrine system. With the exception of the sex organs, males and females have identical endocrine systems. The actions of the hormones are determined by the hypothalamus, an area of the brain about the size of a pea. The hypothalamus sends messages to the pituitary gland, which is directly beneath it. The pituitary gland turns on and off the various glands that produce hormones. Hormones, once released, are carried to their targets by the blood stream, at which point they motivate cells and organs to action. Hormones can influence the way a person looks, feels, behaves, or matures.

The sex hormones that are most important to women are called estrogen and progesterone and are produced in the ovaries. In males, the primary sex hormone is testosterone, which is produced by the adrenal glands and testes. Both men and women do, however, have small amounts of the opposite hormone. Indeed, men need estrogen to have effective sperm. Sex hormones are at work very early in the development of the embryo. When testes are formed, they begin releasing testosterone, which causes the formation of the other male reproductive parts, like the penis. If no testosterone is present, the embryo will develop female genitals. This is true of both natural females and males with malfunctioning testes.

Sexuality

Sex hormones during puberty: At the onset of puberty, the pituitary gland begins to release the hormones that further differentiate between the sexes. Specifically, the pituitary gland releases gonadotropins, which stimulate the gonads to generate the appropriate sex hormones. As these gonadotropins do their work, the secondary sex characteristics are developed. In females, larger amounts of estrogen cause the breasts to enlarge, the hips to widen, and for fat to be deposited on the hips and buttocks. It also causes her external genitals to enlarge, and initiates the processes of ovulation and menstruation. For males, large amounts of testosterone cause the voice to deepen, the penis to become thicker and longer, muscles to grow stronger, and for hair to develop in new places.

Gender differences: It is well documented by science that men and women not only have differences in appearance, but actually think and sense in different ways. In most cases, women have stronger senses of hearing, smell, and taste, while men tend to have better vision. Males tend to be stronger, though females often have better fine motor skills. Brain scans have displayed significant differences in the areas of the brain that are more active in males and females. Of course, there is no telling whether these differences are entirely physiological, or whether upbringing and environment contribute. Most scientists believe that a combination of nature and nurture create the differences between the sexes.

Sexual decision-making: Part of the job of a health teacher is equipping students with the skills they will need to lead healthy, safe sexual lives. The first thing they must have in order to make good decisions is accurate and comprehensive information on the subject. Health textbooks are a good place to start, but students should also be directed to whatever books and authorities are qualified to give them well-researched and thoughtful information. Students should be especially well informed about birth control, pregnancy, and sexually-transmitted diseased before they have any sexual contact. Part of keeping students informed is making sure that they feel comfortable asking questions and discussing their feelings. This can be either with a teacher, parent, or other community leader.

Abstinence: Abstinence can either mean totally refraining from sexual intercourse, or refraining from exchanging bodily fluids altogether. Those who make a point of remaining abstinent throughout their lives are said to be celibate. Abstinence is the only way to entirely avoid the risks of sexual activity, and so many high school students have begun making the commitment to refrain from sex until they are older or in a more committed relationship. Before deciding to engage in sexual activity, students should ask themselves whether it would be in line with their values and moral beliefs. Many people will rush into sex without fully considering the physical, mental, and emotional consequences.

Beginnings of childhood sexuality: It seems odd and even perverse to refer to sexuality in childhood, but many of the foundations for later sexual experience are laid in the early years of an individual's life. For infants, the mouth is the main area for sensual pleasure. By the age of 3 or 4, most children become interested in the differences between males and females, and may start to develop vaguely romantic feelings towards another person. It is very important for parents to discuss these topics with their children, so that the children will have a framework of understanding for these complex and often confusing emotions. Children are likely to have lots of questions, some of them perhaps uncomfortable; parents should do their best to answer honestly and with a minimum of embarrassment.

Adolescent sexuality: As boys and girls enter adolescence, their interest in sex typically intensifies and seeks expression. This makes it essential that health providers give adolescents the necessary knowledge and skills to enter this time in their lives. For teenage boys, it is typical to experience frequent erections, and to begin having nocturnal emissions, or wet dreams. Masturbation is the most common form of sexual expression for adolescents, especially males. Adolescents may also experiment with kissing and petting, oral sex, and even sexual intercourse. At this point, as many as a quarter of all people will experience a same-sex attraction, though this does not predict any future homosexuality. Though American teens are not known to be any more sexually active than teens elsewhere in the world, they do have a higher rate of pregnancy, indicating that adequate birth control information and supplies are not being provided.

Sexual attraction

Sexual attraction is just one of the many factors that contribute to the formation and maintenance of long-term relationships. In most studies, individuals are found to be most sexually attracted to people who share their age, race, ethnicity, and socioeconomic background. Many sociologists speculate that this is because individuals have more access to people that are similar to themselves, and because they intuitively understand that they are more likely to be approved by similar people. In general, men put more emphasis on looks in determining sexual partners, whereas women may value other qualities like dependability and affluence. This may be due in part to the historical need for men to find women who can reproduce easily, while women have sought a man who can provide for them during their period of pregnancy and childrearing.

Mature love relationship

Scientists have marked a difference between passionate love, in which the partners are sexually charged and ecstatic, and companionate love, in which partners are friendly and deeply affectionate. In many cases, relationships that begin with passionate love eventually evolve into companionate love. On the other hand, everyone has experienced or heard of cases in which a long-term friendship suddenly becomes a passionate affair. A healthy and mature love is one in which each partner breaks down the barriers between themselves and the other, while retaining their individuality. Mature partners respect one another's differences, are not threatened by each other's independence, and constantly communicate with one another.

Breaking up

Although people traditionally assume that being abandoned by a romantic partner is worse than leaving a partner, many studies have discovered that the partner who ends a relationship is often more subject to psychological traumas like guilt, uncertainty, and awkwardness. The only real help for the pain of a breakup is time, but the process can be eased if both parties treat one another with respect and kindness. During a breakup, it is important to remind oneself of one's own value as an individual, and not to take the other person's decision as a definitive statement about oneself. Also, it is important to remain engaged with other people despite any feelings of fear you may experience; it is easy to allow feelings of insecurity caused by a breakup to contaminate all the other relationships in your life.

Marriage

Despite claims that the institution of marriage is eroding in recent years, over 90% of Americans will marry in their lifetime. In the past, marriage was as much a business deal as a romantic union; parents often arranged the marriages of their children to advance in society. Though this is still common in some countries, in the United States people are more likely to wed because of a romantic affection for one another. People are increasingly likely to marry someone with whom they share a background and have similar values. Even today, many couples marry because the woman is pregnant, or as a way to escape the authority of their parents. Typically, males are slightly older than females at the age of marriage.

For the most part, people marry someone from the same geographical area and culture as themselves. However, interracial and intercultural marriages are becoming more common and socially accepted. Most studies have revealed that individuals desire a partner with whom they share values and can communicate effectively, and for whom they are willing to make adjustments and tolerate flaws. Many couples undergo premarital assessments to determine if they are truly right for one another. These assessments typically try to measure how compatible the interests, values, and behavior of the two people are. In any case, most couples benefit from some form of counseling before marriage.

According to sociologists, there are two kinds of marriages: traditional and companion-oriented. In a traditional marriage, the two people conform to the prescribed marital roles of their society; for instance, the man becomes the provider and the woman the childrearer. In a companion-oriented marriage, the partnership and the rewards of romantic love are more important than the marital roles. Some sociologists add to this distinction different categories for romantic marriages, in which the sexual passion that originally sparked the union remains present for an abnormally long time, and rescue marriages, in which one partner sees marriage as a way to escape some traumatic event in his or her past.

Marital difficulty: However ideal the beginning of a marriage may be, eventually there will be some conflict. One of the major causes of marital discord is the harboring of unrealistic expectation by one or more of the parties. Sometimes, people assume that their partner will always be just the same, physically and mentally, as they were during the period of courtship. Sometimes they assume that in order to truly be meant for one another, they should always automatically agree on every subject. Of course, both of these assumptions are dangerous for a relationship. In a truly healthy relationship, both parties have room to grow and change without alienating the other, and both feel empowered to speak their minds and to disagree without endangering the union. Many marriages or committed relationships go askew because the individuals disagree about money. Interestingly, fights about money are rarely about how much money the couple has; instead, couples tend to fight about how the money will be spent, and who will keep track of their collective finances. Another subject about which partners often fight is sex. As a relationship matures, one party may lose interest in sex, to the consternation of the other. Marries couples often fight if one party feels they always initiate sex, or if one party feels hurt by the other's indifference. The sex life of a couple will likely change many times throughout the course of a long relationship; the best way to ensure mutual satisfaction is to always be compassionate and communicative.

Extra-marital affairs are about the most devastating thing that can happen to a marriage. If one partner is discovered to be cheating, the other partner is likely to feel abandoned, inadequate, unloved, and angry. When extra-marital affairs are a problem, the parties need to ask themselves whether they really love one another and feel any commitment. In a different sort of way, marriages in which both members work can be difficult. It may be necessary for one party to move for work, or for one to stay home and raise children. When one person's career seems to be more important than the other's, conflicts can often develop. In order to avoid the problems caused by dual-career marriages, individuals should understand their partner's ambitions before deciding whether that person is right for them.

Divorce: In the event that a divorce becomes necessary, there are a few things that parents can do to minimize the damage to their children. First of all, even though it may be tempting, it is inappropriate to indulge children because you feel sorry for them. Spoiling a child so that he will prefer you is not good for the child. It is important to be honest with your children, but without divulging any unnecessarily painful information. Parents should never fight in front of their children. Parents undergoing a divorce should make sure their children know that it is alright for them to love both parents, and that they do not have to choose sides. If parents spend quality time with their kids, and constantly reaffirm their love, their transition through divorce can be eased.

Blended families: More and more families are composed of children and one parent. Though one-parent families are stereotyped as poor and uneducated, many are headed by wealthy and highly educated professionals. Studies have shown that single parents typically spend about as much time with their children as do parents in a two-parent family. Some of these single parents will eventually remarry, creating what is known as a blended family. Extensive studies have been performed on these complicated and often problematic relationships. One recommendation that many doctors make is that children from single-parent or blended families spend time with members of the extended family or community, so that they can acquire other models for behavior.

Dysfunctional relationships

Dysfunctional relationships are those in which the behavior of the participants does not lead to positive communication or honesty. As one would expect, people who have substance abuse problems or addictive behaviors are more likely to be in a dysfunctional relationship. Sometimes, one party may have an inaccurate idea of healthy relationships and will make unfair demands on the other. If there is not trust in a relationship, sometimes jealousy will cause a person to become paranoid and overly dependent on the other. These kinds of unhealthy relationships exist in every section of society, because they spring from personal psychological problems that are universal. Unfortunately, dysfunctional relationships can be very difficult to leave.

Codependence: A codependent individual is one who allows someone with an addiction to use them to achieve satisfaction. Codependency causes a person to ignore his or her own needs in order to serve someone else's. They will change their identity, undergo unpleasant experiences, and even give up their friends and family in order to serve the other. People with low self-esteem and their own set of addictions are more likely to become codependent. In order to escape from a codependent relationship, an individual must realize the worth of his or her own life as well as his or her inability to change the other person. Codependent behavior has at its heart a simple desire for love, though this desire is poorly expressed.

Student Diversity

Components of culture

An important foundation for counselors to broach the subject of culture is to first define what culture is, and what it affects. Below are some of the key components of culture:
- Beliefs or belief systems that define one's place in society, the world, and the cosmos.
- These beliefs can then translate into assumptions and practices regarding social status, personal empowerment, and relation to material wealth.
- Perception of life experiences and how those experiences can impact life choices.
- Value systems including family, career, and education
- Religious beliefs and practices
- Definitions and circumstances relating to belief in life's purpose
- Accepted behaviors for self-validation

It is also important to remember that cultural distinctions are often rooted in historical tradition, supported by generations of practice and affirmation. Working with a culturally diverse population is best approached by recognizing and respecting the roots of culture.

Common parameters of race: In addition to biogenetic factors of race, race can also be defined by a spectrum of factors which may include socioeconomic grouping, distinctive traits and behaviors associated with a particular group, language, traditions and rituals. Individually or as an aggregate, these factors often play a part in racial discrimination and segregation. Members of a school community may segregate other members based on all or some of these factors. These segregation practices may extend to certain groups based on economic status, academic achievement, level of fluency in English, or certain disabilities. In this sense, race can be viewed as a political and psychological concept. Counselors working in the school community to dissipate cultural biases and misunderstandings will be well served to recognize that race is a concept, defined primarily by these behavioral and economic factors.

Parameters of ethnicity: In contrast to race, ethnicity is rooted in national origin and/or distinctive cultural patterns. Ethnicity is based on more easily identifiable factors. Groups of students with the same ethnicity share the same general ancestral background. A group that shares ethnicity will often share religious beliefs, attitudes toward family, school and career, and observations of customs, traditions and rituals. These beliefs and traditions are often reinforced by the fact that individuals who share an ethnicity often socialize together, providing a continuum of culture. However, counselors should be sensitive to the fact that individuals can present degrees of assimilation, developing practices and beliefs that differ from their ethnic origins. Ethnicity is generally associated with family, although it can also be defined by religion, race, and cultural history.

Parameters of oppression: Although oppression may be rooted in cultural or racist biases, it is usually manifested by inequities of power or benefits. The general psychological basis for oppression is a fallacious assumption by one group that another group is intrinsically inferior or unacceptable for a particular quality of life. Unfortunately, these misperceptions often are perpetuated by the vehicles that result from them. Individuals or groups who possess the power or benefits, e.g. better paying jobs, better access to technology, better access to transportation, etc., inherently define oppressed individuals as inferior by their lack of these quality of life indicators. Oppressed groups also often internalize this definition, further perpetuating the oppression and exploitation. Oppressed individuals or groups will often accept their subservient position in the school or work environment because they do not feel empowered to challenge the dominant group. Oppressive tactics include exploitation, intimidation, and occasionally violence.

Oppression can take many forms which fall under five general umbrella categories. The first category is that of individualized oppression, which encompasses oppression stemming from assumptions of inferiority in another person based on race or culture. This process extrapolated to the group level becomes cultural oppression, which is comprised of actions or attitudes toward a cultural group that result in the targeted group changing its behavior to be accepted. Systemic or institutional oppression denotes hierarchical practices that inherently discriminate against certain groups in the distribution of resources. Oppression that is internalized by the targeted group is insidious because it is the dynamic whereby the group believes and acts on its own perceived inferiority. Conversely, external oppression describes actions or beliefs targeting a particular group because they are perceived by others as inferior. Instances of oppression can fall under one or many categories combined.

The terms below identify oppressive belief systems targeting specific groups. Often public schools and other societal entities practice unfair distribution of resources based on these perceptions:

- *Ableism:* Targeting persons identified by different abilities/disabilities
- *Ageism:* Targeting persons younger than 18 or older than 50
- *Beautyism:* Targeting persons who are obese or otherwise fall outside of expected appearance norms
- *Classism:* Targeting persons based on income level or class of work
- *Familyism:* Targeting persons whose family falls outside of expected norms, such as single parents, same gender parents, foster families, etc.
- *Heterosexism and Transgenderism:* Targeting persons who are homosexual, lesbian, bisexual, two-spirit, intersex or transgendered
- *Linguisicism:* Targeting persons because they do not speak the dominant language, or do so with a marked accent
- *Racism:* Targeting persons of another color or mixed race
- *Religionism:* Targeting persons who do not practice the dominant religion
- *Sexism:* Targeting persons of a different sex

Significance and strategies of social justice: Social justice incorporates awareness of inequalities based on cultural, race or ethnicity, and the practices to rebalance the distribution of resources. Counselors who work with diverse student groups will be well served to recognize when and if those groups have been historically oppressed. This historical oppression usually reveals practices and attitudes that have been accepted and ingrained in the larger community as well as the school environment. Counselors can systematically and diplomatically address these practices and attitudes, toward creating social environments that support social justice. Examples of these practices and attitudes can include testing that does not allow for second language learners, lesson plans that use examples that are only familiar to certain cultural groups, etc. Counselors can work with students, school staff, and the surrounding community toward establishing an environment of social justice.

Role of counselor

As America becomes more culturally diverse, the schools will often be comprised of a mix of different races, religions and socioeconomic levels. Counselors need to be cognizant of not only the existence of this mix, but also the significance of these factors in the learning environments of students. One of the factors that counselors should be sensitized to is that certain ethnic groups may be victims of social and economic hierarchies, which can affect the availability of technology and other education-related amenities. Counselors can act as non-judgmental liaisons for students if they are aware and sensitive to some of the situational differences that are often defined by race. They can also work with groups of students on such issues as assertiveness and empowerment. Other factors include issues that arise for second-language learners as well as

- 18 -

religious and cultural premises that may impact student interactions with others and with lesson materials.

The first step in becoming more culturally aware is to recognize the need to do so. Counselors who work with a diversity of races and socioeconomic levels can first recognize those differences in a lateral manner, and invest the time and attention to understand the roots and ramifications of the differences. There are cultural sensitivity training sessions available, possibly through the school district. Although this cultural sensitivity is becoming more commonplace and even required in some districts, counselors and their programs will be best served by a proactive approach.. Some counselors reach beyond the school district to surrounding cultural enclaves, to better understand the nuances of a particular culture. Some counselors take further action by becoming involved in addressing policy and practices that serve to better the overall academic achievement of a particularly underserved group, although the effectiveness of this is not clearly validated.

Role of the counselor in promoting cultural sensitivity in school environment: Cultural sensitivity can provide counselors with not only the ability to recognize culturally-based differences, but also the capacity to recognize culturally-based disparities within the school environment. Counselors can first observe interactions relating to cultural differences, and then address those interactions, maintaining sensitivity to both the minority and the majority cultures. Counselors can involve school staff and administrators in discussions regarding the methods and policies for addressing cultural differences and conflicts among students as well as between teachers and students. Certain school practices can lead to an appreciation and celebration of these differences. These practices can include talking with students, talking with parents, and an ongoing respect of and sensitivity to cultural premises. Increasing cultural awareness within a school environment can lead to a rich, dynamic school environment, and further support the value of a well designed counseling program.

Professional skills and competencies related to cultural awareness: Counselors striving to attain a healthy school environment of cultural sensitivity can begin the process by first presenting a professional demeanor toward all students and other members of the school community. It is important to recognize that cultural and socioeconomic differences can affect behaviors and appearances, and to avoid responding negatively or differently to these manifestations. It is also important to remember that every person, including the counselor, lives with certain presuppositions, and to be cognizant of these presuppositions while developing an increased understanding of cultural differences and misunderstandings. Some of the bases for these misunderstandings include racism, stereotyping, socioeconomic oppression and discrimination. Additionally, cultural differences could be race-based, gender-based, belief-based or based on other distinguishing characteristics. Being aware of these cultural layers and learning to respond with dignity and respect can provide a healthy example for the school community.

Limitations of language: Counselors who have been sensitized to cultural differences, and trained in strategies for addressing these differences in the school environment, nonetheless sometimes experience difficulty finding appropriate terminology to communicate with school staff, administrators, students and the rest of the school community in this regard. There are no clear-cut guidelines to facilitate this, however, counselors can first recognize that cultural differences can stem from historical traditions, racial or ethnic classifications, economic status, and cosmology, to name a few factors. These differences can affect how people view and respond to life experiences, and often divide populations into groups of similar experience and perception. Awareness of some of the roots of cultural diversity and cultural bias can help the counselor develop terminology for addressing issues of diversity, and for integrating cultural sensitivity into various aspects of the counseling program.

Multicultural counseling

In the process of developing the counseling relationship with a student or students, it is important to recognize if it is that of multicultural counseling. Multicultural counseling occurs when the race or ethnicity of the student(s) is different from that of the counselor. The multicultural counseling relationship will necessarily involve two sets of expectations, perceptions, social environments, beliefs and backgrounds, often beyond the usual disparities between two people. Sensitivity to possible culturally-based differences can be helpful with communication, expectations and goal-setting. The five major cultural groups identified by the Association of Multicultural Counseling and Development (AMCD) are African/Black, Asian, Caucasian/European, Hispanic/Latino/a, and Native American. Other cultural groups can pertain to gender, sexual orientation, religious beliefs, etc. Without falling into a biased taxonomy regarding multicultural counseling, it is nonetheless a consideration that can complement other factors in the counseling relationship.

Ensuring counselors are competent in multicultural environments: Counselors who will be working with different cultural or ethnic groups are best served by not only receiving initial training in multicultural counseling, but also to attend workshops and other instruction in the field on an ongoing basis. Many schools and districts with a diverse student body require this of school counselors. Counselors who receive ongoing training in multicultural counseling will be less likely to impose their own belief systems and cultural insensitivity to the counseling relationship, and more likely to consider cultural differences when communicating and setting goals with students. School administrators and counselors can usually recognize when they are incorporating cultural sensitivity in their counseling methods by assessing the success of the sessions. If a counselor or counseling program is operating with multicultural competence, there should be no significant differentiation between success rates based on cultural factors.

Levels of multicultural counseling: Multicultural counseling incorporates three distinct levels of competence. The initial, foundational level is that of awareness. Counselors can begin to build multicultural competence by first becoming aware of the effects of culture on worldview, behaviors, etc. It is also a good first step for counselors to be aware of their own preconceived notions about culture(s), as well as aspects of their value system that are culturally based. Building on this, counselors can come to a knowledge, respect and understanding of other cultures, realizing that cultural assimilation is not always the recommended course of action for students. Cultural sensitivity includes refraining from imposing dominant beliefs and attitudes, as appropriate. Learning to balance social protocol with cultural expression is a valuable skill that counselors can learn and teach to students. Lastly, counselors can increasingly develop skills that enable them to implement effective and appropriate strategies when working with students from diverse cultures.

Knowledge that will enrich multicultural sensitivity: Counselors working with diverse cultures can increase and enrich their sensitivity by understanding the fabric and terminology of a particular culture, as well as developmental theories pertaining to that culture. Understanding culture includes a working knowledge of the history, traditions, strengths, needs and resources of a specific culture. Counselors can act as consultant and liaison by assisting students who are facing misunderstanding and misrepresentation by school staff, students, public media, etc. Understanding the semantics and terminology of specific cultures can be particularly helpful in mediating between cultural groups, as well as encouraging communication and sensitivity between groups. Counselors who approach diversity with a fundamental knowledge of specific cultures and the impact of culture can provide a role model for dynamic multicultural understanding and communication in the school environment. Understanding the impact of culture in particular can lay a strong foundation for multicultural sensitivity, as counselors, students and school personnel begin to recognize the cultural bases for many misunderstandings.

Counseling skills that indicate multicultural sensitivity: Counselors who are cognizant of, and sensitive to, cultural differences will more likely develop strategies and hypotheses that are absent of cultural biases. Developing hypotheses that are not culturally slanted will allow counselors to more objectively plan and assess intervention strategies. Multicultural sensitivity enables counselors to design and deliver lesson plans that are free from stereotypical icons or remarks, as well as when and how to generalize instructions to diverse groups of students. With increased sensitivity, counselors can also design activities and strategies that are inclusive of diverse cultures, or individualize activities as appropriate. An example of an inclusive activity would be one that elicits student responses about a recent event on campus that they have all shared in. An individualized activity could be asking students to write about holiday traditions in their home, which would inherently allow students to respond from a cultural perspective.

Qualitative areas positively impacted with multiculturally competent counselors: Cultural and ethnic diversity in the school environment often results in disparities in peripheral areas, particularly if issues of oppression and bias are not addressed. Some of the peripheral areas which can be impacted by culturally-based hierarchies include academic achievement, literacy competence, AP course participation, career planning, and most significantly disparities in standardized test results which can negatively impact college opportunities, and ultimately income level. Counselors who have been trained in, and operate within a paradigm of multicultural sensitivity can significantly mitigate these disparities by acting as a liaison between the student body and school officials. In this capacity, counselors can act on students' behalf when there is a culturally-based misunderstanding, as well help students develop strategies for bridging cultural gaps. Counselors can also consult with school staff and officials on pinpointing practices that may inherently pose a disadvantage for certain cultural groups.

The need for multicultural and anti-oppression training in counseling programs: Traditional school counseling programs reflect long-practiced curricular parameters based on

Caucasian/Western European culture and history. Consequently, practica and discussions tend to be non-inclusive of other cultures, and particularly diversity and multicultural counseling issues. Counselors who have been trained in a traditional Western European program are usually not adequately prepared to address issues associated with multicultural identities, including practices and environments of oppression. Without infusing additional multicultural training into a counseling program, counselors often unknowingly perpetuate the Western paradigm. The counselors, and the programs they create, will then lack an understanding of oppression, cultural histories, cultural identity and how to strive for and assess multicultural competency. This is why the onus is usually on the counselor to obtain ongoing multicultural training, and to invest in research about multiculturalism and oppression, in order to bring a more comprehensive perspective into the school environment.

Need for additional multicultural training in individual counseling sessions: As with developing counseling programs, counselors who conduct individual counseling sessions can sometimes suffer from a dearth of multicultural knowledge, at least in part because of the limited scope of their training. This can impact counselors' interactions with students as well as strategies for addressing problems. Many graduate programs fail to address cultures other than those with a Western European perspective. This can be a handicap for counselors working with a diverse student body, since they would lack a multicultural understanding of beliefs, terminology, historical oppression and other factors. Understandably, their approach in counseling at best would be irrelevant, and at worst offensive. Counselors working with a diverse student body would be well served to obtain multicultural training, develop relevant strategies for individual counseling, and collaborate with other counselors or school staff as appropriate for working with diverse cultures.

Culture and the counseling process

There are numerous cultural factors that can impact the counseling relationship. One of the primary factors is the differentiation between group-oriented cultures and individual-oriented cultures. Students who come from a culture which values the group above the individual will necessarily approach communication, goal-setting and decision-making from a completely different perspective than one who comes from a culture that values the individual above the group, such as traditional Western culture. Culture can affect how the student perceives the role of the counselor, in a spectrum that may span from helper to intruder. Students from various cultural backgrounds may communicate more with body language than verbally, and could perceive the counselor's communication similarly. Culture can affect students' time orientation, sense of self, and the ability to make decisions. This is particularly significant when counselors are working with students from a historically oppressed culture. Counselors can develop appropriate strategies for developing a student's sense of empowerment in harmony with his/her cultural values.

Group sessions with multicultural students: The dynamics of group sessions can be particularly impacted by cultural factors. Counselors who are forming counseling groups should be sensitive to the cultural backgrounds and premises of its members. Understanding how different cultural groups respond to stereotypes, oppression, discrimination, and prejudice can assist the counselor in forming groups. Likewise, student perceptions of the counselor as facilitator or authority can impact the group dynamics. Although the recommendation is not necessarily to limit groups to similar cultures, and in fact in some cases it might be indicated to blend cultures, it is up to the counselor to be sensitive to the ramifications of multicultural dynamics. It is worth noting that culture can include gender, religion and other criteria. Counselors can refer to literature, research and other resources regarding considerations and practices regarding cultural diversity in group counseling.

Although multicultural groups can benefit from a richness of blended cultures, counseling groups comprised of diverse cultures may also be more susceptible to misunderstandings and conflicts as a direct result of the differences in perspectives. The counselor as facilitator can provide valuable leadership by encouraging the interchange of ideas about such topics as self-identity, self-worth, oppression, responsibility to society, etc. Likewise, if there is conflict in the group, the counselor who has been trained in multicultural sensitivity can better recognize if the conflict is culturally based, and take the opportunity to intervene and work with the students to develop strategies for resolution. It may be possible for the group to work as a whole on culturally-based conflict resolution, allowing other members to contribute newly learned skills or perspectives. Multicultural counseling groups can provide fertile ground for teaching multicultural sensitivity.

Consulting with parents and teachers

Sensitivity to cultural differences can be especially pivotal when consulting with parents and teachers on a student matter, particularly when a student's family is from a different culture than that of the teacher and/or counselor. Often, the consulting/discussion group will be comprised of the student, his/her parent(s), the counselor, the teacher, and possibly a school administrator. Counselors need to be especially sensitive to key factors which may include: a parent who lives in a culturally isolated household or neighborhood, the student who is inherently bi-cultural, the culture of the teacher/administrator, and the culture of the counselor. Counselors should create an environment that is conducive to comfortable communication and open to input from all parties. Counselors should be cognizant of and sensitive to the cultural significance and perception of the issue at hand, as well as to best ways to address the problem within the cultural contexts represented.

Cultural biases or stereotypes

In the process of facilitating a discussion among parents, student, teachers, and other parties in a consulting discussion, counselors may find that one more individuals may be communicating or acting from a paradigm of bias or stereotyping. This may develop into a resistance to resolution, particularly if the problem is culturally based. Any discussion toward resolution may be hampered by one or more individuals acting out of cultural bias. Counselors may need to challenge the individual(s) by pointing out the specific words or behaviors that perpetuate stereotypes, and also the negative effect that these actions have on the intervention process. Counselors can remind the group of the shared desire for resolution, and how stereotyping can detract from the purpose of the gathering. They can remind participants that the well-being of the student will be best served by collaboration and refraining from expressions of cultural bias and stereotyping.

Assessment

In most school environments, there are a number of standardized tests that are administered to assess academic achievement and aptitude. Counselors can provide a valuable service to the school and its students by determining if tests are inherently culturally biased, and suggesting alternate assessment methods as appropriate. Some of the aspects of testing that should be reviewed include references to events or individuals that are specific to particular cultures, language-based assessment that does not allow for second language learners, etc. It may be indicated for the counselor to work with school administrators to develop alternative testing methods, or to work one on one with students from cultures that would be disadvantaged by a test. Counselors will be well served to obtain training and refer to outside resources for identifying culturally biased testing, and for choosing alternative methods. It is also important to understand how to communicate testing results to families of students from diverse cultures.

Counselors should be particularly vigilant about any personal biases that they may have that could obscure the assessment process. In other words, if a test is designed to assess student readiness for academic promotion, and half of the students perform at the readiness level, and the other half at below readiness, the initial reaction might be that the test was successful, and that half of the class is ready for promotion. However, if a counselor finds that lines of success or failure fall in a quasi-line progression toward eliminating or isolating a particular cultural group, s/he should guard against a personal assumption that the test validates cultural differences, and instead review the test and the testing process for cultural biases. Not only can these cultural biases negatively impact individual students, but the continued use of a culturally skewed test can be used to fallaciously document poor achievement by particular cultures, and further perpetuate academic oppression.

Assessment vehicles that are language-based, such as math word problems or reading comprehension tests, may intrinsically put second-language learners at a disadvantage. Counselors should be sensitive to this disadvantage, and offer students alternate testing methods. These methods may include written tests in the student's native language, or an interpreter present for testing. Translators may also be on hand to present the questions in both the dominant language and the student's native language, in order to assist the student in making associations between the native language and the dominant language. It is important that the testing environment is presented in a way that is comfortable, allows ample time for translation, and does not contain any implications of inferiority about second-language learners. Assessing second-language learners should fairly and accurately test students' aptitudes, skills and abilities.

Curriculum

Often counselors are required to speak to large groups of students, and in this capacity can deliver lesson plans to diverse groups of students regarding multicultural awareness and sensitivity. Counselors can effectively improve the cultural climate in a school setting by promoting multicultural sensitivity and educating students about best practices for positive diversity. They can begin by defining and identifying cultural differences, as well as appropriate language and behaviors for addressing these differences. A lesson plan about multicultural sensitivity can first identify that culture may include or refer to race, ethnicity, gender, sexual orientation, different levels of ability, etc. Counselors can illustrate how culturally-biased behaviors and attitudes can lead to oppression and conflict, whereas avoidance of these behaviors can contribute to the richness of a diverse student body. Counselors should also remind students of the negativity engendered by practicing and promoting oppressive behaviors among their families and other members of their own culture.

Counselors wishing to educate students on positive diversity and multicultural sensitivity can include both informational and reflective elements in their lesson plans. Informational elements can encompass the correct usage of multicultural terminology, identification of oppression and oppressive practices, identification of cultural differences and how they can impact interaction, etc. Counselors can explain differences of world view and value systems that are culturally based. Reflective exercises can be group discussions, testimony of personal experiences, or journal exercises exploring personal biases and assumptions. Counselors can also include examples of racism, ageism, ableism, etc. to identify cultural bias and illustrate its negative impact. Included might be identifying cultural bias in historical texts. The class can also discuss ideas for addressing oppressive beliefs and practices throughout the world. Lesson plans can alternate between informational lecture and reflective discussion to best engage the students in the topic.

Community issues

Counselors can offer their expertise and act as liaison to the surrounding community by including parents and neighbors in discussions and events promoting multicultural sensitivity. It is usually the responsibility of the counselor to coordinate this community outreach, and can take many forms. Counselors can develop peer mediation services, family counseling services, or hold workshops in the community to discuss cultural diversity. One of the key goals of a community outreach program is usually to increase multicultural sensitivity and communication, not only within the community but also within and surrounding the school campus. Since school campuses are often diverse, and the neighborhoods often culturally isolated, school counselors can provide the vehicle for transcending cultural differences and encouraging multicultural understanding. Another method for involving the surrounding community is to hold programs, such as talent shows, on campus and invite the parents and neighbors.

Because members of a student body are in many ways required and expected to assimilate the dominant culture, counselors working with these students may be only vaguely aware of the expectations, belief systems and practices of a student's native culture. By developing and maintaining relationships with members of the surrounding community, counselors can be exposed to cultural practices and assumptions that are more pronounced because neighborhoods tend to be culturally isolated. One of the advantages of this exposure is the counselor's understanding of cultural elements that may underlie student attitudes and behaviors. Counselors may also gain insight about cultural identity from adults in the neighborhood that students would be less likely to reveal, partly because of inherent role dynamics between the adult counselor and the adolescent student. Counselors can also find out about cultural holidays, traditions and events in the neighborhood, and be able to talk about these with students.

Empowerment

<u>Impact of counselors</u>
The idea of empowerment encompasses the distribution of resources, but is rooted in a larger context of social relationship and dynamics. Culturally-based oppression often depends on acceptance from both the dominant culture and the oppressed culture to be perpetuated. Historically oppressed cultures sometimes adopt ways of thinking and behaving that originally were enforced by violence or other extreme means, but have continued because of cultural identity. Likewise, historically dominant cultures adopt ways of thinking and behaving that perpetuate a false sense of superiority. Counselors can assist students from oppressed cultures, or in other situations where they feel disenfranchised, in developing personal empowerment by encouraging them to relate to others from a position of recognizing that individuals, and groups of individuals, often share many similarities and are connected at a fundamental level. This kind of thinking transcends the historical relationships, and forges new interpersonal connections, giving empowerment to previously disenfranchised groups.

<u>Development of self-image</u>
There are several key areas of personal dynamics and self-image that are impacted through empowerment:
- Individuals begin to relate to others based on commonalities of experience and belonging, rather than on preconceived notions of difference.
- Individuals begin to recognize social dynamics objectively, rather than to internalize them.
- A sense of empowerment, and a recognition of social dynamics, can significantly reverse students' thinking, from that of victim, to that of change agent for social justice.
- Once individuals understand that it is the dynamics, and not any inherent inferiority, that contributed to their social status, the implications for personal growth can be exponential.

Counselors who work with students toward empowerment are literally giving them back the power that was missing because of culturally-based beliefs, attitudes and practices. Empowerment should be understood as not hierarchical, such that the oppressed group is now the dominant group, but rather as egalitarian, ensuring fair distribution of resources and opportunity.

<u>Helping students feel empowered:</u> Counselors can help students feel empowered by pointing out their membership in the larger community, and helping them to develop ownership and responsibility for their actions. Counselors can begin by discussing the parameters of group membership, noting that each of us belongs to several groups. Students can recognize that they belong to groups identified as students, community, culture, gender, etc. This enables students to transcend limits of identity. Counselors can then point out that social dynamics involve the

whole community, affecting individuals in myriad ways. This allows students to broaden their understanding of social processes. Students should also be encouraged to take personal responsibility for their academic progress, as well as other actions and behaviors. Counselors can work with students in developing new behaviors that reflect a stronger self-confidence, a perception of membership in the larger community, and a realization that they can positively contribute to that community.

Skill-building and developing increased knowledge base

Counselors working with students toward empowerment can first provide them with the knowledge and perspective that will allow them to approach their goals and circumstances differently, allowing them to consider different/better results. Even though students can understand their community membership in theory, often particular events or circumstances become discouraging symbols of validation for the status quo. Counselors can partner with students in confronting these circumstances, addressing them on a problem-specific basis, from an enlightened and empowered perspective. A good problem-solving strategy includes the following key steps:
- Identify the problem
- Work together to set a goal that will mitigate or solve the problem
- Develop incremental actions toward the goal.
- Identify available resources for achieving the goal(s)

Counselors can also provide support and encouragement, reminding students of their strengths, their desire to change their circumstances, and the support and resources available.

Data collection

Utilizing data collected to determine inequities based on race, culture, ethnicity of socioeconomic status should first begin by including appropriate variables. While there may be significant conclusions to be drawn by simply comparing results divided by gender, race, socioeconomic status, second language learners and other major categories, more useful information may be gained by comparing results in different areas within cultural groups. For instance, results of second language learners that perform well on aptitude tests that are number based, but poorly on those that are language based, should be assessed to determine if the testing and/or the curriculum inherently results in a cultural inequity. This kind of data gathering can identify which programs, courses, and strategies are most and least effective for diverse students, and adjustments can be made accordingly. Also, if students do well on standardized tests, and poorly in the classroom assignments and tests, this may be an indication of poor participation in the classroom.

Importance of personal research and reflection: For counselors to be competent in multicultural counseling, it is important for them to develop a sensitivity to the significance of the distinguishing characteristics the define culture(s). A good foundation for this sensitivity is for counselors to conduct self-investigation and self-reflection on their own cultural background. Counselors can develop an understanding of how their cultural and ethnic background has contributed to their value system, their traditions and rituals, their view of the individual's place in the larger society, and many other personal traits. Likewise, cultural history can reveal how particular cultures or cultural traits have played a part in social hierarchy. Counselors who are aware of their own ties to culture will be better able to understand the significance of culture in students who come from a different cultural background.. A counselor with this valuable foundation can be an important liaison for students who need to balance culture tradition with assimilation.

Importance of ongoing workshops and seminars: The issues of diversity in the counseling and school environment are complex and multidimensional. As a society, our collective knowledge of diverse cultures and the issues of multiculturalism is continually evolving. Therefore, it is advisable for counselors to periodically attend workshops and seminars on the subject at least throughout their work as a school counselor. Each workshop or seminar will help to expand a counselor's knowledge of and sensitivity to diverse cultures. From these events, counselors will better learn how to work with students and their families in the school counseling environment. They will learn strategies and terminology that reflect sensitivity and understanding of the scope of culture in general, and the specifics of particular cultures. Fortunately, many professional organizations are aware of the need for ongoing training in multiculturalism, and will usually offer numerous opportunities for the school counselor.

Meeting to work on multicultural competence: The benefits of meeting with other counselors on a regular basis, by joining organizations dedicated to increasing cultural sensitivity, can greatly add to the knowledge base formed from attending workshops and seminars. Also, the knowledge gained from periodic attendance at workshops can sometimes dissipate in an environment where it is not necessarily endorsed. Meeting with peers can repeat and validate this knowledge, and also provide the opportunity to implement and revise strategies, in an environment of learning, before applying these strategies in the classroom as the counselor/teacher. The combined expertise of the group can allow for shared ideas and strategies toward multicultural competency. Also, as a group, an organization of peers can collaborate on methods and strategies for combating oppression in the school and surrounding community through school counseling curricula and programs. These professional organizations include Counselors for Social Justice, The Association for Multicultural Counseling and Development, and others.

Increasing a counselor's knowledge and sensitivity with literature: The ability to read, analyze and critically explore issues of culture diversity through a written medium offers benefits not necessarily present in a seminar, workshop or organizational meeting. Literature about cultural diversity can explore historical and current events through the eyes and perspectives of several cultural groups, because a written text like this is usually the culmination of research and interviews. Reading these texts, counselors can gain a comprehensive understanding of the historical factors and impact of events in relation to race, socioeconomic class, culture, gender and other groups who have been oppressed or victimized because of their particular culture. A good book dealing with these issues is Howard Zinn's A People's History of the United States, which contains personal testimonies and anecdotes about the subject. These personal stories allow for a first-person perspective on issues of social justice, giving the counselor a sense of empathy to bring to the multicultural counseling environment.

The benefits of reading literature addressing issues of multiculturalism are generally two-fold: For one thing, literature on the subject of multiculturalism is always evolving, reflecting current research and other input. As with organizational meetings, literature dealing with cultural diversity is a compilation of the experiences and expertise of a number of people from a spectrum of perspectives. Counselors are well served to become cognizant of this evolving expertise, in multiculturalism as well as other aspects of counseling. Secondly, teaching or counseling in isolation from the continued input of others increases the risk of personal biases and perspectives coloring the curriculum. Any one individual inherently has a limited worldview, and no individual or group of individuals could possibly know all there is to know about other cultures. Consequently, continued exposure to viewpoints and perspectives beyond his/her horizon allows counselors to be aware, sensitive and able to respond appropriately to a diverse student body.

Importance of a checklist in determining one's own multicultural competence: A checklist can provide a rubric for counselors to assess their own level of multicultural awareness, sensitivity and competence. For counselors commencing their own edification in multicultural sensitivity, or those who are relative new and beginning the process of multicultural training, checklists can provide a set of goals to attain in the process of becoming more aware of multicultural issues. Counselors can see which issues or concerns are in need of further work, and can take advantage of the available resources for developing in these areas. Once these goals are attained, counselors can periodically review the checklist to ascertain if they are continuing to incorporate the guidelines and strategies represented by the checklist, and again refer to outside resources if indicated. The Association for Multicultural Counseling and Development, as well as other agencies, publishes appropriate checklists that address such issues as behaviors, knowledge, sensitivity, and awareness.

Teaching multicultural classes

One of the great aspects of teaching in most American classrooms is the diversity of the student population. This diversity can be a great advantage to a class, though it can also be an obstacle if it is not handled properly. Too many teachers take the easy way out and make their instructional methods the same for all students, when it would be to their benefit to modify their methods to best suit the student. Research has found that teachers are most successful when they focus on academic achievement, and allow their students to maintain their cultural differences. The best teachers are also those that attempt to cultivate in their students a fair-minded view of diversity; that is, a pride in their won culture and respect for the cultures of others.

There are many resources available for teachers who would like to improve their sensitivity to differences in culture. The Center for Multicultural Education at the University of Washington maintains a comprehensive on-line library of multi-cultural information at http://depts.washington.edu/centerme/home.htm. Brigham Young University publishes Culturegrams, a series of summary descriptions of various cultural beliefs and practices. Teaching Tolerance is a biannual publication designed especially for teachers, and includes projects and activities that will encourage cultural literacy and appreciation. The International

Multicultural Education Association publishes the Mulicultural Messenger, with reviews of multicultural resources and news updates.

Factors Affecting Students

At-risk Students

Counselor intervention with at-risk youth

Counselors can provide at-risk students with opportunities to develop healthy dynamics and self-validating experiences among their peers as well as with significant adults. Threat assessment teams can be formed and trained which are developed to focus on preventative strategies. Peer mentor groups should be established that will allow both at-risk students and students not considered at risk to interact under the guise and facilitation of the counselor. These groups can provide an insulated environment for learning healthy strategies for coping with bullying, neglect and other forms of abuse. Counselors can teach healthy interpersonal skills within these groups. Counselors can also collaborate with local authorities and community groups to provide opportunities for at-risk youth to have positive experiences with adults and outside groups. At-risk students can be encouraged to join community support groups such as Big Brother/Sisters. Counselors can also encourage family members to develop connections with available support groups and resources.

Community resources

Many schools will have ongoing relationships with community groups as a part of a general philosophy of community outreach. However, for at-risk students to receive any direct benefit from these groups or relationships, counselors may have to initiate and coordinate auxiliary relationships for the purpose of addressing specific needs of at-risk students. Understanding that at-risk students are often overwhelmed by a variety of life challenges, counselors can collaborate with a number of community resources, including: businesses, families, recreational centers, police departments, and universities. Counselors should cultivate these relationships, possibly in tandem with existing school relationships, and coordinate resources available with the complex needs of at-risk students. With the counselor's facilitation and coordination, these resource groups can cooperatively address many of the needs posed by at-risk students. This comprehensive coordination of resources can provide a significant hedge against students dropping out.

Interventions for diverse cultures

Counselors who work with at-risk youth from diverse cultures are in a pivotal position that both allows and calls them to reduce the gap between intervention strategies designed for the dominant culture, and those that address the needs of minorities. Counselors need to first be aware, and to communicate to school officials, that under the umbrella of at-risk students may be ethnic groups whose problems are defined or exacerbated by their marginalized status.

Counselors can consider cultural differences of at-risk students, and how they will interpret different activities when creating preventative and intervention programs. If necessary and when appropriate, counselors can act as a liaison on behalf of students from diverse cultures, by making recommendations for program changes to better accommodate cultural diversity. Counselors can make significant and important changes in the school system, to the benefit of present and future students.

Documenting intervention outcomes

In the absence of available success/failure rates for many intervention strategies, the onus is often on the counselor to document the outcomes of strategies used. In order to authentically and effectively produce this outcome assessment, it is at first important to document student responses during and/or after an intervention. In keeping with the assessment model, counselors should produce documentation that either quantifies or clearly identifies specific outcomes. Counselors should also be mindful of their role as an advocate for the students by realistically reporting successes and failures, so that program improvements can be made if necessary. By doing so, they can also provide a model for reflection and willingness to change. Counselors who provide authentic documentation and are willing to revise strategies are excellent candidates for added funding or other resources, and can provide comprehensive parameters for the role of school guidance counselor.

Empowerment modeling

Recognizing that at-risk youth are generally overwhelmed and under-supported, counselors can be particularly effective by providing students with numerous opportunities to develop empowerment and self-confidence. When setting goals with and for students, it is important to set achievable, short-term goals, to best ensure success by the student(s). Each success should lead to further and larger successes, and counselors can provide scaffolding goals and challenges. Counselors can also encourage listening and cooperation among family members by their own willingness to take a back seat and emphasize the importance of collaboration and teamwork, facilitating when appropriate. In terms of advocacy, counselors may be aware of policies or procedures within the school system that inherently poses an obstacle or inequity for at-risk students, and may need to intervene on behalf of the student(s). This is another way that counselors can model empowerment.

Factors and behaviors

It is important for counselors to be cognizant of the events and influences contributing to at-risk students, as well as the potential ramifications of their behavior and mental state. Counselors should be aware of changes in student behavior that may signal depression or other mental or emotional fragility. It is worth mentioning that the leading cause of death for young people is suicide, and therefore counselors are in a pivotal position to notice and respond to these symptoms. Some students may need more intensive, outside treatment other than school counseling. Some of the factors that can contribute to emotional vulnerability of at-risk students can include rising levels of poverty, substance abuse of the student or parent(s), domestic violence, and community violence. Other kinds of behavior problems may be a result of ADHD or other behavior disorders and may indicate the need for the student to be referred to special education resources in the school.

Although the factors and behaviors of at-risk students fall within a rather large spectrum, there is an umbrella definition that can be used as part of an overall set of guidelines for identifying these at-risk students. Generally speaking, if a student shows decline in any or all of the areas of physical, mental, social, spiritual or economic health, then the student is considered at risk. Also, community and social circumstances may contribute to a student's sense of isolation, increasing the possibility of deterioration in one or all of these areas. Students who are at risk in any or all of these areas often face a diminished likelihood of becoming productive members of society. Counselors are encouraged to refer to guidelines from professional organizations or literature to identify and appropriately respond to at-risk students. Counselors can provide the support, resources and encouragement that can significantly mitigate deteriorating factors.

Curriculum considerations

Counselors are generally responsible for addressing the academic as well as career and social development needs of students. To that end, they should be well versed in the areas of leadership, advocacy, systemic change, and collaboration. Also, they should develop and continually refine the skills to teach in these areas to diverse groups of students which include not only cultural differences but also at-risk students. Within the category of at-risk students are included those students whose behavior and performance are a result of family or socioeconomic factors, as well as students who come from a more stable background but suffer from physiological disabilities. Although the scope of the necessary preparation may be daunting, it can be more generalized to say that counselors should be cognizant of the subject matter, as well as the perspectives of the students, and choose a framework or frameworks for the curriculum delivery accordingly.

Cautions

There are five key areas of caution to consider when identifying a student as at-risk:
- Students who fall within the guidelines of at-risk may nonetheless be very resilient with strong coping skills, and therefore at-risk may be a temporary status for that student.
- If a student is overtly and obviously treated differently than other students because of the at-risk category, this may have the reverse effect of discouraging any creativity or confidence that student may have otherwise displayed.
- The term at-risk can easily become a label rather than a status, and therefore there is no mechanism to identify when the student is no longer at risk.
- The term by itself encompasses so many situations and behaviors, the responsive strategies may be also very generalized and not address the issues specific to a particular student.
- Cultural factors should always be considered, as possibly contributing to or masking an underlying issue.

Cultural issues

When a student is identified as being at-risk, the identification is usually made based upon overt behaviors or shortcomings. These may include poor academic performance, or inappropriate behavior. An initial assessment may point to the need for more native language materials or conflict resolution workshops. However, for some first- or second-generation immigrants, these outward circumstances may be noticeable, but not the underlying or most problematic issue. Often, the underlying issue can be masked by overt behaviors, until the need for treatment is long past due. Students from diverse cultures may be contending with issues related to isolation, sadness for loved ones left behind, bridging the gap between cultures, and other issues directly related to poor cultural assimilation. Although there are no clear guidelines per se for identifying such cultural factors, counselors should be aware of the possibility of precipitating circumstances when dealing with at-risk students from other cultures and/or countries.

Peer association

Adolescent students between the ages of 14 and 17 are particularly at risk for peer association and influence. Youth in this age group generally gravitate to groups that they can join and belong to, other than their family. Often, young people join groups that are formed around a common ethnicity. Unfortunately, if a good portion of the members of the group engage in violent or illegal activities, those who join the group often mimic this activity in order to be accepted. Consequently, students who participate in violent behavior or drug use engage in a lifestyle that leads to the decline of their physical, mental, social, spiritual and/or economic health, which places them clearly at risk. Although counselors need to refrain from making assumptions based on associations, they nonetheless should be aware of student's association, particularly as it relates to at-risk behaviors and attitudes.

Current versus declining trends

Within a large student body, there will be a small percentage of students engaging in at-risk behaviors, for which counselors should be on alert. At-risk youth commit various crimes after school, generally between the hours of 3 and 8, in fact closer to 3, right after school. Robberies are sometimes committed by youth, usually during the week and usually after 9 p.m. Today's students still face problems with premarital sex and unwanted pregnancies, which can significantly put them at risk for poor academic performance. However, the incidences of student suicides are on the decline, as are those of students riding with drunk drivers, and students carrying weapons to school. Although these activities and behaviors still occur, counselors should be aware of rising and declining trends in at-risk behavior to best be aware of the signs and symptoms associated with them.

Rejection by school system

Students who are displaying at-risk behavior often pose a challenge to educators who are striving for academic objectives and good classroom management. The at-risk behavior can cause a disruption on both fronts. This can be compounded by multiple at-risk students in multiple class periods.. Teachers and school administrators faced with this disruptive activity will first attempt to remedy the behavior, using known strategies. However, if this proves unsuccessful and the disruptive, at-risk behavior continues, teachers in particular can become discouraged and begin to develop an attitude of complacency about the behavior that can grow into complacency about teaching in general. Consequently, faced with this possibility, administrators will sometimes make the decision to remove a student or students from the school. Unfortunately, the short-term problem is solved in this case, but a longer-term issue arises of underserved youth becoming unproductive adults. Counselors can provide a valuable service in preventing this downhill slide in at-risk youth.

Counselors partnering with educators

Since schools are the primary focal point for issues relating to adolescents, often counselors and educators work with other community entities in discussing and developing strategies for addressing the needs of youth. Some of these entities include libraries, police departments, private schools, recreation centers, and other community-based programs as well as national- and state-based organizations. One of the ways that counselors can work as liaison between students and these entities is by dispelling the idea that the onus of at-risk behavior lies with the student. They can work with community representatives who feel that students are solely or primarily to blame for their behavior. Counselors can collaborate with educators to develop programs that are designed to address the needs of not only mainstream students, but also at-risk students. These programs can incorporate the needs and concerns of the larger community as well as academic goals identified for the student population.

Many educators have not addressed the needs of at-risk youth for some or all of the following five reasons:
- Funding has not been allocated for programs focusing on at-risk youth. Counselors can assist appropriate entitles in reevaluating the need for programs to address the needs of these students.
- Existing systems and programs do not include strategies for at-risk students, and changing the systems can be very challenging. Counselors can work with educators to broach this challenge.
- There is a stigma associated with at-risk youth that presupposes they will always be at-risk. Counselors can implement goal-setting strategies that guide and encourage at-risk students to productive behaviors.
- Social and community groups usually do not have programs that focus on at-risk students. Counselors can increase awareness for the need to do so.
- Graduate programs do not always include pedagogy focusing on at-risk youth. Counselors can collaborate with their peers by educating each other about at-risk youth.

Government funding and allocations

Funding resources and governmental mandates to assist at-risk youth exist at both the state and national level, although this assistance may be found under the auspices of umbrella categories. Program initiatives from the federal and state levels through federal or state departments of education or mental health have developed the 1967 Elementary and Secondary Education Act (ESEA) that provides for continuing public education through grade 12. There is also funding allocation for disadvantaged children, focused on the goal of drug-free schools and the availability of after-school care. The National Defense Education Act (NDEA) of 1958 authorized schools to hire counselors who encouraged students in the areas of math and science and other related areas. Counselors and other educators who are committed to assisting at-risk youth can find government support that relates to a guaranteed education for all youth, safer schools, and improved academic performance.

Crisis intervention

School or community trauma

Numerous kinds of traumas can affect a student population, from individual crises to those affecting the entire student body. Counselors need to be cognizant of the types and levels of trauma, and how they impact students. It is prudent for them to be aware of the possible ramifications of trauma, how to identify these effects, and strategies for intervention. Counselors need to be aware of the scope of trauma, and the scope of the needed intervention. School-wide traumas can include natural disasters, school shootings, widespread gang activity, etc. Individual traumas may encompass family illness, depression, domestic abuse, and even suicide. Sometimes an individual crisis can escalate into a school-wide trauma, by culminating in a school shooting or a suicide. Counselors should be well versed in types of trauma, and how to assess and treat its victims. This information should be ready knowledge, in the case of a trauma or crisis.

School environment crisis

A crisis is defined in part by the event, and in part by the response to the event. Generally speaking, a crisis is a situation that is perceived as overwhelming and intolerable by the individual(s) facing the crisis. Crises can affect people cognitively, psychologically, behaviorally and even physically. For an individual, a crisis may fall somewhere in the spectrum between failing an exam to full-scale disasters affecting the entire community. Although full-scale disasters necessarily impact entire populations, and inherently pose overwhelming circumstances, counselors also need to be aware of the levels of crisis facing students vis-à-vis their coping skills. For most crises, which fall significantly short of full-scale disaster, counselors can employ intervention strategies to help students through the present crisis as well as to help them develop coping skills for future challenges. Early intervention will mitigate the possibility of traumatic response to a crisis.

Parameters of crisis intervention: Since crisis by definition is a situation that is overwhelming and intolerable, crisis intervention serves to provide immediate support, and assist the individual(s) in developing the coping skills to meet the present crisis and similar crises in the future. It is good to remember that one of the factors that can contribute to a crisis is that the situation or event poses a new challenge to the individual(s). Some of the components of crisis intervention include:

- 35 -

- Defusing emotions to allow for exploring solution options.
- Interpreting the event or situation causing the crisis.
- Organizing the situation in terms of information, resources, etc. Proper preparation calms the student to better be able to handle the situation.
- Integrating the event into personal experience. Assist the students in recognizing the life lessons to be realized.
- Recognizing the positive impact gained from a crisis, e.g. the coping skills gained, new awareness, etc.

Crisis response plan: Counselors can work with school staff and administrators, both at the school level and at the district level, to develop a crisis response plan, to be prepared for any crisis that may occur. Counselors should facilitate regular meetings with school personnel, parents and other professionals as appropriate, to educate them on crisis intervention both at the school and at the community levels. Crisis response teams should coordinate campus-wide and community-wide services as part a critical response team. Counselors can educate and prepare the team on strategies and methods for handling the crisis. The team should be versed on methods for crisis prevention, strategies to employ during a crisis, and post-crisis needs. The team should work together, with the counselor usually as facilitator, to develop a well organized, systemic response plan. The coordination of the team and the crisis response plan should be implemented as a matter of preparation, and preferably not in response to an immediate crisis.

Crisis response plans need to address the possibility that normal logistical operations may be suspended, particularly in the case of a school-wide or community-wide crisis. Therefore, a good crisis intervention plan will allow for the following needs:
- *Location needs:* It may be necessary to establish a location for temporary counseling offices. This should be addressed by the team in anticipation of a possible crisis. Locations should also be established for a communication facility, first aid/treatment, emergency personnel, storage of supplies/food, and a break room or safe room.
- *Communication needs:* Crisis response teams will need to communication with other members of the team. They may also need to communicate with parents, as well as with the press. Part of the communication requirement will be the oversight and monitoring of team activities.
- *Other considerations:* An overall plan and assigned personnel for assessing the situation and assigning intervention tasks.

Suicide

School counselors need to be educated on potentially suicidal behaviors, and be prepared to intervene if necessary. These behaviors can include ideation, or any other behaviors that may indicate a student is contemplating suicide. All threats of suicide should be taken seriously. Counselors should consult institutional directives and state laws regarding responsibility for notification. In some cases, parents should be notified immediately, and may even need to pick up their child from school as soon as possible. In any case, students who are at risk for suicide should be in the presence of an adult at all times during the school day. Since the possibility of suicide can be extreme and immediate, intervention may include referral to an outside agency or institution. Counselors can work with parents and consultants in order to transition to treatment facilities and should be familiar with community services available.

Counselor's role in addressing the possibility of suicide: Suicide is very prevalent among young people, and has been deemed the moist common cause of death for adolescents. School counselors working with youth need to be well versed on the factors and behaviors contributing to suicides. There is no guaranteed strategy to prevent suicide, and in fact suicide may occur despite the best efforts in the student's network of support. However, counselors can take the stance of being informed and prepared in the event of suicidal behavior. It should be noted that suicidal ideation may be expressed differently among different cultures, and therefore counselors should respond to every potential ideation seriously. Some of the common circumstances precipitating suicide are alcoholism, depression, and a sense of hopelessness or helplessness. Counselors who observe suicidal tendencies should meet with the student regularly to discuss and work on the student's problems and state of mind.

Counselors and students with suicide ideation: Working with students who are presenting suicidal ideation includes reconnecting that student to his/her network of support. In the process of working with a student, a counselor can glean which activities and people in his/her life provide meaning, and contribute to an attitude of hope and resiliency. If a counselor deems that suicide is an imminent threat, the first consideration is the student's safety. This may include involvement of the parents, within the parameters of privacy mandates in this situation. Counselors can also encourage the student to reach out to his/her network of support for encouragement. This network could include parents, friends, church, coworkers, etc. As the student's ideation begins to subside, this network can also provide a grid upon which the student can reestablish positive connections. Counselors can remind students of their responsibility, purpose, and place in this network and in the larger community.

Warning signs of suicidal ideation: Although there are infinite manifestations of suicidal thoughts, there are seven key identifiers that counselors should take note of:
- Communication, either spoken or implied, which incorporates suicidal thoughts and possibly includes themes of escape, punishment, or self-harm.
- Well-thought-out plans for dying. If the plans are feasible, concrete, detailed and specific, this may be a good indicator that the student is seriously contemplating suicide.
- Well-thought-out plans for self-harm or for murder. Remember, suicide is self-murder.
- An association of completed business, closure, or a note with the idea of dying.
- Extreme stress such as a traumatic loss, illness, failure, etc. Counselors should also be wary of significant anniversaries in a student's life representing past losses.
- Mental state indicators pointing to alcoholism, depression, or any recent changes in attitude.
- A sense of overwhelming hopelessness or helplessness.

Statistics: Although suicide is not considered in itself to be a psychiatric disorder, it is the unfortunate result of many of these conditions. Every year about 30,000 Americans will take their own lives, and about ten times this number will make a serious attempt. The rate of suicide among citizens between the ages of 15 and 24 has tripled over the past thirty years. Men are about three times as likely to commit suicide as women, though women make the attempt far more often. The majority of suicides, especially those committed by young people, involve firearms. Suicide is more common among whites, though it appears to be rising quickly among African-American males. Health professionals believe that as many as 80% of those who are at risk of suicide can be helped with immediate therapy.

Risk factors: There are a number of factors that can contribute to make an individual consider taking his or her own life. About 95% of those who commit suicide have some form of mental illness, most commonly depression or alcoholism. Individuals who for whatever reason have lost hope that their life will improve are at a high risk of suicide. There appears to be some hereditary influence, as well: about one in four who tries suicide has a family member who has killed him or herself. Autopsies have shown that suicidal individuals often have a low level of the neurotransmitter serotonin. Finally, it is well documented that individuals who have easy access to firearms are far more likely to commit suicide.

Violence and aggresion

Causes of aggression: *Biological causes:* Oftentimes, individuals who have suffered some traumatic brain injury are more likely to display aggressive behavior. The abuse of alcohol or drugs will also increase an individual's tendency towards explosive rage. Scientific evidence has shown that many prescription medications, especially painkillers, anti-anxiety drugs, anti-depressants, steroids, and over-the-counter sedatives, may increase the risk of violent behavior. Males who commit violent crimes appear to have lower levels of serotonin in their brains, and males with a high level of testosterone are thought to be more prone to violence. As one would expect, individuals who suffer from psychological problems like schizophrenia are more likely to become violent.

Developmental causes: Children of abusive parents are much more likely to engage in violent behavior as they grow older. Although scientists believe that this is in part because such children fail to learn other coping mechanisms, there is also speculation that aggressive tendencies may be inherited. However, even if a child grows up in a nonabusive home, if they live in a violent community they are more likely to become overly aggressive. Children who perform poorly at school or are ostracized by their peers are also more likely to become violent. Individuals who display violent behavior at a young age are often rejected by their community, which only exaggerates the problem.

Society and the media: There is a great deal of research to suggest that the portrayal of violence in television, films, and music can incite impressionable individuals to commit similar acts. According to some statistics, the average American child will be exposed to about 40,000 deaths and countless more acts of violence during his or her childhood and adolescence. It has also been clearly illustrated that poverty, unemployment, and gang involvement often lead to violent acts. The risk of violence seems to be inversely proportionate to the chances that an individual has for success in society. It should be noted that violence seems to be tied to economics rather than to race; no racial or ethnic group has been shown to have a greater predisposition to violence.

Sexual violence causes: Although sexual violence must ultimately be blamed on the offending individual, there are a few social factors that contribute to its prevalence. First, there is an unhealthy tendency for individuals to accept male aggression as natural, and to suggest that women should be receptive to all male advances. It is also a myth that the male sex drive is somehow unstoppable. Too often, our society seems to blame the victims of violence as if they had somehow provoked others to act out against them. Similarly, many aggressive tendencies of feelings are condoned if they are part of a "joke" or "prank." This only serves to trivialize behavior that can be very painful to the victim. Finally, the prevalence of media in which sexual violence is condoned or even glorified sends the wrong message to would-be offenders.

Indicators: Often, students who feel disenfranchised will act out by bullying or otherwise victimizing other students. This sense of separation can result from a student feeling isolated from peer groups, cultural groups, family, or other groups from which the student feels excluded. This sense of exclusion may precipitate the student attacking other students, with bullying, ignoring, harassment, etc. This sense of isolation may also be a precipitator of suicide, or attacking the self. Students may intensify this attacking behavior by bringing weapons on campus, or inciting physical fighting. Recent years have seen more covert and more violent victimization on school campuses. Counselors and other school personnel need to be attentive to any incidents of bullying, which can escalate into more intense forms. Bullying and other victimization may be more prevalent among certain groups of students, and should provide the counselor with the opportunity to address ubiquitous attitudes and behaviors.

One of the factors that makes it difficult to predict violent incidents is that many students who display violent behavior do so on an impulse, resulting in most violent incidents being unplanned. Generally speaking, students who feel disenfranchised, helpless, or threatened will sometimes act out by perpetrating violent acts or behaviors. Often, violence will be perpetrated by feelings of desperation or an irrational fear that others may be threatening harm. Males are generally more likely to commit violence than females, and the highest incidents of violence fall between the ages of 15 and 24. Lower socioeconomic status is also a common factor in violent tendencies. Also, if a student has a history of violence, s/he will be more likely to commit violence. Lastly, students who have disorders related to conduct, ADHD, hallucination, delusions, etc., will be more likely to commit violence.

Types of violence and abuse: *Partner abuse:* Sadly, about one in five women will be abused by a romantic partner during her life. Indeed, domestic violence is the largest cause of injury among women. Women are considered to be battered if they are the victims of repeated and persistent physical abuse. This is usually accompanied by a tremendous amount of psychological stress. Battered women are often unwilling to admit that they have been abused, and so the health care professionals who treat them are unaware of the abuse. Alcohol and stress are the reasons most often given by men to explain why they abuse their partners. Many of these men are not violent anywhere but in the home. Partner abuse seems to become more common the poorer a family becomes, and the more crowded their home becomes.

- 39 -

Child abuse: Although statistics have shown that impoverished parents seem to abuse their children more often, child abuse remains a problem among every socioeconomic group. Child abuse can be physical, psychological, or sexual. Sexual abuse includes virtually any sexual contact between an adult and child, whether it is kissing, fondling, oral sex, sexual intercourse, or just suggestive conversation. Pedophilia is the clinical term for any sexual abuse of a child that is perpetrated by an individual other than the child's parents. Incest, on the other hand, refers to sexual contact among members of the same family. Oftentimes, children that are psychologically or sexually abuse may develop physical symptoms, or begin to act out in society.

Bullying: Any act of bullying or other victimization implies a power hierarchy. The victim is perceived and treated as powerless against the perpetrator, and each act of victimization further endorses that hierarchy. Often, social injustices and inequalities in a community or school environment provide fertile ground for bullying and victimization, which perpetuates the inequalities. If a comprehensive program to balance inequalities is not implemented, the bullying and victimization will most likely continue. Counselors can begin to address chronic victimization problems by educating students and pertinent adults about how to effectively break the cycle of victimization. Victimization can also take the form of gossiping or excluding certain individuals from group activities. Although some schools have rules specifically prohibiting victimization, counselors can provide a valuable service by working with the parties involved to recognize and stop the cycle of victimization.

Dating violence: The definition and parameters of dating violence vary between studies. However, the overall incidences of dating violence have been steadily increasing in recent years. The figures of violence occurring in a dating environ range from a few incidences to a significant portion of the student body. As indicated by the term dating violence, the general parameters define an individual victimizing another individual in a dating environment. This can occur with middle school, high school or college students. Most of the victims are women. The impact of this dating violence is felt at the individual level, often throughout the students' school, family and community network. The victim often is left with feelings of helplessness, which can expand into depression, substance abuse, and risky sexual behavior. These behaviors and mental states understandably the student/victim's family, friends, academic performance, etc. Counselors need to be aware of the possibility of dating violence in a student who is presenting at-risk behavior.

Sexual harassment: Sexual harassment is any inappropriate verbal or physical conduct of a sexual nature, specifically when it is directed at an individual because of his or her gender. The Supreme Court has determined that sexual harassment violates the protections for employees that were set forth in the Civil Rights Act of 1964. There are also state laws against sexual harassment. In order to prove that sexual harassment has occurred, a plaintiff must be able to demonstrate that the alleged harassment was either severe or consistent enough to affect their work, and that the employer is liable because of their knowledge of the harassment. In many cases, the courts have leveled extremely harsh punishments against businesses that neglect to stop or punish sexual harassment.

Most sexual harassment cases are either built on the idea of quid pro quo (literally, "this for that") harassment or the existence of a hostile work environment. In order for a plaintiff to prove that quid pro quo harassment has occurred, he or she must be able to demonstrate that harassment was considered a necessary part of having the job, that tolerating harassment affected the employee's progress in the company, or that the harassment clearly affected the plaintiff's ability to work. In order to make the case that harassment created a hostile work environment, the plaintiff must prove that he or she was discriminated against on the basis of gender, that this discrimination was pervasive and regular, that he or she was negatively affected by this discrimination, that any reasonable person would have been similarly affected, and that management either knew or should have known about the harassment, and did nothing to stop it.

Impact of abuse or neglect: Students who have been abused, neglected, or who have been witness to abuse within their family are inherently at risk of decline in any or all of the areas of physical, mental, social, spiritual or economic health. Often students with a history of neglect or abuse display chronic behavior problems including anxiety, depression, substance abuse and/or other emotional or mental disturbances. Further, victims of childhood abuse or neglect often feel a deep-rooted sense of shame or embarrassment, which translates to chronic social and emotional isolation. They often exhibit poor academic performance, and retreat from normal activities with friends and fellow students, particularly if they have been helpless bystanders to abuse which has been perpetrated against a parent or siblings. Counselors fine that there is often a clear correlation between at-risk behavior in school and abuse or neglect in the home.

Preparation: Counselors should first be assured that incidents of campus-wide student violence have declined in recent years. Nonetheless, there is always some possibility of a student or students committing violent acts that harm or impact the campus as a whole. Unfortunately, there are not always clearly identified indicators of potential campus-wide violence. Most experts agree that this type of wide impact violence is usually the culmination of several factors in at-risk students. The best preparation strategies for counselors include both individual intervention for at-risk students and developing an intervention plan for the school. On the individual level, counselors should always work with students to mitigate their violent tendencies or fantasies, regardless of whether or not they appear to pose a threat to others. On the campus-wide level, counselors can work with school officials to develop a rubric for threat assessment, as well as an intervention plan to minimize the casualties should a campus-wide event occur.

Threat levels: *FBI classifications for threats of violence:* Most of the research completed on the violent tendencies of students has been completed by governmental and FBI profilers and analysts, and made available to counselors and other educators to mitigate the possibility of future occurrences. There are four basic classifications of threats of violence identified by the FBI:

- *Vague threats that imply violence:* The threat is implied in the terminology, but not specified. Time and place are not generally specified.
- *Veiled threats of violence:* The terminology is more specific, but time and place are still not specified.

- *Conditional threats of violence:* The terminology refers to violence if certain conditions are not met. A common example of this is extortion.
- *Direct threats of violence:* These threats are clearly stated and straightforward. The terminology is in the form of a warning, specifies a target, time and place.

Determining the three levels of threat seriousness: According to government publications, the likelihood or seriousness of a threat can be generally divided into three sets of criteria:
- Low-level threats are generally categorized by vagueness, a lack of specificity, etc. Students may make a general, indirect statement of threat with little or no detail, and little or no specific plan to carry it out. Minimal risk is associated with low-level threats.
- Medium-level threats are more direct and plausible but do not appear to be realistic. They may contain details about time and place, but lack evidence of comprehensive planning. A medium-level threat may include phrasing that indicates seriousness, but lack the specificity to make it happen. The risk level of a medium-level threat is higher than a low-level threat, but generally does not pose imminent danger.
- High-level threats are distinguishable by their high levels of specificity, and comprehensiveness and plausibility of a plan. High-level threats should be taken very seriously, and school officials should always contact the local authorities.

The FBI's four-pronged assessment model for threat assessment: The FBI has developed a four-pronged model of threat assessment that focuses on the student making the threat(s) and his/her particular circumstances:
- Prong 1 assesses the behavior and emotional dynamics of the individual, including signs of alienation, poor anger management, poor coping skills in general, lack of trust, or marked changes in behavior.
- Prong 2 assesses the circumstances of the family and home of the student, including a lack of limits or lack of monitoring, access to weapons, lack of intimacy and/or volatile relationships within the family, particularly between the student and parent(s).
- Prong 3 assesses the student's perceived marginal place in the school community, evidenced by bullying, a lack of attachment to the school, inflexibility about culture, and a pecking order among the students.
- Prong 4 assesses the student's other connections, including peers at school, use of drugs or alcohol, and other outside activities or interests.

CDC findings

<u>Adolescent findings:</u> *Suicide:* The Center for Disease Control (CDC) acknowledges that the rate of suicide among youth has declined during the past decade. However, the CDC still believes that the rates are still too high. Many adolescents become overwhelmed by stress, confusion, and depression, and consider taking their own lives. In fact, suicide is the third leading cause of death among people between the ages of 15 and 24. The majority of suicides among adolescents are males. Firearms were used in the majority of these suicides. An individual may be at risk of suicide if he or she is impulsive, aggressive, has a history of mental disorders or substance abuse,

has a physical illness, has access to some means of committing suicide, or has recently suffered some personal loss.

Young drivers: Unfortunately, two of every five deaths among American teenagers are caused by an automobile accident. Studies have shown that having teen passengers increases the risks for teen drivers, and the risk increases along with the number of passengers. Teens are more likely to underestimate the dangers of driving, and are more likely to speed, run traffic lights, drive while intoxicated, or ride with an intoxicated driver. Teens also have the lowest rate of seatbelt use. Most of these accidents occur on the weekend. The CDC recommends that parents restrict adolescent driving and work hard to ensure that drivers are sober and obedient to traffic regulations.

Youth violence: Youth violence is a major problem in American society; homicide was the second leading cause of death among people between the age of 10 and 24. Youths may be at risk of committing violent acts if they have antisocial beliefs, a low IQ, poor behavioral control, a history of aggressive behavior, or an involvement with alcohol and drugs. Oftentimes, adolescents become violent if they were raised by an authoritarian parent, if they come from a low economic class, or if they have been witness to violence in the home. Adolescents can minimize their risk of being involved in violence if they maintain strong, positive ties with their family and school, if they stay involved in community activities, and if they display an intolerant attitude toward violent behavior.

Obesity: The Center for Disease Control maintains that the instance of obesity among adolescents between 12 and 19 has more than tripled in the past twenty years. This problem is blamed on simple caloric imbalance: individuals are consuming more calories than they are burning off. These problems can be exaggerated by a genetic predisposition to obesity as well as by bad health. Many overweight children also have high blood pressure or a high cholesterol level. Children who are obese are more likely to develop bone and joint problems, sleep apnea, low self-esteem, and social dysfunction. As they age, obese children are also more likely to develop heart disease, diabetes, cancer, and stroke

HIV and AIDS: The Center for Disease Control asserts that a tendency to have unprotected sex and multiple sex partners places adolescents at a greater risk of contracting HIV and the AIDS virus. The risk seems to be especially bad for minority adolescents. Individuals are considered to be at special risk of contracting HIV if they are regular substance abusers, do not have much awareness of the risks of HIV, come from a poor and/or uneducated background, or have dropped out of school. In order to combat this problem, the CDC has developed a number of programs to continue providing education to students both in classrooms and community centers. Many of these programs specifically target minorities.

Alcohol abuse: The Center for Disease Control not only considers alcohol destructive to adolescent health in itself, but believes that it contributes to other behaviors that are damaging to adolescent health. Specifically, the CDC suggests that alcohol contributes to unintentional injuries, fights, academic problems, and other illegal behaviors. Over time, alcohol is blamed for liver disease, cancer, cardiovascular disease, neurological damage, depression, anxiety, and antisocial tendencies. The rate of alcohol abuse among adolescents has fluctuated a bit in the past years: whereas 50% of high school students admitted to regular drinking in 1999, only 45% said that they were regular drinkers in 2003. Of these, 28% stated that they engaged in regular heavy drinking.

Drug abuse: The Center for Disease Control maintains that adolescent drug abuse is an ongoing problem that needs to be addressed. Besides the health risks associated with the drugs themselves, the CDC asserts that persistent drug use contributes to failure in school, fights, antisocial behavior, and unintentional injuries. Prolonged drug use can also be responsible for depression and anxiety. The CDC also maintains that drug use contributes to the HIV epidemic, insofar as those who share needles are liable to contract the virus, and drug users in general tend to engage in risky sexual behaviors. The statistics kept by the CDC state that marijuana use among teenagers decreased from 26% to 22% between 1997 and 2003.

Tobacco: According to the Center for Disease Control, every day about 4000 American teenagers try smoking for the first time. Assuming that conditions remain as they are today, about 6.4 million of today's children will eventually die from a smoking-related illness. The CDC reports that in 2003 22% of high school students smoked cigarettes regularly, and 15% smoked cigars on a regular basis. In addition, about 10% of high school students were users of smokeless tobacco. For the most part, students seem to be more likely to smoke cigarettes of they are from a poor background, and if they have parents or friends who are smokers. White males are far more likely to use smokeless tobacco than are any other demographic groups

Unintended pregnancy: According to the CDC, teens who become pregnant immediately decrease their chances for success in life. Teen mother have a reduced chance of finishing high school, and are more likely to spend their lives in poverty. The good news on this subject is that better contraceptive practices and more responsible behavior by adolescents have led to a reduction in the number of teen pregnancies, abortions, and birth rates over the past decade. However, these rates are still higher in the United States than in other developed countries, and they are especially high among African-Americans and Hispanics. The CDC has approved a number of programs that they say do a good job of educating and encouraging teens to make the right decisions.

Sexually-transmitted disease: Because they are more likely to engage in risky sexual activity with multiple partners, adolescents are more likely to contract a sexually-transmitted disease. The CDC believes that adolescents are particularly at risk if they are frequent drug users and if they do not have access to contraceptives or to sex education. In order to meet the ongoing needs, the CDC has developed programs to present important information to adolescents so that they can protect themselves, as well as so that they can seek treatment if they do contract an STD. Part of the CDC's mission is to increase the level of parental involvement in the lives of adolescents. The CDC has published a number of statistics indicating that when parents actively supervise their children's lives, the children are less likely to engage in dangerous sexual behavior.

Substance abuse

Since the prevalence of substance abuse among youth is increasing, and the spectrum of illegal substances includes many possibilities, counselors should be at least generically educated on common legal and illegal substances and behaviors associated with substance abuse. Counselors should also be aware of local resources available for students involved in substance abuse. Although school guidance counselors cannot be expected to be experts on substance abuse, it is nonetheless a good idea to be cognizant of behaviors and other signs of possible substance abuse and be able to discuss the possibility with the student. However, students will not necessarily readily admit or discuss substance abuse, so the counselor should still be prepared for referral if necessary. Also, counselors should be aware of how substance abuse impacts academic performance and mental ability, in order to best address these issues in a student for which substance abuse appears to be a contributing factor.

Strategies to encourage students to self-report substance abuse
Although students may be hesitant to self-report or even to recognize substance abuse, counselors can facilitate this recognition and self-reporting through a series of questions. The following questions target alcohol abuse and are identified by the acronym CAGE:
- C – *Questions about cutting down.* Ask the student if s/he has thought s/he should cut down on alcohol/substance use.
- A – *The annoyance factor.* Ask the student if s/he becomes annoyed when people criticize his/her drinking.
- G – *The guilt factor.* Ask the student if s/he ever feels guilty about the amount of alcohol/substance consumed.
- E – *Alcohol as the eye opener.* Ask the student if s/he ever needs alcohol to get going in the morning, or to calm his/her nerves.

Counselors should also have regular access and referral to the Physician's Desk Reference to maintain current knowledge about drugs, alcohol, and possible side effects.

The following questions can be used as a guide for encouraging students to recognize and self-report substance abuse. Counselors can ask the following of students that may have a substance abuse problem:
- If they are taking over-the counter or prescription medications.
- The reason they take the medications.
- Any other medications/drugs they take.
- How long they have been taking these medications.
- Side effects, including severity and when they noticed the effects.
- If they drink alcohol.
- How they are affected by alcohol.
- About their drinking and substance habits – alone, with friends, etc.
- If their alcohol/substance use has impacted their personal, financial, professional or legal circumstances.
- If anyone in their network of family/friends has asked them to stop using drugs/alcohol.
- If they attempted to quit alcohol/drug usage.

- If an attempt to quit caused withdrawal symptoms.

Grief and loss

Types of losses: One thing for counselors to remember is that a loss is still a loss, even though it may be as severe as the loss of a parent or as seemingly trivial as failing a class. Divorce of parents can be a particularly devastating but unfortunately a commonly experienced loss for young people. Also, friendships are very important at this age, and the loss of a friendship can be very upsetting and be experienced as a major loss. What is significant about these different types of losses is that students/young people feel loss just as intensely as adults, and that each loss needs to be grieved and processed. Students need to move through the grief, and on to acceptance. By understanding that a sense of loss can be experienced regardless of the precipitating event, and by knowing about the grief process, counselors can provide the support and the guidance to move students through the loss and on to acceptance.

Stages of the grief process: The grief process encompasses the following five major stages:
- Shock and denial usually define the first stage of the grief process. Counselors can guide students toward identifying their fears.
- The second stage is usually anger which involves an indignation and questioning of why this loss was perpetrated on them. It may include thinking they did not deserve the loss.
- Guilt is generally the third stage, evolving to a sense that the student's actions or inaction may have caused the event leading to the loss, and therefore they did deserve the loss.
- The fourth stage is that of hopelessness and depression. This tends to be the longest stage and may include feelings of sadness. As this stage becomes less intense, this is usually a signal that the student is nearing readiness to move on to acceptance.
- Acceptance is the fifth stage in which the student adjusts to his/her new life circumstances.

Assisting students through the grief process: Throughout the process, counselors can assure and remind students that these feelings are normal, and that life will resume to normalcy for them. This is not intended as a denial of their feelings, but rather as an assurance that the grief process is a process, and not a permanent state. Counselors can work with students in the grief process, remembering that there are four major tasks that are accomplished during grief:
- Accept the reality of the loss, both emotionally and intellectually.
- Experience the pain, both internally and externally.
- Acclimate to life after the loss, accepting help from others as appropriate.
- Assimilate the loss and reinvest energies elsewhere.

Counselors should be watchful for the stages and tasks involved with the grief process, and be prepared to refer to the student to outside or specialized resources if the situation becomes overwhelming or too complicated for the counselor to be of assistance.

Dropping out of school

Counselors should be particularly alert and responsive to the plausibility of students dropping out, if they present any or all of the following:
- High rate of absenteeism
- Low or dropping grades
- Low participation in extracurricular activities
- Limited parental support
- Evidence of alcohol or drug problems

Following are recommended intervention strategies for students at risk for dropping out:
- Tutoring services – either peer tutoring or other trained assistance
- Career and skill training for success after high school
- Expressing high but reasonable expectations for students
- Additional general/foundation classes for students with disabilities, or as needed

Continued support and resources are recommended for at-risk students who stay in school, including:
- Relevant curriculum
- Significant support and assistance from teachers and others as appropriate
- Useful and accessible textbooks and other classroom materials

For all interventions with at-risk students, counselors should address interpersonal skill-building and self-reflection. It is important for counselors to encourage students to develop strong relationships with peers and school staff/administrators, which often increases their sense of community and belonging. Throughout the intervention, counselors should always assure students that they can discuss personal issues in both individual and group sessions. Often, at-risk students are struggling with numerous issues in several arenas of their lives. There are four key areas that are possibly involved when students are at risk for dropping out:
- *Personal/Affective:* Counselors can offer retreats or other groups to encourage interpersonal participation
- *Academic:* Counselors can arrange for tutoring and/or other individualized methods of instruction
- *Family Outreach:* Encompassing increased feedback to parents
- *School Structure:* Possibilities include class size reduction or alternative school options
- Work/Career: *Vocational training*

Other disorders

Eating disorders: Eating disorders in youth commonly manifest as either bulimia nervosa (BN) or anorexia nervosa (AN), or both. Because both of these disorders result in extremely poor nutrition, and bulimia nervosa can result in esophageal injury, students who are suffering eating disorders are at risk for poor health, poor intellectual and social development, and in some cases death. Counselors can implement intervention strategies through a complete medical assessment and multifaceted therapeutic assessment. In particular, the combination of behavioral therapy and cognitive therapy can be very effective in treating eating disorders. Cognitive therapy can addresses issues of control and self-esteem, while behavioral therapy can promote healthy eating habits and discourage destructive behaviors like purging. Group therapy may also be quite helpful, and in some cases family therapy may be indicated. Medical assessment may also be indicated, to ascertain if the student is in immediate physical danger from an eating disorder.

Tic disorders: Tic disorders are defined by recurrent, non-rhythmic sequences of movements and involuntary sounds from certain muscle groups. These disorders can include Tourette's tic, transient tic, and not-otherwise-specified (NOS) disorders. Counselors should initially garner enough information to accurately diagnose the condition, and educate the student and the parents more fully about the disease. Therapy can include identifying any underlying stressors as well as assessing family interaction and understanding regarding the disease. Various therapeutic strategies can be effectively implemented for tic disorders. Cognitive-behavioral therapies can address stress management. Self-monitoring, relaxation training, and habit-reversal training are effective strategies to consider, once initial data about the tic have been collected. Habit-reversal training is more commonly indicated, which requires the student to relax the affected muscles and introduce a competing response. If students present with frequent or explosive outbursts, counselors should collaborate with a physician to determine if medication is indicated.

Mood disorders: Mood disorders are generally defined as those in which students externalize feelings of depression, sadness, guilt or other negative emotion, possibly including thoughts of suicide. Students with mood disorders may present with somatic complaints. Counselors should take care to not misidentify a mood disorder when a student may just be experiencing temporary sadness. On the other hand, counselors should be cognizant of the signs of mood disorder, especially symptoms that may signal the risk of suicide. Effective therapeutic strategies for mood disorder include cognitive and behavioral interventions as well as psycho-educational programs that focus on improving social skills and promotion of rewarding activities. Some students suffering from mood disorders have improved with antidepressants. However, studies regarding the efficacy of medicinal treatment of depression are inconclusive, and therefore the use of antidepressants should not be immediately considered, if at all.

Substance-related disorders: One of the initial intervention steps for substance abuse is to identify the abuse, and the substance(s) involved. A strategy is for parents to conduct drug tests at home, although students may also self-report. An important factor to remember is that students with substance abuse may also have family members with substance abuse, since the correlation is very strong. In addition to individual counseling and education, counselors can conduct school and community workshops that address the benefits of early detection, the risk factors involved, and treatment options available. Based on the type of substance abuse, duration and intensity, treatment models are available, ranging from outpatient therapy to intensive inpatient treatment. The spectrum of treatment options encompasses very restrictive models as well as more participatory models. Treatments include detoxification, contracting, self-help groups, behavior therapy, family therapy, social skills training, as well as nutritional and recreational counseling.

Generalized anxiety disorder: Generalized anxiety disorder (GAD) is defined as a pervasive anxiety that is characterized by excessive, uncontrollable and often irrational worry about everyday things, which is disproportionate to the actual source of worry. Physical, somatic symptoms may include shortness of breath and/or muscle tension in other parts of the body, both of which can be difficult to control. Although GAD is not limited to adolescents, it does present problems particular to students in that the physical symptoms and the irrational worry can overshadow attention to academics, and therefore negatively affect performance. Students who are chronically anxious are unable to focus on their lessons. Counselors can use cognitive-behavioral strategies to mitigate the intensity of the anxiety and the accompanying physical symptoms. Students can be taught coping strategies such as identification, modification of anxious self-talk, education about emotions, modeling, relaxation techniques, and related self-regulating models.

Exceptional children: A great deal of time is spent trying to equip teachers to handle students labeled "exceptional" for one reason or another. Furthermore, Public Law 94-142 mandates that schools must identify those students that require special treatment, whether from being extremely gifted or because of a disability. Many schools, however, feel that the best way to handle exceptional students is simply to include them in the regular classroom. Advocates of this program assert that specialists can come in to the class and help exceptional students as necessary, and that otherwise these students will benefit from being in contact with students of a wide range of ability. However, many classroom teachers feel overwhelmed when they are asked to instruct a very wide range of students.

Learning Disabilities

Learning disabilities: Learning disabilities are physiological disorders that may damage a person's ability to store, process, and retrieve information. For the most part, learning disabilities affect reading and language skills. It is important to note that learning disabilities do not indicate that a student has a lower level of intelligence, or is more likely to be emotionally disturbed. Teachers should be aware of their students with learning disabilities, so that they can avoid discriminating against them for their handicaps. The most common learning disability is dyslexia. One reason why learning disabilities can be so frustrating is that they are so specific, so that a student who excels in almost every area of school may be terrible in one particular area.

There are a few common ways for teachers to minimize the problems their learning-disabled students face in a normal classroom. One way is to break complicated tasks down into a series of small steps; often, students with learning disabilities have a difficult time imagining the chain of tasks they will need to perform to accomplish some larger goal. Establishing a regular routine is also a good way to keep students involved in class. Learning-disabled students may need to learn abstract concepts through drawing, movement, or conversation. Finally, teachers can help remove some of the anxiety associated with having a learning disability by assuring their students that it is alright to make mistakes, as long as the best effort is given.

- 49 -

Some students may struggle for years without ever realizing that they have a natural learning disability. For this reason, secondary school teachers should be familiar with the signs that a student may be learning disabled. One sign of a disability is spelling the same word several different ways in the same document. A teacher may also become alarmed if a student is unable to answer open-ended questions, or accomplishing basic reading and writing tasks. If students seem to be consistently misreading information, or having a hard time grasping abstract concepts, they may be battling an undiagnosed learning disability. Finally, students with learning disabilities frequently have a hard time focusing on details and working at a fast pace.

Legal issues

As defined by the ASCA, the school counselor should address the following functions in his/her role as facilitator and advocate for student needs:
- Lead and facilitate activities of the comprehensive school counseling program.
- Collaborate with other student support personnel to deliver appropriate services.
- Provide services to both students with disabilities and traditional students.
- Provide individual and group counseling.
- Work with staff and parents to develop an understanding of students' special needs.
- Refer students as appropriate to auxiliary resources in the school system or in the community, to address needs not met in the context of the counseling program.
- Advocate for the rights of students with disabilities in the school and the community.
- Assist school staff with issues related to students transitioning between grade levels.
- Serve on interdisciplinary groups that assess students who may have undiagnosed special needs.

IDEIA: The Individuals with Disabilities Education and Improvement Act (IDEIA) was enacted to ensure that eligible school-aged students receive the opportunity for a reasonable education. Eligible students are defined as those students who exhibit any single or combination of 13 identified disabilities. Reasonable education is distinguished as allowing students to make reasonable educational progress, and not necessarily to achieve highest possible performance. Eligible students can receive a free appropriate public education (FAPE) under IDEIA. The Act stipulates that these eligible students receive an education that is designed around their intellectual and physical levels. Also mandated as that ,the curriculum delivery is specially designed to meet students' particular requirements. If the disability presented by the child has minimal or non-negative effect on learning, then the student may not be eligible for IDEIA resources, but may be eligible for reasonable accommodations under Section 504.

Types of learning disabilities

Attention Deficit Disorder: Teachers should have little trouble identifying those students who may be suffering from attention deficit disorder, as the behavior of these students will probably be disruptive. Students with ADD usually make careless mistakes in their work and have a hard time sustaining their attention during long lecture periods. They are typically disorganized and are often losing things. They may fidget a great deal with their hands, and just seem to have a great deal of nervous energy. They often talk too much and out of turn. They often have a difficult time working quietly and keeping their hands off of the other students. Many students are so afflicted by attention deficit disorder that they almost seem to be possessed, or driven by some internal motor.

Although dealing with students that have attention deficit disorder can be a challenge for teachers, there are a few ways to manage this behavior effectively. It is essential first of all to provide a consistent schedule and routine for students, so that they will not have idle time in which they are not sure what they need to be doing. Students with ADD may need help keeping themselves organized. As a teacher, one should always allow kids with ADD to take frequent movement breaks, so that they can work out some of the nervous energy that may drive them to distraction. It is also a good idea for teachers to maintain good communication with parents, so that both can determine the best strategies for dealing with a particular student.

Attention deficit/ hyperactivity disorder: Attention deficit/ hyperactivity disorder is the diagnosis given to a range of conditions in which the individual has a hard time controlling motion or sustaining attention. Although ADHD is typically thought of as a disorder that affects children, new research suggests that it is not outgrown, and that adults may be just as likely to suffer from it. Individuals suffering from ADHD are impulsive, constantly in motion, and easily distracted. They may feel perpetually restless, may be unusually forgetful, and are likely to be socially immature. Although there is no specific test to determine whether someone has ADHD, most doctors are trained to recognize the condition. Most of those who suffer from ADHD are benefited by behavioral therapy and medication.

Autism: Autism is a disability that impacts social interactions as well as verbal and non-verbal communications. It can present with repetitive activities, stereotyped movements, resistance to changes in routine or environment, and unusual responses to stimuli. Most autism is evident in children before the age of 3. Academic performance may be mildly or severely impacted by autism, depending on the range and intensity of the symptoms.

Deaf-blindness, deafness, hearing impairment: *Deaf-blindness* refers to significant impairment in both hearing and vision. The combined impairments can result in severe suppression of development, learning and communication, well beyond that which would result from deafness or blindness alone.
Deafness refers to a hearing impairment that is sufficiently significant to affect the processing of linguistic information through hearing, with or without amplification. Academic participation and performance are affected accordingly. *Hearing impairment* refers to a permanent or fluctuating condition that adversely affects the educational performance but does not qualify as deafness.

Developmental delay, emotional disturbance, and intellectual disabilities: *Developmental delay* refers to a significant cognitive lapse between ages 3 and 9 that cannot be accounted for by any other identified disability. *Emotional disturbance* refers to a spectrum of symptoms that encompass a general inability to cope or learn, which presents over a long period of time and to a marked degree. Symptoms include: an unexplainable inability to learn, inappropriate behaviors or feelings under normal circumstances, a tendency to develop physical symptoms or fears that correlate with personal or academic problems, the inability to foster satisfactory interpersonal relationships with peers or teachers, and a general mood of unhappiness or depression. This condition adversely affects educational performance accordingly. IDEIA includes schizophrenia in this category. *Intellectual disabilities* refers to a significantly sub-average intellectual functioning that may exist with deficits in adaptive behavior and manifest during the developmental period.

Multiple disabilities, specific learning disability, orthopedic impairment, and other health impairment: *Multiple disabilities* refers to a combination of impairments such as intellectual disabilities with either blindness or orthopedic impairments whereby the student's educational needs cannot be accommodated in the traditional classroom. Excluded from this group is deaf-blindness. *Specific learning disability* refers to a disorder whereby one or more of the basic psychological processes inherent in using or understanding spoken or written language causes a person to have difficulty in linguistically communicating or in performing mathematical calculations. *Orthopedic impairment* refers to physical impairments that adversely affect a student's academic performance. Included in this category are loss of a limb, clubfoot, cerebral palsy, and disease-related conditions like poliomyelitis and bone tuberculosis. *Other health impairment* describes the presence of such chronic or acute health problems as diabetes, epilepsy, ADD, heart conditions, or sickly cell anemia, that adversely affect the student's educational performance.

Other Learning disabilities: Learning disabilities are physiological disorders that may damage a person's ability to store, process, and retrieve information. For the most part, learning disabilities affect reading and language skills. It is important to note that learning disabilities do not indicate that a student has a lower level of intelligence, or is more likely to be emotionally disturbed. Teachers should be aware of their students with learning disabilities, so that they can avoid discriminating against them for their handicaps. The most common learning disability is dyslexia. One reason why learning disabilities can be so frustrating is that they are so specific, so that a student who excels in almost every area of school may be terrible in one particular area.

There are a few common learning disabilities that teachers are likely to encounter. Apraxia is the inability to plan motor activity; that is, the inability to move correctly to accomplish a particular task. Dysgraphia is difficulty in writing, and difficulty with spelling. Dyslexia is difficulty with language that extends beyond just reading. Dyssemia is any difficulty an individual may have distinguishing social cues and signals. Problems with auditory discrimination mean that a student has a hard time telling the differences between sounds and their sequence. Problems with visual perception are those in which a student has trouble identifying and assigning meaning to the things that he or she sees.

There are a few common ways for teachers to minimize the problems their learning-disabled students face in a normal classroom. One way is to break complicated tasks down into a series of small steps; often, students with learning disabilities have a difficult time imagining the chain of tasks they will need to perform to accomplish some larger goal. Establishing a regular routine is also a good way to keep students involved in class. Learning-disabled students may need to learn abstract concepts through drawing, movement, or conversation. Finally, teachers can help remove some of the anxiety associated with having a learning disability by assuring their students that it is alright to make mistakes, as long as the best effort is given.

Some students may struggle for years without ever realizing that they have a natural learning disability. For this reason, secondary school teachers should be familiar with the signs that a student may be learning disabled. One sign of a disability is spelling the same word several different ways in the same document. A teacher may also become alarmed if a student is unable to answer open-ended questions, or accomplish basic reading and writing tasks. If students seem to be consistently misreading information, or having a hard time grasping abstract concepts, they may be battling an undiagnosed learning disability. Finally, students with learning disabilities frequently have a hard time focusing on details and working at a fast pace.

Gifted students: Not all exceptional children are designated as such because they are disabled in some way. Many students are considered exceptional because they are more intellectually advanced than their peers. Gifted students may be able to think faster and to solve more complex problems than their peers. They may be able to think creatively and empathetically, and to have profound insights. According to the Education Consolidation and Improvement Act of 1981, gifted children are those that surpass their peers in reasoning, leadership, artistic, and academic fields. These students, according to the government, are entitled to special treatment from the school so that they can fully develop their abilities.

There are three basic types of programs designed to serve gifted children. Enrichment programs are those that extend the regular classroom work, either by providing more topics of study or giving a deeper treatment of the material covered in the normal class. Enrichment seems to work best when it capitalizes on the interests of the student. Acceleration programs are those in which the student moves ahead to content that normally he or she would receive later in life. This may involve grade skipping or early entrance to school. Affective programs are those that are designed to address the social and emotional needs of gifted students. These students may have greater trouble assimilating into social groups because of their intellectual differences.

Teachers may find that helping gifted students work to their potential is just as difficult if not more than helping their disabled students achieve. One way to help gifted children succeed is to give them some independence, and allow them to determine enrichment materials. It is also a good idea to partner gifted children with one another, so they can work on social development while not sacrificing academic difficulty. Gifted children should be challenged; sometimes it may be good to let them struggle with advanced subject matter rather than continually gliding through less complex material. Gifted students should not be required to spend too much time going over material they have already learned. Finally, gifted students should be given the chance to develop their critical thinking skills through independent study.

Implementing special education

Generally, the steps involved in appropriating special education accommodations for a student include:

- Student will be recommended as needing special accommodations or additional instruction by parents/guardians, the school system, school personnel, or a state agency.
- History of student learning problems will be reviewed with parents/guardians, school administrators, school educators/special educators.
- Counselor should request written consent from parents/guardians to conduct further, formalized assessment.
- Students is formally assessed through tests administered by psychologists, special educators, specialists such as audiologists, etc. to determine the specific special needs and the extent of the special needs.
- Student eligibility for special accommodations is determined from results of assessment.
- If student is eligible, counselor will develop an individualized education plan (IEP) that will address student needs.
- Counselor will implement an FAPE in the least restrictive environment (LRE) as determined by the parents/guardians and educators.

Inclusion

A great deal of time is spent trying to equip teachers to handle students labeled "exceptional" for one reason or another. Furthermore, Public Law 94-142 mandates that schools must identify those students that require special treatment, whether from being extremely gifted or disabled. Many schools, however, feel that the best way to handle exceptional students is simply to include them in the regular classroom. Advocates of this program assert that specialists can come in to the class and help exceptional students as necessary, and that otherwise these students will benefit from being in contact with students of a wide range of ability. However, many classroom teachers feel overwhelmed when they are asked to instruct a very wide range of students.

Planning and Implementation

Program Management

Principles and Goals

Instruction principles

There have been times when the principles of effective instruction have been described as art and not something taught to teachers in college. A teacher must possess certain qualities about themselves in order for their instruction to be effective. One quality is the teacher must show an honest interest and enthusiasm for the subject they are teaching. If the teacher is not interested the students won't be either. In the classroom they must also show respect and interest in each student. The students should be allowed time to ask questions and discuss with others about the subject matter. The objectives should be clear and the students should know what is expected of them. Any class activities, homework or projects should reflect what has been discussed in class and graded appropriately and fairly. The tests and papers should accurately measure what has been accomplished through the course objectives.

Instructional objectives

Instructional objectives are very specific and describe what the student is expected to do. Therefore, it is important that when deciding what the objectives are going to be, teachers and administrators know exactly what they expect from their students. Instructional objectives are also determined by what the outcome will be. They will state what the student should be able to accomplish after the teacher has finished his or her instruction. It is important to make sure the objectives are used to ensure that learning is clearly focused on a goal and that both students and teacher are on the same track. When determining instructional objectives, it is also important to ensure they line up with the lesson plan. It does not make sense for a teacher to teach a lesson on a certain topic, but the objectives do not follow the same topic.

When choosing learning activities that reflect the instructional objectives, it is important to remember that these activities should encourage students to have meaningful interaction between other students and the instructor. Activities can include anything from writing papers, doing projects, group discussion and hands on activities. It may be difficult for the teacher to decide which activity is best; therefore after deciding the instructional objectives, a teacher should keep them near by and use them as a source for deciding which activity to use. There are different levels of objectives and the instructor will want to choose the activity or activities based on that particular level. It is important to remember that what ever activity is chosen, it must support the student in learning the instructional objectives. It must also align with what the lesson is about.

One of the most crucial steps an administrator needs to implement in order to have an effective school is to have clear goals and objectives for curriculum, instruction and learning outcomes. It is imperative to the school's effectiveness that these goals are explained and well known to everyone that is involved with the student's learning. However, the goals can be well known but, how does an administrator know they are being achieved? One indicator of achievement is student assessment. Once the data has been collected on these an administrator can carefully examine the data and see if there are still weaknesses in the same areas or if there has been an improvement. Another indicator of achievement is the staff's opinions and attitudes. An open line of communication is crucial to any administrator wanting to achieve something more in their school. The staff can be able to tell if a curriculum is working or if there is still room for improvement.

Proper expectations

An administrator should set high expectations regarding students. However, it is important for the administrator to remember every student is different and the expectations should be set accordingly. One of the first considerations to take is the student's developmental level. An administrator needs to be aware if the student has any learning disabilities or is developmentally slow. Expectations should not be set too high especially if the expectations are not developmentally appropriate for the students. Another factor to consider is the instructional level for the students. Expectations should not be set so high that they go beyond the instructional level. A kindergartener can not be expected to perform on the same level as a sixth grader. The opposite is also true; expectations should not be set too low that the students will be performing below grade level and not want to achieve anything higher than that.

Determining educational needs

In order to construct an appropriate needs assessment, a department head needs to first conduct a gap analysis. After this is done, though, he or she needs to identify priorities for the department and rank them in importance. Sometimes a cost-benefit analysis is helpful in figuring out which are the most important actions that the department can take. Next, teachers will try to identify whatever problems may be keeping the department from reaching its potential. Possible problems might include under-trained staff or a failure to make department goals clear. Finally, the effective needs assessment will identify solutions to these problems, as well as any chance for improvement in other areas. The completed needs assessment provides a basis on which the whole department can work in the future.

Assessing community needs: When an administrator is trying to determine which educational needs are the most important to meet, it is important that he or she looks at the community needs. Some communities need to know that when they send their children to school they are going to be safe; others may need to know that their children are getting the best education possible. Different communities have different needs. Administrators need to get involved with the parents and find out what they expect from their child's school. Ignoring the parent's expectations can have a negative effect on the administrator. The parents could start to complain and the leadership status of the administrator could suffer from it. It is also important to look at the population projections. These types of population projections can help give an indication of how fast the school is going to grow and which ethnicity groups are coming in. This is important because different ethnicity groups also have different needs.

Specific needs of diverse populations: Administrators need to look at what the population is regarding their school. If there is a diverse population then there could be diverse educational needs as well. In a diverse population there are people of all races and ethnicity groups and each race and ethnicity group has different expectations. It is so important that an administrator recognizes this and ensures that the groups know they are important and their voices will be heard. Another population group that should be recognized is the mobile population. If a school services a mobile population group, for example, a homeless shelter, it is important to recognize their needs may not have anything to do with education. Their needs may be just to keep their children fed. Another important factor in determining educational needs is gender. Boys and girls are different emotionally, mentally and physically and their educational needs are different too.

National perspective: It is vital that administrators are aware of the national perspective concerning education. They need to know what is expected of them, their staff and their school.

Administrators should know what the expectations are and make sure they are trying everything to meet those standards. The nation has certain goals that they expect schools to achieve and administrators need to know what is expected of them and ensure their school is moving in that direction. When an administrator knows what the national expectation is, they can look at their school and ask whether or not they have the means to achieve those expectations. If they do not then they will know what their educational needs are and find the means they need to achieve those goals.

Research: It is important for administrators not to rush and implement programs that do not have solid research and results. Many times new programs can just add more activities to the curriculum and not fit the needs of the students or they can conflict with what the school's mission is. Many research articles and journals can say that a certain program can bridge the learning gap however; it may not work in every school. Administrators need to stay focus and remember what works best for their school and stay on that course. An effective administrator should only use programs that can produce solid research-based results. It is always important for an administrator to know what the needs are for their students and school before making any huge program change.

Assessment of student achievement: Assessing students allows administrators and teachers to understand at what level their students are on, whether it is reading, math, science or social studies. Assessments can give an indication of what area students are achieving and in what areas they are struggling. If there is an area of great achievement then administrators can take that information and decide what exactly it is that this school is doing right in order to get these results. They can also ask themselves if there is anything else this school needs in order to help students keep achieving in a particular area. The same is true if after an assessment there is an area where students are struggling. Administrators can look at this data and ask why are students struggling and what are the needs that need to be met in order to achieve improvement. After all this data has been collected and needs have been identified then administrators can start setting priorities to ensure improvement will be made.

Consensus building

After schools have determined what their educational needs are, then it is time to decide what the plans are to meet these needs and how they will be implemented. There will be many opinions and ideas from many people, and one way to decide what the best plan is, is through consensus building. Using this technique will allow everyone to have an opportunity to speak their opinion and have their voices heard. The goal is to persuade others to decide with a certain party. It is important that it is understood that everyone will get a chance to speak and their opinion will be respected even if others do not agree with it. Consensus is achieved when one party's viewpoint is preferred over the others. The one big disadvantage with this technique is that it can be extremely time consuming.

Change

- 57 -

Assessing need for change: There will be times when an administrator is forced to face the pressure of making changes within the school. The first and most important stage in the process of change is using a needs assessment plan that provides important information about the strengths and weaknesses about the various educational programs and activities the school is currently using. If the administrator does not occasionally assess the current educational program then most likely he or she will be unaware of any needed change and assume all programs are working well and meeting the needs of everyone. This assessment will also help others understand the need for change. Once there has been a decision to change the program, alternatives need to be selected. One alternative is to replace the current program or just modify it. The administrator should choose the alternative that will best help to improve the school.

Reducing resistance to change: There are certain groups who will be affected the most when there is change; the faculty, the students, the parents, the school board, the administrator's superiors and the state department of public instruction. These groups can also provide the most support or the most resistance to change. Administrators must remember every group will have their opinions, and the most professional thing to do is respect, listen and accept those opinions even if they are not agreed upon. One of the most important groups an administrator needs to consider during the change process is the faculty. It is crucial to get the faculty involved because if the faculty does not understand why there needs to be a change, there will be less support and in return an implementation of a new program might not be successful.

Adopting innovation: The first stage an administrator will go through is the awareness stage which is becoming aware of a new innovation, but not having enough information about it. Many times an administrator may not even have a strong enough interest in finding out more information about the subject. At the interest stage, an administrator is beginning to show signs of interest and desire to gather more information and may even begin to develop negative or positive feelings. At the mental stage, the administrator has decide this is something worth trying and is evaluating the innovation and deciding how it will be implemented. They may also ask respected members of the school community to assess it. During the trial stage the innovation is implemented on a trial basis. Next is the adoption stage and this is the point when the innovation is implemented fully. The last stage is the integration stage and the new innovation is now a routine.

Teachers and change: Teachers will worry when there is going to be a change, however administrators can ease those fears by providing adequate information about why the change is being made. Administrators should still be sensitive about teacher's fears and ensure they are provided with reassurance. One of the first fears teachers will have is wondering how the change will affect them personally. If these fears can be eliminated then there may be concerns about whether or not they will know how to perform the tasks that will be required of them. After those concerns have been eliminated, next will come questions about how the new change will affect the students. The best thing for an administrator to do is to listen and ensure the staff that their concerns are important and being heard.

Unsuccessful innovations: Many times innovations are unsuccessful because teachers feel they do not understand what their responsibility is in their new role regardless if they had the orientation before the process began. Administrators should never assume that teachers will fully understand their roles after one or two orientation sessions. Receiving feedback is crucial in the beginning. Teachers may also feel they lack the knowledge and skills to fulfill their duties. Administrators must ensure teachers receive the proper training and assistance needed to fulfill their duties. Another reason innovations fail is due to the lack of materials the teachers need. If an administrator wants an innovation to succeed, it is their responsibility to make sure material is available in a sufficient quantity. Innovations are often unsuccessful because certain aspects of the school program were not changed to assist the teacher's new role.

Conflict resolution

<u>Group process conflict resolution:</u> Using groups to resolve conflict can be extremely resourceful to an administrator. Individuals in groups can provide a variety of opinions and offer creative ideas on how to resolve issues. It is important to first establish the rule that everyone's opinion will be valued and respected. If there are too many individuals involved, it could become a chaotic situation and nothing will be achieved, therefore, it is important for the administrator to keep order and structure. It may also be wise to keep the amount of people involved to a minimum. Once an idea has been agreed upon on how to solve an issue it is now time to decide on how to implement the plan. Everyone will have their own opinion but it is important for the group to come to an agreement on which plan best meets the needs of the school.

<u>Conflict management techniques:</u> In most cases, when an administrator is deciding which technique is the most appropriate to resolve conflict, they would choose a contingency approach, which is choosing the technique based on the nature of the situation. However, an administrator should also consider the individual personal needs of the staff in selecting a conflict management technique. Other important factors to consider are the people involved in the conflict, how serious the situation is to them, the type and intensity of the conflict, and the authority that some individuals possess. An administrator is likely to encounter several different types of conflicts and therefore there will be a number of alternative techniques to choose from. One technique will not be suitable for all situations.

<u>Conflict initiation:</u> In most cases, administrators will want to prevent conflict from happening and may find it impossible to prevent conflict. However, if an administrator finds themselves in a situation where an individual or group is not performing at the level they should and does not want to change; it may be cause for the administrator to actually initiate conflict. If an administrator is in a situation where he or she observes a problem with a teacher and the teacher disagrees, the avoidance of conflict will not be possible. It is the administrator's responsibility to ensure that all staff members are performing to the best of their abilities, and conflict may be needed in order to bring about improvement.   It is important that all possible outcomes are considered before conflict is initiated and that conflict is absolutely necessary for improvement.

<u>Dealing with conflict:</u> Administrators can choose from four different options about how to deal with conflict. One option is to use the cooperative approach which means to hear other's points of view and show empathy toward that group's feelings. After this has been accomplished then

the administrator can attempt to find a compromise that will lead toward a mutual solution. Another approach is confirming, which means the administrator communicates to the groups that he or she feels they have a great deal of competency and they are highly respected for it. Another option is to use the competitive approach, which views conflict as a win-lose battle. One of the groups at conflict must back down from the conflict and it is only then that the conflict will end. The last option an administrator has is to use the avoidance approach. This approach is when the groups stop discussing the situation and end the conflict but do not resolve any issues.

Research has shown that administrators who use both the cooperative and confirming approaches have much more success in resolving conflict. Those who choose to use the competitive or avoidance approaches are less likely to succeed in conflict resolution. The cooperative and confirming approaches are considered to be more successful because when an individual feels they are recognized for their competence they feel a sense of security and value and more likely to want to resolve the conflict. The competitive approach seems to be less effective because many times the administrator will use this approach when he or she thinks they can win the conflict and they use the avoidance approach when they are uncertain of how to handle the situation. The cooperative and confirming approaches requires the administrator to have strong interpersonal skills and if they are lacking these special skills, then it is best for the administrator to designate someone who does posses these skills.

Power struggle bargaining: An administrator can possibly find themselves in a situation where they feel strongly about their objectives and conflict cannot be avoided, and chances are an agreement is impossible. This situation is called power struggle bargaining. The administrator will do everything it takes to resolve this conflict; however they may be convinced the solution must go their way. This can cause hurt feelings and destroy many personal and professional relationships with individuals that may be involved with this situation. Many times conflict may seem to be resolved, however it will reappear in future situations. However, the advantage to power struggle bargaining is that the conflict may end in complete favor of the administrator. It may be necessary for an administrator to get involved in this power struggle; however, if they want the conflict to end in their favor they must assess their power and authority accurately or there could be disastrous results.

Conflict avoidance methods: Other techniques that can be used for conflict resolution are techniques called conflict avoidance methods. One of these techniques is called the withdrawal method in which an administrator will not argue in a certain situation and just accept the outcome. The other method is indifference, this is when an administrator makes it seem as though an issue does not matter to them personally. An administrator can also avoid any circumstances that would cause conflict, this method is called isolation. Using the smooth over method would mean the administrator accepts the situation and minimizes any arguments. The consensus method allows others to discuss their views and try to persuade others. Although these methods avoid conflict they do not resolve it. These methods may be necessary to use, especially in situations when one group feels powerless in changing the views of the other group.

Problem-solving approach: The problem-solving approach is another method of conflict resolution and can be the most effective. However, this method is most likely to be successful if the parties are willing to compromise and an agreement is possible. It is also important that both parties can contribute something valuable and they are reassured and confident that the solution will made that will not exclude their interests. Each group should be allowed the opportunity to state their opinions and their conflicting positions. The group members should also state the opinions and position of the opponents as way of assuring their opponents that their points of view were heard and understood. This way the administrator can also ensure each group is clearly listening to the other. An administrator should then clarify with the groups if there is still conflict. Group members should state why their opinions and views are valid to them. When all members are through stating their viewpoints, the members should be asked if they have anything that needs to be added. There is a possibility that conflict may still be unavoidable.

School-based community: A school-based community involves everyone in the decision making process including teachers, parents and students. Each team is responsible for a certain part that will improve the school and with all three teams working together it will promote a school-based community that focuses on trying to continue to improve the school. This type of community will help student behavior, performance and will encourage parents to take an active part in their child's education. When the teams are able to work together and make decisions it creates a feeling of ownership and responsibility. Everyone is aware of the school's goals and will know what direction they want to take the school. It may be difficult at times for everyone to agree on certain issues, however, the conflict may be reduced if individuals can agree on issues by using a "no fault" problem solving, collaboration and making decisions by consensus. These methods work better than voting because with voting there is an increased chance of individuals taking sides.

Fact finding during conflict: Once the administrator has heard each party's point of view about the dispute, it is important for the administrator to then validate the facts of the situation. Many times individuals will consider their opinions to be the facts and the absolute truth; however those facts need to be verified. It is very common that a person's emotions can distort their memory and the true facts of the situation. The administrator must also recognize that individuals in the conflict can agree on the facts; however their interpretations are complete opposite. The administrator's goal while in the process of fact finding is to clarify the areas that the parties do agree upon and narrow down the issues that are at disagreement. The administrator is put in the position to act as mediator; this role will be much easier to play if he or she is not one of the parties at conflict. If they are, then it is best if a neutral person acts as mediator.

Arbitration: There will be many times when conflict cannot be resolved using mediation; it may be necessary to use arbitration. This process involves the parties at conflict explaining their point of view to a third party who is the arbitrator. Each party must agree to accept the third party's decision and they must commit to carry out the arbitrator's decision when they agree to discuss the issue with the arbitrator. The best way to choose the person to be the arbitrator is to base the decision on the type of conflict and the circumstances surrounding it. Using an outside party for arbitration is not common; it is more common to use a superior in the organization.

The growing trend of arbitration is a reflection on the fact that traditional means of conflict resolution is failing to achieve results.

<u>Conflict between formal and informal leaders:</u> When a school has a number of different leaders, there is a strong potential for conflict. There could be a disagreement on a wide variety of topics, and any type of conflict could make it harder on the administrator to build a unified organizational culture. The important issue an administrator needs to remember is to listen effectively to both sides in order to understand the main issue of the conflict. There should be an opportunity for both the formal and informal leader to be able to voice their opinion and ensure they feel they are important. An administrator can use their influence to persuade one party into the direction that is more suitable to the overall school organizational culture, however this may not work every time. There is not a correct way of handling a situation like this; however, an administrator with strong conflict resolution skills can change a difficult situation.

Staff Development

<u>Priorities:</u> An effective administrator realizes that teachers do not know how to do everything on their own. There needs to be critical training for each teacher however, not every teacher needs help in every area. Setting staff development priorities should be based on the staff's needs. These staff developments need to be arranged to improve the teacher's skills in a particular area. This is extremely important, especially if the school is implementing a new program. The teachers should not be expected to know how to teach it without the proper training. Many times teachers feel as though staff development is something they have to go to in order to fulfill their staff development requirements. These training times should not be something they have to go to, these should be times when teachers actually find ways to improve their teaching skills. Priorities should be set according to what is important for the school.

<u>Staff development activities:</u> In order for a school to achieve success, an administrator should involve each teacher in the planning and implementation of staff development activities. Staff development activities not only enhance a teacher's skills but it is also a tool to get other teachers to help each other. An administrator's responsibility is to help teachers assess their needs and ensure they have the necessary tools and support to carry out their duties. Staff development activities can provide wonderful ideas to enhance student achievement, however, if a teacher does not have the necessary material to perform these lessons, then goal will be harder to achieve. Administrators should also provide each teacher with classroom management and teaching models of these activities. This may make it easier for the teacher to perform them instead of just hearing about them during one staff development session.

<u>Communication:</u> If an administrator can communicate in a certain manner, this can create a more encouraging environment. If an administrator can open a meeting by just stating their true feeling or their reaction to a certain situation, then this can create a more secure environment. Opening with these kinds of statements can put a staff at ease because they know there is a common ground that has just been developed. It is always crucial that an administrator talk to the staff in a non threatening manner; nothing will cause a person to become defensive faster than if they are under the assumption they are being attacked personally. An administrator must

also learn how to become accepting of others and that includes their personality, opinions and approaches. Another important consideration is to remember that an administrator can control the attitude of the group. If he or she comes in and is positive about a situation, then the chances are the group will be more positive.

Changing behavior

Using referent influence: If an administrator possesses a referent influence, this means others are able to identify with the administrator as a person. Certain characteristics that others can identify with are a strong character, outspoken personality and compelling leadership style. Characteristics like these may enable an administrator to gain cooperation from others even if teachers, parents and students may question the decisions made by the administrator. The qualities are positive and tend to make people want to react positively to another. However, there are no certain types of character traits that have a positive impact on everyone. While some groups respond positively to certain traits others may view them as a sign of weak leadership. Another issue with referent influence is that if an administrator is in a position of leadership, their authenticity has already been established, and if certain traits are not there, then the probability of them developing is unlikely.

Using reward influence: This type of influence means an administrator has certain rewards that can be given out to certain individuals who act and obey certain decisions an administrator makes. One issue with this type of influence it that an administrator may not have enough rewards to be able to distribute equally. There may occasionally be a time when rewards may be offered to an individual or group without having to distribute the same reward to others. However, this may seem like preferential treatment and in the education field this is not viewed favorably. Another problem that may arouse is the administrator may receive very little rewards to give from the school board and other bureaucratic agencies. Although these problems may occur, an administrator can develop their own variety of awards. These rewards can include a free period, an additional lunch break or support a new activity a teacher wants to implement.

One reward that an administrator has an abundant amount of and is often overlooked is positive reinforcement. This reward can be given out in the form of written or verbal communication. Taking the time out of the day to go to a teacher or other staff member and tell them they are doing a great job can have a major impact. Many times an administrator may think they are already giving out plenty of positive reinforcement, but in fact they are not. Any administrator can give positive reinforcement, but an effective one knows that reinforcement must be clearly related to a certain task the staff member is doing. If compliments are given out randomly, then they seem meaningless and not valued as much and in return the behavior that is desired may not occur.

Administrator's role

Promoting parental involvement: Parents are often hesitant about getting involved with the school functions because they often feel they are not important and their opinions do not count. In some cases parents may have had a negative experience involving a principal or other school functions, therefore, it is the responsibility of the administrator to make those parents feel valued and important not only to the school but to their child before discussing any type of involvement. An effective administrator knows the value of parental involvement and realizes they must invite, recruit and motivate all parents to get involved. Many times when these efforts do not work an administrator may have to offer incentives or rewards in order to get parents to take that first step toward involvement. Involving a parent does not mean they have to speak in public or put on a carnival, it could as simple as donating time to repair something in the school.

Building a school culture: When an administrator is striving to build a school culture it is important to have certain characteristics. School culture consists of everyone; teachers, students, parents and other staff members. One of these important traits is paying attention to the values of its members. These are the ideas and opinions of the member and what they feel is needed for the improvement of the school. One sign of an effective culture is the behavior of the members, whether or not they are positive and upbeat. Another sign is whether or not teachers are interacting with students and parents in a positive and effective way and vice versa. A strong culture also respects the written and unwritten policies and procedures. In order for the administrator to truly understand the school's culture they should take the time and perform group interviews, this way they can accurately understand the issues of the school.

Group meetings: Group meetings are a common occurrence in the educational field. In most cases the administrator will be the lead the group and be in charge of planning and conducting the meetings. However, there will be times when someone else will be responsible for carrying out those functions however; administrators are responsible to make sure the functions are carried out in an effective and productive way. Many times administrators believe their meetings are meaningful and productive, however, many times staff members see them as a waste of time. Teachers often feel meetings do not provide resourceful information and the planning of them is unsatisfactory. Administrators must make sure the information given is valuable and meetings are planned for a purpose and not to just hand out papers.

Negative reactions to authority: When an administrator is faced with a negative reaction to authority, their first reaction may be to become defensive or become upset. However, the appropriate way to handle this situation is to investigate and examine the reasons why others are responding this way. This may be a difficult reaction to have for many administrators. The feelings of hurt and anger are normal, however, an effective administrator knows how to put those feelings behind them and move on to the problem solving stage. The challenging of authority can be a positive situation, especially if the causes are understood. The key to diagnosing the reasons for the negative reaction is to have a discussion with the parties involved. Every effort should be made to avoid putting anyone on the defensive and every attempt should be made to understand the person's point of view.

Exercising authority: There are numerous reasons why people question and challenge authority. However, if an administrator follows certain guidelines, then this issue can be overcome. Administrators are obviously going to have to make some very difficult decisions and give directives to others. One consideration an administrator should decide on is how and in what style the directive will be given. It is important for an administrator to remember that regardless of how professional the directive was given, if the person who received it does not feel that it is in their best interest, there is going to be an issue of resistance. An administrator should also consider the strengths and weaknesses of the person before giving a directive. Issuing an order for someone who is not motivated will result in failure. They should also explain the rationale behind the directive and remember not everyone may understand the value in it.

Community volunteers: Effective administrators know that in order to build a successful school culture, community volunteers need to play a vital role. Asking community members to volunteer their time will help boost their self esteem and make help them realize they can have a major impact on the student's learning. If there is a strong volunteer program then parents and community members can become actively involved in their child's education and feel their skills are useful and important. This bond will help break down the barriers between teachers and parents. Community volunteers can also have a major impact on the teacher's lives. If volunteers are actively helping to meet the student's needs, then this can give the teachers more time to plan other activities in the lesson plan. Their scheduling can become more flexible.

Nurturing themselves: Administrators have an extremely difficult job; they must motivate, coach, lead, attend meetings and maintain the mission and goals of the school. These job duties can feel rewarding, however, they can also be emotionally draining. Many times this can cause burn out among many administrators and in return have a negative impact on the rest of the school. In order for an administrator to perform their responsibilities effectively they must remember they are individuals too, and need to take care of themselves. It is important for administrators to find a healthy balance between a work and personal life. Sleep, relaxation, fitness and a healthy diet will enable an administrator to be a well-adjusted person. When an administrator has found a way to balance their responsibilities, they become a healthier individual and in return a wonderful role model for staff members, students and parents.

Empowering teachers: When administrators empower teachers they allow them to have a voice in the decision making process. This makes them feel valued and in return will improve their performance. Administrators are still the leaders and facilitate the school goals and encourage teachers to create their own ideas. However, the more power teachers have the more responsibility they will have to take the burden for. Administrators should make it be clearly known that each teacher is solely responsible for carrying out their duties and performing them to the best of their ability. However, administrators should be responsible for providing the necessary training and education for each teacher that informs them of the appropriate decision making skills. In order to make this empowerment successful the school board members have to be in support of it as well.

Barriers to effective communication: Every message an administrator sends out will be interpreted in different ways from every person who receives it. Many times the message will not be successfully communicated simply because of factors that are not in the control of the administrator. Many times an administrator will send out a message they believe is extremely important and the persons receiving it do not share that same opinion. Many times the person receiving it may have a lack of interest of what is being said. Another factor is the person receiving the message lacks the background knowledge needed to understand the content of the message. Certain phrases or words require a certain degree of knowledge in order to understand it. Understanding the group who will be receiving the message can help the administrator with how the nature of the message should be written in order to help reduce the misunderstanding.

Social barriers the may deter from a message include factors such as age, sex and position in the hierarchy. Teachers who teach different subjects or grade levels may misinterpret the message. The same is true for men and women teachers as well as new and experienced teachers; each one will develop their own interpretation of what the administrator was trying to say. Men and women each have their own way of communicating with others. Males can often be misinterpreted as arrogant or harsh whereas females can come across as weak and lack leadership. Different communication styles carry into the different cultures. Administrators should be aware of the different ways of communicating that may be inappropriate. Certain cultures may find it inappropriate to stand too close or to use a certain voice tone.

Enhancing school culture: Before an administrator can enhance a school culture, he or she must first achieve a good understanding and full knowledge of what the organizational culture is. After this has been achieved then the administrator can move on to the next step of enhancing it. If the school culture is not an effective one, it will be a challenge for the administrator to change it. The administrator must envision the future of the school, what is the goal that will make the school improve. An administrator must also make it a priority to meet the needs of the teachers and students. Enhancing the school culture will more likely be achieved if the administrator views a problem as an opportunity to find solutions not another burden. It will also be enhanced if teachers are encouraged to use creative practices and they are given opportunities to share their ideas and made to fill they are a vital part of the improvement of the school. The most important factor that will enhance school culture is staying focused on student achievement.

It is well known that effective administrators know how to shape and lead an effective school culture. Administrators can easily get the impression that the school is under one culture. This is highly unlikely because of each school will contain a wide variety of personalities and opinions. A school can have multiple organizations that make up a culture, subculture and even countercultures and each one is the one who wants to define who the school is. The most common example of this is in secondary schools where there are several departments and subjects. Many of the departments make up a culture and possibly within the department are subcultures. This can be an extremely difficult challenge for an administrator trying to understand and gather information about the school's culture and trying to set goals and expectations.

Building character: One of the many responsibilities of an administrator is building the character of the students. They should always set high expectations for good behavior in the lives of the students. However, if students are expected to behave and act in a certain way then they must see examples of good behavior happening in the environment around them. What happens at home cannot be controlled but what happens at school can. Students should be able to see staff members using caring words and having a positive attitude. Changing student's attitudes can have a major impact on their work habits and achievement. Character building is something that can be carried with a student for the rest of their life. Responsibility, kindness, caring, trustworthiness, and integrity are character traits students will need as they continue on through school and adulthood it does not stop in elementary school.

Communicating through symbolism: It is important that the entire school community understand the expectations and sanctions of the school. These can be communicated through symbolism and can be done in the form of a slogan, group rituals or awards banquet. Values and expectations can also be communicated by symbolic activity through behavioral change. If students are expected to act in a certain way then staff members and the administrator should be expected to perform that same behavior. The goal of symbolic activity is not what is said but rather what actions are taken to reflect the desired behavior. If students are expected to read then they should see teachers reading. Administrators should also apply this strategy for staff members. If something is expected of them then as the leader, the administrator should demonstrate the behavior as well.

Developmental Guidance Program

Career Counseling

Career advice and counseling

One of the common tasks of a business teacher is to provide students with career advice and counseling. Because of a business teacher's area of expertise, students have a right to expect that teachers will be able to dispense valuable information about careers. In order to do so, a business teacher must stay apprised of changes in the job market, and must be knowledgeable on the responsibilities and functions of various professions. This is not to say that a business teacher must be an expert on every career; on the contrary, one of the most valuable functions a teacher may perform is directing students to on-line or text resources on a certain profession, or setting up a meeting between a student and a member of the community currently working in the student's area of interest.

Job-shadowing: Job-shadowing is one of the many ways that students can gain some experience in the workplace. In job-shadowing, a student simply follows along with a worker in the field in which they are interested as that worker goes through a normal day. Through shadowing a real worker, students can learn first-hand what skills they will need to hold a certain job and what exactly a job entails. Sometimes, students may discover that they are not as interested in a particular job as they originally thought. For instance, a research study showed that students that originally were interested in fire-fighting often changed their minds once they realized the real, day-to-day life it would involve. One of the limitations of job-shadowing is that students only observe; they do not actually practice any job skills.

Career development

Career clusters: In this extremely specialized modern economy, it is useful to consider various "clusters" of careers that have similar attributes. The United States government has established sixteen career clusters: agriculture and natural resources, arts/audio/video technology and communications, architecture and construction, business and administration, education and training, finance, government and public administration, health science, hospitality and tourism, human services, information technology services, law and public safety, manufacturing, retail/wholesale sales and services, scientific research and engineering, and transportation distribution and logistics. These clusters have been created in part to aid vocational educators, who may be overwhelmed by the variety of potential careers and can benefit from a system of summary.

One of the main uses of the system of career clusters as devised by the United States government is to provide vocational educators with a simplified way to look at the skills and standards for various types of jobs. The government has developed extensive paperwork regarding each of the sixteen skill sets, complete with specific training required and skills that must be acquired. Oftentimes, vocational teachers will administer a questionnaire to students that determines which career clusters best suit their interests and aptitudes. Then, with the help of the available literature, the teacher can work with the student to develop a plan for attaining the skills necessary for employment in their chosen field.

Employee concerns: *Work standards for employees:* It is very important that an employer enforce clear standards for employees. In order to do this successfully, the employer needs to make sure that standards are posted visibly and that employees are introduced to them during orientation. Employers should also lead by example by following all the rules themselves. Employers should strive to present the image to their employees that their business prizes accuracy and honesty. Finally, a good way to ensure that employee work standards will be attained is to set certain performance goals and reward employees for reaching them. Work standards may have to do with customer service, accuracy in bookkeeping, cleanliness, punctuality, productivity, or safety.

Employee rights: There are four main categories of employee rights: rights associated with collective bargaining and unions; rights having to do with working hours and pay; rights having to do with workplace safety and worker's compensation; and rights having to do with discrimination in the workplace. The rights that employees have today have been codified by federal legislation. Before that, however, employee rights were established first by state law, and later by negotiation between unions and employers. Some of the specific rights enjoyed by employees are the rights to distribute union literature, the right to negotiate wages and working conditions in good faith, and the right to work without being treated differently because of race or gender.

Employee attitudes: There are some business analysts who note a mismatch between the passion for personal liberty in the United States and the authoritarian hierarchies of American business. Over the course of the twentieth century, statistics have shown a gradual decrease in the trust of the American worker in his or her employer. At the same time, the average age of American workers and management has decreased, so there is reason to suspect that communication between employer and employee may improve. One means of increasing employee satisfaction is through the formation of quality circles, groups of people that meet together to discuss work-related issues. Many statistics show that workers are now more concerned with being challenged and feeling important than with earning money to survive; the modern manager will have to do more than pay his employees to make them feel their work is worthwhile.

Legal issues: *Nondiscriminatory discrimination:* Screening is always the first part of the recruiting process. Some companies have recruiting officers that travel to universities to interview potential employees. In any case, it is important that the firm have a good set of minimum requirements, and that they do not bother to interview just anyone who is interested in a job. An able recruiter should establish close relationships with people at the place of recruiting, so that he or she will have an available reference for candidates. Usually, resumes are used to screen candidates at first. Business analysts all agree that it is best for a company to have an immediate idea of a candidates weaknesses; being placed in a job for which one is unqualified is as bad for the individual as it is for the company.

Civil Rights Act of 1964 and EEOC: The United States government has set up some laws to ensure that all citizens are given a fair chance at available jobs. The Civil Rights Act of 1964 decreed that it is illegal to discriminate against candidates based on their race, ethnicity, religion, or gender. Title VII of this act established the Equal Employment Opportunity Commission (EEOC), which has its goal an increase in job opportunities for women and minorities. Since its inception the EEOC has been enhanced by the Equal Pay Act of 1963, the Age Discrimination in Employment Act of 1967, and the Equal Employment Opportunity Act of 1972. These are laws that apply to business, state and local governments, labor unions, and educational institutions.

Laws affecting employee compensation: The Consolidated Omnibus Budget Reconciliation Act (COBRA) requires employers to allow employees who have lost their jobs for certain reasons to continue receiving health insurance at the company rate. The Equal Pay Act prohibits employers from paying two people who perform the same job different wages because of gender. The Fair Labor Standards Act requires employers to pay the minimum wage and to pay overtime wages to all employees that earn them. The Health insurance Portability and Accountability Act of 1996 regulates the health information that employers can require from employees, although it does not strictly forbid employers from viewing employee health records under certain circumstances.

Family and Medical Leave Act of 1993: The *Family and Medical Leave Act* was passed in 1993. It enables employees to take up to twelve weeks of unpaid leave for certain family or medical emergencies without risking the loss of their job. This law was created because of the tendency of employers to be rather callous in dealing with employees who have legitimate personal crises.

Drug Free Workplace Act and OSHA: The *Drug Free Workplace Act* allows employers to discipline or terminate employees who are using or distributing controlled substances in the workplace. The *Occupational Safety and Health Act* requires employers to meet certain standards regarding safety in the workplace. OSHA also created an agency to survey businesses and ensure that these standards are being maintained.

Worker's compensation laws: Worker's compensation laws are those statutes that require employers to pay workers or the dependents of workers who are injured or become ill on the job. These laws, which are typically enacted at the state level, also establish that employers are liable for illness and injury that occurs in their workplace. Generally, employers will be required to pay medical bills, disability benefits, and lost wages. In exchange, workers are prohibited from suing their employers for any more damages. One important piece of federal legislation relating to worker's compensation is the Occupational Health and Safety Act of 1970, which established standards for safety at various workplaces. Since then, there has also been federal legislation requiring employers to notify employees in advance of any major layoffs.

Ethics: One of the most important missions of the modern business education teacher is to show students what constitutes ethical behavior in the workplace. Put simply, ethical behavior is just good business sense; customers that are lost to unethical behavior are a much bigger concern to a company than any short-term profits that may be gained from the behavior. Companies work hard to earn reputations for ethical behavior because they know it will help them in the market. To this end, they discourage lying to customers, employee theft, and misuse of company time. If a business teacher can instill a good sense for business ethics in his or her students, then he or she has given them perhaps the most valuable tool for success in the contemporary workplace.

Utilizing and maintaining a specific code of ethics in the workplace: In order to ensure that all employees understand and can abide by the basic principles of business ethics, the manager s of a business should set out a concrete code of ethics for their company. In doing so, they should consider the general principles that will lead to fair business practice in their industry, and then confer with any similar organizations. The managers should then write out a specific code of conduct for employees, using examples from the business itself and making sure to square the code with company policy. Some businesses may find it necessary or advantageous to provide employees with specific training in ethics. Finally, the managers of a business should recognize that ethical decisions are not always easy to make, and therefore they should resolve to continually monitor adherence to the company code, and update the code if necessary.

Although every business will have a unique set of issues that are relevant to its operations, there are certain topics that are generally applicable to business, and should therefore be covered in any company code of ethics. These include the company policy for handling checks and cash from customers, as well as the forbidding of any preferential pricing for personal friends. Employees should know whether they can accept gifts from suppliers and business associates, as well as how they should deal with shoplifters or damaged merchandise. A company code of ethics usually includes provisions for making accurate advertising promises, handling problems with employee performance, the accounting procedures that will be used for cash sales, and how to deal with the return of purchased merchandise.

Job-hunting: As part of preparing students for entry into the job market, teachers need to show them the various places to look for jobs. One of the best places to find a job is still the classified ad section of the local newspaper. However, there are now many on-line listings for jobs as well. These are constantly changing, so business teachers will want to keep abreast of the most popular sites. Many part-time and odd jobs will be advertised on bulletin boards and message boards at local supermarkets and libraries. Magazines and trade journals often have job listings, too. One of the most obvious yet often overlooked ways to get a job is simply to ask for one. If students are interested in working for a particular company, they should have the skills and wherewithal to call and inquire about openings.

Resumes: A resume may be the most important document that students will ever compose in their lives, so it is essential that business teachers give them the skills to construct thoughtful and effective ones. It is essential first of all that students have an idea of who the target audience is for their resume. If they are applying for a babysitting job, for instance, they would want to highlight different aspects of their background than if they were applying for an internship with their local congressman. A student should think of the resume as a marketing tool, in which the product being sold is him or herself. To this end, a resume should make clear the unique and positive attributes of the student, without going into too much detail. After all, a resume aims to earn an interview, not necessarily a job. Too many resumes are overloaded with accomplishments, to the point where they are either unbelievable or unreadable.

Stylistic points: There are a few stylistic points that students should keep in mind when they are composing a resume. First, they should always use short, bulleted statements rather than lengthy descriptions. After all, they can expect that their potential employer is going to be looking over a large number of resumes, and so they need to make the information immediately accessible. A resume should try to use as many "action" words as possible, rather than using forms of "to be" or passive verbs. If the student is applying for a job in a particular field, then it may help to demonstrate some knowledge of the terminology associated with that field, as well as to display any experience doing the kind of work that will be required. Finally, and most obviously, a resume must contain no grammatical or spelling errors!

One of the quirky things about writing a resume is that, even though it lists your past achievements, it is actually supposed to be a document about your future. That is, an effective resume should be designed to suggest your ability to do whatever work you are aiming to do, rather than show your past successes in their best light. So, the accomplishments that you list should be those that will be the most impressive to your desired employer, not those that you happen to think are noteworthy. A good resume should always lead off with a statement of purpose, so that whoever reads it knows immediately what you would like to be doing. Then, you should design the rest of the resume as if it were an advertisement for yourself, showing how you can fill the role you desire.

Some students will have been a part of many organizations, received many awards, and just generally have acquired a number of tings to list on a resume. They should be discouraged from including everything. A proper resume will take its cues from its statement of purpose; in other words, if a certain achievement doesn't support your desire to do the work you are aiming for, it has no place on your resume. Including too much information will only confuse whoever reads the resume, and may result in that person not reading it any further. This may be of particular concern if you are applying for a job for which you feel overqualified. Many times, individuals in desperate need of a job apply for positions that are below their level of training. They may feel concerned that their full resume will put off potential employers; it is perfectly alright in such a case to omit certain data, as long as the resume remains truthful and doesn't contain any large gaps in the employment history.

Too often, resumes include long, detailed descriptions of the duties and responsibilities the applicant held at a previous job. For the most part, these summaries should be avoided in favor of lists of achievements at that job. The main reason for this is that a simple job description does not convey to the resume reader that the applicant is particularly good at his or her job; in many cases, it may simply tell the reader things about a certain job that he or she already knew or could have guessed. It is much better to alert the reader to whatever success you may have had in a previous position, or to indicate any special privileges or duties that would not normally be considered part of the job.

Honesty: In order for a resume to net the desired job, it should be oriented to promote the idea that you are capable of performing that job. In other words, you should avoid bragging about skills you no longer wish to use, or describing jobs you no longer wish to perform. Say, for instance, that you had a managerial job in a restaurant in which you were frequently called upon to wash dishes; it would be foolish to apply for another managerial position by mentioning how great your dish-washing skills are. This is not to say that one should lie about one's job history, but simply that one should only advertise what one has an interest in providing to a future employer. Nondisclosure (that is, not mentioning something) is not the same things as lying.

One of the most important things a student can learn about composing a resume is how foolish it is to ever lie on one. Resume lies can take a number of forms, from misrepresenting your duties and position at a former job to claiming to have degrees that you haven't obtained. No form of misrepresentation is acceptable on a resume; besides being immoral, it is bound to catch up with you. The advent of high-powered search engines has made it quite easy for companies to check up on the claims that their applicants make, and any candidate who lies on their resume can be assured that if it is discovered during the selection process they will be disqualified, and if it is discovered after they have been hired they will most likely be terminated.

Job objective: Every resume should begin with a job objective. The job objective sets the tone for the rest of the resume by answering three key questions: what position you are seeking to find, who should be reading your application materials, and how to interpret your resume. In order for this to work, of course, a job objective must be clear and precise. One should not say something like, "I want to improve myself and work as part of a cohesive team." Of course this may be true, but a potential employer needs to hear exactly what you want to do for his or her company, so that he or she can be start visualizing you in that position as he or she reads the rest of the resume. A strong objective, with action verbs and precise terminology, immediately separates a quality resume from the pack.

After a job objective is given, an effective resume will provide a brief Summary of Qualifications; that is, a list of the three or four best reasons for you to be considered for the job. This is the place to mention whatever you consider to be the most impressive, and most relevant, attribute that you have. This might include your experience, your credentials, your particular expertise, your work ethic, or your personality. Note that a summary of qualifications does not have to reference specific achievements. This is not to say, however, that it should be general. On the contrary, you should take this opportunity to highlight any skills that make you different from every other applicant, and worthy of special consideration.

Work history: The work history section of a resume is your opportunity to showcase whatever experience and training you have already acquired, so long as it is pertinent to the job for which you are applying. Even if a job you have had is not directly relevant to your desired job, however, it is a good idea to briefly list it so as to avoid giving the impression that you have been unemployed for long periods. If there are gaps in your employment record, it is a good idea to indicate that you were not just lying about during this period by entering something like "student" or "personal travel," and then giving a brief summary. Job candidates should avoid mentioning rehabilitation, unemployment, or personal illness unless it is absolutely necessary.

If you have been promoted at a past job, the work history section of your resume is the right place to indicate it. Future employers will naturally be impressed by candidates who have apparently thrived in their past jobs. In order to effectively show these promotions, you can create separate entries for each position you have held—just make sure to list the name of the company for each, so that people reading your resume won't think you simply changed businesses often. If in fact you have worked for a number of companies over a brief period of time, you should try to minimize the impression of flightiness this might give by simply listing the employment agency you were working with, or indicating that you were performing strictly contractual work by including a title like "consultant" or "contractor."

Every resume should include a list of whatever achievements either indicate particular skills relevant to the job or general personal qualities that will be appreciated in an employee. In fact, a successful resume will simply frame every job description in terms of achievements; that is, instead of describing responsibilities held and tasks performed, a good resume will list skills acquired and advances made. The idea that you are trying to convey by listing achievements is that you have the skills to do the job, you enjoy and are proud of these skills, and you hope to do more of the same in the future. For this reason, it is a good idea to downplay any achievements that may seem irrelevant to the job for which you are applying, and especially those which may make it seem as if you are overqualified.

Since business managers will read many letters of application, business students need to be equipped with some tools to help their letters stand out from the pack. The most important place to distinguish oneself is in the opening paragraph. Rather than use some formulaic introduction, students should be encouraged to pique the reader's interest with an anecdote, or a clever way of mentioning how the job came to his or her attention. Certainly, a letter of application should stay on the subject, but too many students damage their chances for employment by merely filling in the blanks of some cover letter model. Instead of doing this, the savvy applicant will indirectly demonstrate his or her intelligence and familiarity with the company without boring the reader with empty praise or false modesty.

<u>Cover letters:</u> In order for a letter of application (or cover letter) to have the desired effect, it must be tailored to its audience. This means finding out the name and title of the person who

will read the letter, even if it requires a bit of research to discover this information. A proper cover letter should also give the reader a bit of insight into the author; including some personal experience or anecdotes is a good way to distinguish one's letter from the rest. In this line, it is important to try and disguise whatever letter form the author may be using. Many applicants are helped by using available models of application letters, but it should never be apparent to the reader that a cover letter "formula" is being used. A cover letter should always strive to represent the individuality of the person it represents.

There are a few essential tips that concern the composition of all letters of application, and that any business class should be sure to impart to students. First, a cover letter should always refer the reader to the applicant's application, or to any other documents that may be contained in the same envelope. A cover letter should always end with a clear and courteous offer for an interview, and should of course include the same contact information as the resume. It goes without saying that any letters of application should be scrutinized closely for spelling and grammatical errors. An accomplished cover letter will be professional without being boring and interesting without being too casual. Students should be encouraged to always have a friend or mentor read their cover letters before submission.

Job interviews: In order to be fully prepared for a job interview, a candidate must have considered three areas. First, the candidate must have a general understanding of his or her own skill, strengths, and weaknesses. This is essential so that he or she can decide whether the job is truly an appropriate one for him or her. Next, the candidate must have prepared for the questions he or she is likely to be asked, both those that are standard to a job interview (for instance, why he or she would like the job, or what he or she already knows about the company) and those that are unique to the company. So that these last questions may be answered effectively, the candidate should also have spent some time researching the business as well as the job that is available. If possible, it is good to know a bit about the person who will be conducting the interview.

Too often, students assume that a job interview is always given with an eye towards getting a particular job. While this may be the usual case, it is also perfectly appropriate to interview for a job so that one can discover more about it, as well as about one's place in the job market. Many time, individuals will interview for a number of jobs they have no intention of taking, for the sole reason of polishing their interview skills. It is important to decide before an interview just exactly what your objectives are. One danger that candidates run when they interview only to seek information, however, is that they will discover mid-interview that they would like the job and they have not done adequate preparatory work for the interview. For this reason, it is best to always be as well-prepared as possible, and settle the question of objective before the interview begins.

One common misunderstanding of job interviews is that they are simply opportunities to go through a rehearsed monologue of one's skills and achievements. In actuality, one's ability to listen well may be more impressive to a potential employer. The candidate should make sure not to interrupt the interviewer, or fill in blanks in their sentences. If one is not sure about something the interviewer has said, it is always better to ask for clarification than to pretend comprehension. Too often, candidates are so focused on what they intend to say that they do not pay adequate attention to the tone and nuance of the interviewer; a well-prepared candidate should never have to worry about forgetting his or her lines.

Any candidate who hasn't got any questions about the employer during the interview is, whether intentionally or not, conveying the idea that he or she does not really care about the company. A candidate should always inquire about a few key areas. First, who are the business' chief competitors, and how does the business distinguish itself? What is the leadership structure of the business, and how long has the present leadership been in place? What particular issues or problems is the business dealing with at present? Does the company have a particular set of values? What is the "culture" of the company? Have there been any major changes in the business or in the industry as a whole that will affect the business in the near future? Questions like these convey to a potential employer that the candidate has a real interest in the business.

Once an individual has scheduled an interview with a particular company, he or she should seek to find out as much about that company as possible. There are a number of ways to go about this. First, he or she can simply ask the company to send along any brochures or promotional literature that might be helpful. He or she might also try to contact other businesses that work with the company, to ask them their opinions. A very simple way to procure some information is to do an internet search of the company, or to search at the local library for articles about the business. Finally, one can make use of one's own business network, to try and discern what the reputation of the business is in the local community.

Questions: In a job interview, closed questions should be the easiest to answer, although they may not necessarily be the most pleasant. Closed questions are those that require just a one or two word answer. Such questions might include whether the candidate has a college degree, what their grade point average was, or whether they have ever done similar work before. Usually, these questions are asked simply to verify information that is listed in an individual's resume, or to introduce lines of conversation that will then be developed more fully. As a candidate, one should avoid elaborating too fully on these kinds of questions, particularly if such elaboration might be seen as making excuses or qualifying negative aspects of a resume. One should simply answer these questions and move on.

Open questions are those that require more than just a simple one-word answer. An open question might invite a candidate to describe a past work experience, or to detail what it is about the company that interests him or her. These are good questions for well-prepared candidates, because they give him or her a chance to accentuate positive aspects of his or her resume, as well as to avoid mentioning qualities that might be viewed less favorably. One of the common dangers of these questions, however, is that they may lead to vague responses. If the candidate feels unsure exactly how to answer an open question, there is nothing wrong with politely asking the interviewer to narrow it down, or breaking it down him or herself into some simpler parts.

Leading questions are those which the interviewer poses with an eye towards introducing some further line of conversation. Leading questions can be very dangerous for a candidate if he or she is not well prepared. As an example, an interviewer might insinuate that one of your previous bosses was unfair or incompetent. While this may or may not be true, sometimes interviewers will use such a line of questioning to determine whether a job candidate is likely to be overly critical of authority, or to pass the buck. The best thing to do in an introductory interview is to try and remain diplomatic when presented with opportunities to be critical. A good candidate will not suggest that he or she is incapable of criticizing others, but will always emphasize his or her own responsibility as the most important concern.

Appropriate clothing: Perhaps the most important thing a job candidate can do is present a positive image with his or her dress. Although what is appropriate clothing will vary from job to job, it is generally agreed that a successful candidate will ensure that no aspect of his or her appearance will be uncommon for people in that profession. This may seem a rather soulless idea, but one should remember that the point of a job interview is to convey the impression that one can easily assume the role and responsibilities of the job. Even if one is supremely qualified otherwise, it will be difficult to convince a potential employer of this if one's first impression is wildly outside the norm. In a similar line, it is crucial that a candidate have performed the appropriate hygiene regimen before the interview; bad breath and body odor can kill job chances before the interview even starts.

Screening interview stage: The first in the series of job interviews is the screening interview. During their screening interviews, a company is just trying to narrow down a large field of potential candidates. These interviews may not be performed by the same individuals that will conduct later interviews, and they may even be performed over the phone. For this reason, candidates should always be prepared for a screening interview. This means having a copy of one's resume and cover letter close to the phone, and being able to provide succinct answers to basic questions. The main point of a screening interview is to ensure that candidates have the basic qualifications and skills to be further considered for vacancies.

Selection and confirmation stage: After the initial screening interview, a candidate should assume that his or her basic skills and achievements are known by the company. So, in the next interview (known as a selection interview), the goals should be to make clear what other skills the candidate will be able to bring to the business. If the selection interview goes well, there will be a final interview, the confirmation interview. In some cases, the confirmation interview may be simply a formality, in which the top executives get a chance to meet candidates who have already been approved for hire by the human resources department. Candidates who make it to a confirmation interview should just try and be polite, and not try too hard to sell themselves.

Business education program

Teaching problem-solving: Unfortunately, making ethical decisions in the business world is often quite difficult. Business teachers should recognize this fact, and equip their students with a good decision-making process. The first step in the process should be defining the problem; students may often jump to conclusions about a problem without ever really articulating it to themselves. Next, students should be trained to consider the various alternative solutions to the problem. Making a list on paper is a good way of externalizing choices. After this, students should get in the habit of identifying the consequences of the various proposed solutions. Consequences may be both short-term and long-term; as every businessperson knows, losing a customer in the name of short-term profit is always a bad decision. Finally, students should determine whether they have enough information to make decision, and if not they should have the discipline to acquire the information they need.

Promoting the program: Teachers should be familiar with some ways of promoting their classes to the local community, so that they can develop helpful relationships with local businesses. One good way to do this is by interacting with the community advisory councils from local businesses and municipal groups. These are committees whose only purpose is to discover ways in which the business can create positive connections with their community. Obviously, a great way for them to do this is by setting up relationships with local schools, and so they can become a wonderful resource for business teachers. Through partnerships with community advisory councils, business teachers can set up mentoring, job-shadowing, or internship programs, organize class trips, or simply acquire useful information about contemporary business practices.

In an effort to promote their programs and to establish relationships with local businesses, business teachers should avail themselves of every possible resource. One good way to access the outside community is to create a business class newsletter. This kind of document can be created with any basic desktop publishing program, and sent home with students or through the mail to local businesses. Often, the parents of business students are leaders in the business community themselves, and will be glad to help out if the class' needs are made clear. Business teachers may also find it helpful to advertise their requests for community involvement in the school newspaper, the school bulletin, or the newsletter for the local parent-teacher association

Typical equipment: Most business classes currently have a broad array of technology available to them. Teachers should anticipate having several computers (if not one for every student), a printer, a scanner, a television with VCR and DVD player, and a projector. Typically, all of the computers will have broadband access to the internet, so students can receive up-to-the-minute information. Students will probably also have access to graphing calculators, which can be used to demonstrate economic concepts as well as to calculate accounting data. Some teachers may want to make use of the telephones that most classrooms are equipped with in order to help their students with proper telephone etiquette.

Interpreting research: Many teachers find it useful to include in their curriculum any modern research and topics that can help enliven their subject matter for students. There are always new studies of business behavior being published in magazines, journals, newspapers, and on the internet, and it is wise for students not only to have access to this information, but to have learned the proper way to interpret it. Business teachers should strive to inculcate the same sort of skills in regards to research as they do in their consumer education program; that is, students should be trained to determine the quality of research, the source of that research, the potential interest of the source in presenting information of a certain type, and the usefulness of the research to the student.

<u>Vocational education:</u> Vocational education is the training of individuals to perform certain jobs. Often, large communities will have separate schools whose sole purpose is to cultivate workplace skills. These schools may work in conjunction with local industries to tailor the students' education to the anticipated job market. Vocational classes and schools may also offer cooperative training opportunities, in which students gain first-hand experience in their field of interest. As industrial work becomes more and more specialized, companies are requiring extensive vocational training and on-the-job experience for their employees. Public vocational education is designed to enhance the entire life of the worker; to this end, non-vocational classes are required so that students can earn a secondary degree as they gain work skills and experience.

<u>Competency-based instruction:</u> Most vocational classrooms now feature what is known as competency-based instruction. Loosely defined, competency-based instruction is a style of teaching in which progress is determined by students' mastery of skills rather than some arbitrary time limit. For example, in a business class, the teacher will ensure that every student is reasonably adept at making a basic budget before moving on. In a teacher-based classroom, a certain number of days would be allotted to each subject, and the teacher would adhere to this schedule whether students learned or not. Research has shown that a more learner-focused style of instruction, like competency-based instruction, ensures that students will retain the most of the curriculum. Teachers using competency-based instruction methods will be required to issue periodic assessments, so that they can gauge whether students have mastered a particular concept or skill.

<u>Computer technology:</u> In deciding when and how to use technology in a business class, teachers should bear in mind a few things. First, they should consider their degree of access to equipment. It is important that there be enough equipment for all students to remain involved throughout the course of the program. Teachers should also consider the amount of time available for the activity; most teachers have found that short, specific activities encourage the best use of time and equipment. It is important that teachers take into account their students' experience with the technology to be used, so that there is no delay and confusion over how to do the work. In this same line, teachers should have a back-up plan in case of technical malfunction. Finally, the teacher should ensure that students will be monitored, and that, particularly when the internet is involved, that all the subject matter will be appropriate to the age group.

<u>Educational acts:</u> The Vocational Education Act of 1963, also called the Carl D. Perkins Act of 1963, broadened the government's conception of vocational education. It established some procedures to provide part-time employment to students, and established a federal advisory council on vocational education. It also set aside some federal money for the construction of local vocational schools. This act also established some work-study programs enabling students to get real-life experience while earning some school credit. Some amendments were made to this act in 1968, including some direct support for cooperative education and a renewed emphasis on postsecondary education. The amendments also included new provisions for funding an expanded vocational curriculum.

The Carl D. Perkins Act of 1984 was issued in the hopes of improving the basic skills of the labor force and preparing students for the job market by enhancing vocational education. Specifically, the Perkins Act sought to establish equal opportunities for adults in vocational education, and to aid in the introduction of new technologies in vocational instruction. In order to meet its objectives, the Perkins Act set aside money for research into vocational education, as well as money to ensure access to vocational studies for people with disabilities, adults in need of retraining, single parents, and ex-convicts. This act was enhanced in 1990 with the issuing of the Perkins Vocational and Applied Technology Act. This act sought to integrate academic and vocational studies, as well as to fund better technology in vocational classrooms and better cooperation between the business and education communities.

Curriculum development

Curriculum goals: Before an administrator can decide which curriculum to use or design it is important to first decide what the curriculum goals are going to be. These goals should not be determined by only the administrator but also the staff and parents. They should use data that has been collected through assessments and decide what the areas are that need improvement. It is crucial to ask teachers what they want out of a curriculum and in what direction do they want their students to go. Parents should also be asked what they expect their children to learn when they are at school. A curriculum should be based on a group effort. It should focus on what everyone wants the students to achieve and what is best for the school. Many times the district will already have goals and the school can just add to those.

Interdisciplinary approach: The interdisciplinary approach is used to encourage learning across the curriculum. Lessons are set up to make thematic units in all learning subjects. Each subject will be connected to this thematic unit. The teacher is making links between each subject. When this method is used the student is able to learn without fragments during day and at the same time have a stimulating learning experience. The teacher chooses a topic or theme and then brainstorms activities to do in each subject area that revolve around this topic. Questions are then thought of in order to serve as the scope and sequence. The teacher can determine a grade by evaluating standards of performance levels or by using rubrics that evaluate the students completed work assignments.

Instructional resources: When an administrator is deciding what the curriculum needs are, he or she has several resources they can turn to. One of the best resources is the personnel. The teachers and teacher aides are vital to this decision. They are the ones teaching the curriculum and they are experts at knowing what additional needs there are. They will know if there needs to be more activities or if there should be an integration of another curriculum. There could also be a need of more materials. Many times there is a material shortage and not enough for each teacher to give to the students. The finances are another useful resource to use. Administrators need to be extremely careful and use the finances wisely when it comes to curriculum. Advisory groups, community agencies, and institutions can also be extremely resourceful when deciding the needs. These can give their opinion on what they think will best for the students.

Functions of the state: The development of curriculum at the state level involves creating guidelines concerning the development and implementation of curricula and ways of assessing student achievement. The state also creates the tests and other performance measures that are required for each academic subject. They should take a limited approach and focus assessment on language arts, social studies, science and math. There has been a movement toward assessments to test the student's ability to complete projects and open-ended problem solving rather than the tradition pencil and paper methods. It is also the responsibility of the state to provide the needed material and resources to local school districts. Often times the most desired resources are monetary support and technical assistance. The state must also decide the graduation requirements in terms of credits and competencies. These functions are general and allow the district more ownership in deciding what their needs and strengths are.

Functions of the district: Each district can implement any program of study they feel is necessary for their schools, however, it would be to the district's advantage if the program is consistent for each grade level and uniform for each academic subject. If the district ensures a consistent and uniform program of study this would help guarantee equity that all students across the district are getting an equal education. Another advantage is it makes it easier for a student to transfer within the district. A parent will not have to worry that their child is not on the same level with other students simply because they changed schools. The school district should create a mastery core curriculum that will explain the subjects that all schools will offer. A mastery core will also explain the goals and objectives of each subject. However, there is still the freedom and flexibility for each school to development their curriculum using the mastery core for guidance.

Functions of the school: After the school has received the curriculum's goals and objectives from the state and district, it is time for the school to make choices. The school's decisions will be made under the leadership of the principal and teacher leaders. The school will also collect the appropriate input from parents and then build a curriculum that is guided by the mastery core. The school should identify their goals and needs and then supplement any classes they feel are necessary to add in order to meet the student's needs. As a team, there will be a decision about the schedule, curriculum integration, and how to align and implement the curriculum. If this process is to be successful, it is important that the principal has strong leadership skills and is well informed and active in the development process.

Counseling

Theories and Principles

Learning theory

Behaviorism theory: The theory of behaviorism states that if a new behavior pattern is repeated so many times it will become automatic. This theory is associated with the Russian physiologist, Pavlov. He performed an experiment on a dog. The dog would salivate when it saw food, so Pavlov would ring the bell seconds before he showed the dog his food; therefore, he trained the dog to salivate after hearing the ringing of the bell. Another famous psychologist associated with this theory is an American, John B. Watson. He performed an experiment on a young boy named Albert. Albert was initially not afraid of a white rat, but when the rat was shown to Albert along with a loud noise, he soon became afraid of the rat. Skinner is also associated with behaviorism except he studied operant behavior. According to his studies the learner behaves a certain way according to the environment.

Cognitivism theory: This theory states that learning involves using certain information that has been stored in the brain. One of the most famous psychologists associated with this theory is Jean Piaget. A key concept of the cognitive theory is schema; existing internal knowledge that has been stored in the brain and compared to new knowledge. There is also the three-stage information processing model, which means information is inputted through a sensory register, then is made into short-term memory and last is made into long-term memory and used for storage and retrieval. Other key concepts are a meaningful effect, which means information that has meaning is easier to remember and learn. Serial position effects mean that a person can remember items on a list if they start from the beginning or end. Some other effects that are associated with this theory are; practice, transfer, interference, organization, levels of processing, state dependent, mnemonic, schema, and advance organizers.

Constructivism theory: The theory of constructivism states that a person develops their own knowledge based on their past experiences. This theory states that each learner is unique because every learner comes from a different background and experiences. Social constructivism encourages the unique traits in each individual learner. The learner should become involved in the learning process; therefore, the responsibility of learning does not solely rest on the instructor. The learner will take and active role rather than be passive. This theory also states that the learning environment should be set up in order to challenge the learner to their full potential. The instructor's role is not to just give the information and answers according to a curriculum, but rather to encourage the learner the find conclusions and answers on their own. The goal for the instructor is to help the learners become effective thinkers and challenge themselves.

Motivation

Behavioral views: There many behavioral learning theorists that have created techniques of behavior modification based on the idea that students are motivated to complete an assignment because they have been promised a reward. This reward can be praise, a grade, a ticket that can be traded in for something else or it can be a privilege of selecting an activity of their choice. There are also operant conditioning interpretations that explain why some students like a certain subject while others have a strong dislike for it. For example, math, some students love it and others hate it. The students have love math, may have been brought up to love it. Their past experiences may have shaped them this way because they have all been positive. On the other hand, the students who hate math may have had negative experiences.

Cognitive views: Cognitive theorists believe people are motivated because their behavior is influenced by the way some think about themselves and the environment around them. This view of motivation is heavily influenced by Jean Piaget who developed the principles of equilibration, assimilation, accommodation and schema formation. He stated that children naturally want equilibration which means a sense of organization and balance in their world. The cognitive theorists also believe that motivation comes from one's expectations for successfully completing a task. John Atkinson proposed motivation can also come from a person's desire for achievement. Some are high-need achievers and will seek out more challenging tasks, while others are low-need and will avoid challenging tasks. Those who avoid them do so because they have a fear of failure and that alone outweighs the expectation of success. William Glasser stated that for someone to be motivated to achieve success they must first experience success in some part of their lives.

Humanistic view: The humanistic view of motivation is heavily influenced by Abraham Maslow, most famous for Maslow's five-level hierarchy of needs. He proposed that everyone has five levels of needs and each level needs to be fulfilled first before moving on the next level. The bottom level is physiological needs, needs people need to survive, food, water, air and shelter. If this level is satisfied then people will be motivated to meet the needs of the next level, which is safety. After this level comes belongingness and love and after this level is esteem. These first four levels motivate people to act only when they are unmet to a certain point. The highest and last level is self-actualization, which is also called a growth need. Self-actualization is often referred to as a need for self-fulfillment. People come to this level because they have desire to fulfill their potential and capabilities.

Decision-making

Involving stakeholders : In order to involve stakeholders in the decision-making process, an administrator must first identify them. Stakeholders in education can be any group involved with education; however, the most notable groups are students, faculty members, teachers, administration, parents, school board members, legislators and community leaders. All these groups have a powerful impact on education. Many stakeholders want to take an active part in education while others choose to take a more passive role. Allowing stakeholders, especially parents, to be a part of the decision-making process can have a positive impact on their child's educational achievements and emotional development. Their ideas and opinions can be extremely helpful and it creates a unity between parents, teachers and administrators. However, there can be drawbacks, for example, if one group of stakeholders takes an active part, they can have too much power. There is a chance that this power could be used to create conflict.

Rational model : The rational model for decision-making is viewed as a process that first begins with the administrator admitting they are facing a problem. Then the administrator addresses this issue through a series of steps which in return comes out with an effective decision. This model focuses on what should be done and requires the administrator to follow certain actions that have already been designed to help achieve the best solution. It is assumed that the administrator is a rational administrator that works in an environment that functions rigidly and in a bureaucratic nature. Obviously, many school administrators do not work in this type of environment. This model does have some advantages; it clearly states the actions an administrator should take in certain situations and forces the administrator to decide which actions are most appropriate. However, this model has also shown that administrators are too quick in making decisions and do not attempt to try and find the true cause of the conflict.

Shared decision-making: Shared decision making, which is also known as participatory or site-based decision making is also built on the idea of choice. This model states that choices are made by the administrator in order to satisfy constraints. The focus of this model is on consensual decision making that is based on the values of the members in the group. The members of the decision making process also have open communication and everyone's status is equal. The whole idea of a participatory decision-making theory centers on the idea of the way administrators make decisions versus how they should make decisions. Some critics believe this way of making decisions limits the control of the decision maker and they believe administrators are influenced by other's personalities and values more than their own reason or intelligence.

Strategic decision-making: When an administrator uses this model, they are making a decision based on information they have gathered for their own knowledge and evaluating the internal and external environment. The environment is made up of interest groups, negotiation, and informal power. In order for this model to work, the members need to identify what the obstacles are as well as what challenges may impact the decision choice. An administrator will want to use this model if they are interested in making a plan that has room for change, is flexible and has a long term effect. It is important that the individuals involved with this decision have the same philosophy and purpose in common. There will situations when unexpected events occur and an administrator may find themselves making decisions based on these unexpected events despite trying to strictly use the strategic decision making model.

Differentiated or situational decision-making model: This decision-making model does not follow the traditional way of thinking. The administrator needs to take into consideration a variety of points and each point will affect the decision choice in some way. Certain situational variables can have an impact on how the administrator will make their decision choice. This model recognizes that administrators may need to take a different approach in deciding what is best for the school. A decision can be made regarding the goals of the school itself or just about the whole process. Other factors that administrators should take into consideration are ethical considerations, values, culture and climate. It is important that administrators are prepared that different situations will arise and the need for a decision may be needed immediately. The process will not be the same each time, different situations call for different decision making processes.

Process of decision-making: Making a decision is a process that takes valued information and opinions from others and in return make a choice that you think is best. This whole process follows steps in order to achieve that decision. The first step is defining the situation that needs a decision. This is the time to fully investigate and gain an understanding of what the problem is. The next step is identifying the alternatives that can be used to make a decision. It is important for the administrator to know there can be more than two alternatives. After identifying the alternatives, the next step is to assess them. When the administrator is at this step, they should consider if they have the resources or power to implement a certain alternative and what kind of reception will they receive. When a desirable alternative has been chosen, then it is time to implement it. An administrator may encounter resistance or complete acceptance. After it has been implemented, the administrator should evaluate the decision and see if any other decisions need to be made.

Assessing decision-making: Assessing decision-making effectiveness is an important process in order for an administrator to improve as a decision maker. Administrators are extremely busy people and this can be a challenge to complete, therefore, often times this step is overlooked. It can be difficult for an administrator to be objective about their decision, especially since they have invested so much of their time. It might be helpful to involve outsiders who do not have vested interest in the assessment process. There is a chance that the decision's effectiveness could reflect negatively on the administrator. However, if the administrator wants continued improvement for their school, they should occasionally asses the effectiveness of their decision. Many times there will not be enough time to assess every time a decision is made; however, if he or she wants to improve their decision-making skills, a periodic check will be in their best interest.

Intelligence theories

Recent research: Too often teachers recognize intelligence solely in terms of verbal and mathematical ability. Recent research has shown that there a number of different ways to be intelligent. with these various ways of expressing knowledge so that they can best work with each student. Instead of focusing on reading ability alone, teachers should try to identify creativity, innovation, group maintenance, visualization skill, strength and dexterity, reasoning skills, problem-solving skills, curiosity, and persistence. These are all forms of expressing intelligence. By becoming attuned to their students' various strengths and weaknesses, teachers can determine the best way to present their material.

Benjamin Bloom: Benjamin Bloom and his team of researchers redefined education by declaring that it is not simply the acquisition of knowledge, but the development of three distinct spheres of knowledge-based skills. These spheres are the cognitive, affective, and psychomotor, and they are known collectively as Bloom's taxonomy. The cognitive sphere is the ability to make a sequential reasoning, and depends on the individual's knowledge and comprehension of a given topic. The affective sphere has to do with the way the individual reacts emotionally, and their ability to imagine other emotional states. The psychomotor sphere has to do with the ability to physically manipulate a tool or instrument.

According to Bloom, the development of every sphere of knowledge (that is, the cognitive, affective, or psychomotor) passes through six successive levels. At the first level, knowledge, one can recite facts or concepts from memory. The next level of knowledge is comprehension, in which one can demonstrate an understanding of facts through organization and comparison. After comprehension comes application, in which the individual can use the acquired knowledge to solve new problems. One then acquires the ability to analyze the new information, breaking it down into parts and identifying causes or motives. After analysis comes synthesis, in which one can compile information in a different way, and propose alternatives to some of its parts. Finally, one should be able to evaluate the new knowledge, developing opinions about it that can be supported with reasonable arguments.

<u>Howard Gardner:</u> The renowned Harvard psychologist Howard Gardner determined after long research that there are eight major forms of intelligence. They are logical-mathematical (ability to reason deductively and inductively, or to see rational patterns), linguistic (ability to read and write easily, and to appreciate subtle differences in language), musical (ability to discern pitch and rhythm), spatial (ability to create visual-spatial representations of the world), bodily-kinesthetic (ability to use the body to solve problems, make things, and convey ideas), interpersonal (ability to work effectively with others and empathize with them), intrapersonal (ability to work effectively by one's self), and naturalist (ability to distinguish among and use effectively the various features of the environment). Gardner is currently exploring a ninth intelligence: existential (the capacity to reflect on questions of life, death and ultimate realities).

Counselor's Role

Explaining counselor's role

Counselors are not only responsible for explaining their role in the session, but this explanation can and should serve to establish a relationship of trust and collaboration with the student. It is important for counselors to be sensitive to a student's age when explaining his/her role. In other words, for a younger student, the counselor might couch the discussion with the explanation that s/he wants to help the student feel better, whereas for an adolescent this type of explanation could easily be deemed condescending. For adolescent students, it might be advisable to first begin by asking the student of his perception of the goals and purposes of counseling, and then elucidate or clarify from there. Counselors will often be also responsible for explaining the role and purpose of counseling to parents, and need to be sensitive to this approach, particularly in relation to explaining to the student.

Individual Counseling

Counseling concerns

Through addressing such issues as relationship issues, anger or stress management, family dynamics, sexual topics and academic goals, the counselor acts as a guide and mentor for students in their academic and personal lives, as well as in the process of choosing a career. Since students may be referred by school officials, family members or other students, the counselor should anticipate varying levels of openness by the student and/or the family. It is vitally important for counselors to be trained in the strategies and techniques necessary to recognize and address issues in a manner that will capitalize on the counseling session to the maximum benefit of the student. The first step in this process is recognition of the key issue or issues, which may take more than one session to determine. Beyond that, counselors can use various strategies focusing on the particular situation as well as the individualities of the student.

Individual counseling

Foremost in the school counseling model is the establishment and also the perception of a trust relationship between counselor and student. This includes, but is not limited to, developing a relationship of trust and cooperation. This trust and cooperation sometimes needs to be established over a period of several visits, and is augmented by a strict policy of confidentiality by the counselor, further contributing to the safe environment. The dynamics of identifying and addressing key or underlying issues can be very positive and productive in a counseling setting when the relationship between the counselor and student is established, during as many sessions as is reasonable. An added benefit of numerous sessions can be the student's receptiveness to the counselor's recommendations, ideally working with the counselor on possible resolutions.

Responsibility to individual student: It is important to remember that the primary responsibility of the counselor is to the student body and the school community as a whole. This community includes parents, teachers, the student body and even other counselors. Within this context, counselors can and should strive to address the needs of individual students who will most benefit from individual counseling, particularly as it relates to their academic development and success. The counselor's role is to assess individual students to determine if one-to-one counseling would be beneficial, and then to implement that counseling if it appears it would be helpful to the student, particularly as it relates to his or her academic success. If a counselor feels a student is in need of additional therapy or therapy beyond an academic context, it is recommended that the student be referred to outside agencies or other appropriate resources.

Criteria to be addressed: An initial consideration for the school counselor is that of scheduling the session at a time that is least intrusive to the academic day, tempered by factors that are most beneficial to the student. Although the primary consideration is that of respect to the academic setting, the counselor also should be sensitive to student nuances, such as students who may be more receptive after school hours as opposed to during a time in the middle of the day. Beyond that, within the session format, the counselor needs to strategically incorporate the particular needs of the student within the context of developing and implementing therapeutic goals. It is important to couch counseling techniques in a way that will be most effective, such as considering a student's developmental or situational hindrances. Further, the counselor should develop rubric for assessing the success of the therapy.

Group counseling

Adolescents as a rule tend to learn better and respond more when interacting with peers. Therefore, group counseling that augments individual counseling can be beneficial for several reasons. In group counseling, students have the opportunity to both experience and contribute support for positive behaviors. Likewise, group counseling provides immediate feedback for negative behaviors and thought patterns, allowing the student to reflect on his or her choices. The format of a group counseling session can also serve as a microcosm of larger society, providing a venue for students to experiment with behaviors in a controlled environment, and to experience the feedback of peers with whom they have developed a trust relationship. The group counseling, in tandem with the more remedial individual counseling, provides a comprehensive therapeutic environment for the student. Counselors who utilize both formats reap the benefits of opportunities for preventative therapy, as well as a richer school counseling program.

Basic types

Group counseling sessions are generally categorized by their focus and purpose. Task groups focus on an activity or activity, bringing the members together for a common purpose or activity. Some typical tasks for this kind of group may include peer assistance groups, crisis response teams, etc. Other students who need to focus more on specific issues related to life management and may be better served in either a psycho-educational group or a counseling group, both of which usually take place in a classroom setting. Some of the issues to be addressed can include skill development, major life changes, or working on personal values. More severely affected students will likely be in a psychotherapy group, which addresses chronic or severe issues of maladjustment. These sessions generally take place in the setting of a mental health institution rather than a school.

Psycho-educational groups

To appreciate the distinctions between psycho-educational and counseling groups, it is a good idea to first identify the similarities. Either group can function to address life management issues such as loss, stress issues, academic success, etc. Either group can be categorized into developmental, remedial or school environments. Where they differ lies in the focus within the groups and group sessions. Counseling groups tend to address matters of managing crisis in their focus areas, targeting issues of process more so than specific content issues. Psycho-educational groups, conversely, apply a more concentrated focus on particular content. Counseling groups tend to be less structured than psycho-educational groups. The effect and impact on students of the two groups is often perceived as distinctively different, although counselors tend to view them as similar in format and purpose.

Psycho-educational groups serve to address and develop personal growth factors within an academic or educational setting. The academic setting provides a framework for targeting common adolescent issues such as emotional development, self-image, identity definition, and interpersonal social skills. The student in the psycho-educational group develops socially and emotionally in tandem with addressing academic skills. The counselor in the psycho-educational setting can take advantage of the opportunity to provide students with increasingly developmental tasks toward optimum benefit for the student. An important added benefit of this model is that it provides students with an array of resources, contributing to an increased feeling of self-worth and self-confidence. An effective psycho-educational counseling group can contribute positively to the futures of the students involved, by both mitigating future problem occurrences, as well as providing a cache of resources that will be useful in career planning.

The initial consideration for choosing topics for psycho-educational groups should be the age and developmental levels of the students involved. While adolescent and pre-adolescent groups will respond better to groups focusing on social and interpersonal skills, groups of younger students would find more to connect with in a friendship or play group, or one focused on problem solving. These topics or themes can provide a framework for students to address peripheral issues. It might be advantageous to refer to the school's agenda for academic and social skill development, in order to glean topics or a series of topics for psycho-educational groups. Some typical topics, particularly for adolescents, could include stress management, romantic relationships, time management or career planning. It is also a good idea to ask the school if there are any survey instruments that they have utilized in identifying topics of interest among their students.

The first step in creating a psycho-educational group is to define the following: purpose of the group, anticipated membership, focus of the group, and interventions and expected outcomes.

Secondly, the counselor should clearly identify both long-term objectives and measured short-term steps toward those objectives, applicable to each session. It is important to delineate the steps necessary toward achieving objectives. Develop content and exercises that use an experiential framework which will incorporate and address the following:
- The demographics and targeted needs of the group
- Educational content that fits within the students' academic agendas
- Opportunities for students to learn from experience
- A format that allows students to make connections between tasks and skills addressed
- Exercises that generate group discussion and response

Lastly, evaluation of the success of the group should include evaluation of each session and process involved in achieving the long-term objectives.

Focus and student population

Counseling groups are generally formed to address personal issues that hinder or prohibit academic success. The groups can target behavioral problems such as outbursts of temper, disruption of class, social maladjustment, etc.; or they can target specific life-altering events such as a death, a pregnancy or other event precipitating a personal crisis. The groups are formed to specifically work on the personal issues aside from any academic issues that have resulted from the personal situation. Students referred to counseling groups have demonstrated an inability or significantly lessened ability, particularly in the case of a personal crisis, to manage and positively respond to their academic responsibilities. Within the counseling groups, facilitators can provide an environment for students to benefit from peer support, including buffeting a sense of isolation. Benefits include a stronger sense of self-worth as well as healthy strategies to handle emotions.

Parameters

The counseling group provides a venue for students to express and process overwhelming emotions in a controlled environment. The overall tone of the group should be one of caring, compassion, and empathy. Many of its members will have experienced, or will be experiencing, similar events and emotions. The format of the group should be one of support, trust, and understanding. Members of the group should feel a sense of camaraderie with the other members. Acting as facilitator, group counselors can encourage peers within the group to provide support and suggestions for emotional healing to the other members, contributing to the general benefit of all its members. Counselors should also be cognizant of each student's need to address both actions and thought patterns in the process of working through their issues or trauma with the group.

Crisis-centered groups: A crisis-centered group is formed in response to a traumatic precipitating event. The event could involve a few individuals, or could be school-wide, such as a shooting or other crisis involving a population. The overarching purpose of a crisis-centered group is that of providing a controlled venue where students can express their feelings. In the case of an issue involving a few students, such as a disruptive conflict between students, an additional goal of the crisis-centered group is to facilitate resolution of the conflict. In this case, the group will form for the purpose of resolution, and at least until the matter is resolved. In the case of a large population trauma, the group will form to assist the students in coping with the trauma and/or loss. In both of these instances, additional meetings could be held to work on personal development issues for the student members.

Problem-centered groups: Problem-centered groups are often an outgrowth of crisis-centered group, formed after the crisis has passed or been resolved, for the purpose of addressing issues that could erupt in future problems or crises, and may have been one of the precipitating factors. The students in these groups come together to focus on specific issues that may be hindering their academic progress, or their general well-being. Some of the issues that are addressed in problem-centered groups include such issues as managing stress, conflict resolution strategies, academic or career goals, and possibly substance abuse. The effectiveness of the groups depends on the receptivity of its members to resolution. Participation in problem-centered groups is usually an option chosen by the students involved. The members of these groups, which are usually smaller than crisis-centered groups, benefit from the support and input from other members in resolving an issue that may feel overwhelming when faced alone.

Growth-centered groups: Similar to problem-centered groups, growth-centered groups often form as an outgrowth of another group. While a preceding group, such as a crisis-centered group, might be formed to address a shared crisis or situation such as anger management, the growth-centered groups instead address each individual student's issues and concerns, which may be peripheral or contributory to the group topic. Under the umbrella topic of a common issue such as anger management, students may be dealing with low self-esteem, stress as a result of poor time management, conflicting value paradigms, etc. The tone of the group is supportive, and empathetic, allowing students to develop healthy responses to their situation in a controlled environment. The group as a whole works on positive behavior dynamics, as a group and addressing each individual in the group. Growth-centered groups allow counselors to identify and address students on an individual basis.

School setting groups: Once a counselor perceives a need to form a group, based on input from teachers, parents, and/or students, the following parameters need to be explored and established:
topic and purpose of the group, group meeting schedules and time allotted for sessions,

proposed members of the group, including group size, and stablished process and rubric for recruiting and screening potential members. The focus and purpose of these groups should be primarily for the benefit of the students, within the context of the therapeutic paradigm. Counselors should discuss the group's formation with teachers and other school personnel as appropriate before launching the group. Issues of confidentiality should be clearly and firmly established, and communicated clearly to students, parents, and school personnel. Although the groups are generally established for the benefit and well-being of the students, the issue of confidentiality and other counseling ethics continue to apply.

Group size and length of sessions: Both group size and session length are primarily determined by age and developmental level of the participants. One of the key deciding factors is the ability for certain age groups to focus on a topic for a specific period of time. Since younger elementary children have shorter attention spans, a rule of thumb for them is to have group sessions lasting about 20 minutes, with about 5 members. Older elementary students, roughly grades 4 through 6, can meet for periods of time spanning from 30 to 45 minutes, in groups of 7 or so. High school students will benefit from an expanded length of session, but still fare better with smaller numbers. The ideal group size for high school students is 6 to 8, meeting for 40 to 50 minutes. If a counselor feels that a particular group could extend the recommended time or group size, s/he should refer to research regarding both the topic and the group size.

Group dynamics can be very much impacted by the size of the group. There need to be enough participants to provide for peer feedback and support as appropriate, but not such a large group that individuals are eclipsed by it, or that focus becomes dissipated. In addition to consulting published standards regarding ideal group sizes for age group, counselors can determine effective group sizes by considering the age or developmental level of the group, for instance the short attention spans of the participants. The topic being addressed is also a factor. If the strategies indicated for a particular topic, for instance individual exercises versus group exercises, that will impact the choice of group size, of course smaller group sizes allowing for more individual participation. Further, counselors can consider the individual participants in the group, including their modes and likelihood of participation, when determining group size.

Scheduling: It is important to remember that the responsibility of the school counselor is simultaneously for the student as well as the school community. Because of that, the counselor should work with school personnel and school schedules when developing group counseling schedules. This is particularly pivotal in high school and middle school because counseling sessions that are scheduled at the same time every day, or every week, will necessarily impact that same school subject because of the way classes are scheduled. Collaboration with teachers and other school personnel is probably the first best approach, soliciting their input about best and worst times to schedule counseling sessions, such as avoiding sessions on days when standardized tests are administered. Beyond that, it is always a good idea to stagger group counseling sessions, especially in the middle or high school setting, although this may be the case in an elementary school also, if indicated by the teachers.

Collaboration

An effective counseling group is reliant on the support, endorsement and collaboration of parents, teachers and school administrators. It is important that these individuals and administrative groups understand and support the importance and goals of the counseling groups. Counselors can work with parents and school personnel to sensitize them to the importance of counseling groups. One of the common concerns is that counseling groups ask students to spend time that could otherwise be spent in the classrooms. It is important to stress to parents and school personnel that the time students spend in the classroom is generally more effective if students are allowed to address personal, time management and other issues in counseling sessions, that can hinder their performance and success in the classroom. Once counselors have established this understanding with parents and school personnel, they can unite in a partnership for the students' benefit.

It is important for individuals advocating the creation of counseling groups to first emphasize the comprehensive nature of a counseling program within the school setting, pointing out that an effective counseling program works collaboratively with parents and school groups. It should also be stressed that counseling groups serve to address personal issues that can hinder academic performance. Developing a counseling program also should include vehicles for input from school personnel and parents in particular. It might be advisable to hold meetings in tandem with PTA or other parent groups, providing a forum for open communication about the need for and implementation of a counseling program. It is recommended that these presentations be held early in the academic year, to allow for the process of discussion and consensus. It is also important for these meetings to be facilitated by professional counselors who can appropriately address questions and concerns. Regular communication with parents and school personnel provides continued interface regarding both future and existing counseling groups. Some of the channels for keeping this communication open include:

- Regular, informative meetings with school administrators discussing current counseling groups, future plans, and any peripheral activities occurring.
- Distribution of surveys assessing specific needs for groups, or for topics to be addressed
- Share information about groups needed as well as groups being formed, as appropriate, to parents and school personnel.
- Be available on a regular basis to hear from school personnel regarding student issues or concerns, that may precipitate the need for a counseling group.
- Speak with students in their classrooms about the availability of counseling groups, and provide a clear and confidential process by which they can bring concerns forward.
- Develop and communicate clear procedures for group formation, group participation, and parental and school permission.

Topic determination

Choice of topics for counseling groups should be representative of the needs of the school community and/or student body. Many topics to be addressed will arise out of regular meetings between counselors and the school staff, or from meetings with parents. Others may be revealed through the surveys that are distributed to parents, students and school staff. Students themselves can also be a source of potential topics, particularly if they are provided with a clear and confidential process for bringing these concerns forward. Counselors can be proactive in the process of choosing topics, and ask groups to suggest topics, or to choose from a series of topics that might be of interest. Once the counselor has established him/herself as a responsive conduit for topic suggestions, there should be a body of recommendations available from which to determine best topics to be addressed in counseling groups.

Another resource for assessing the need for counseling groups and topics is that of school records. These records can produce profiles that may reveal patterns of low retention, poor attendance, low test scores, or other identifiable areas of need. Counselors can also research commonalties of specific age groups to determine which topics would most likely be appropriate and well received. These topics can range from healthy social behavior to career planning. Some of these general areas can be addressed through specific focus on life experiences, such as beginning a college prep program in high school. It is important that development of groups and group topics be well researched in terms of not only common topics for a particular age group, but the applicability of these topics to the particular student body, as documented by school records and the input of school personnel.

As a part of a comprehensive counseling program that includes addressing specified needs, counselors can also include topics that are generally relevant to particular age groups. Some of these age-specific topics include:

- *Elementary students:* Students in this age group are dealing with issues relating to such topics as friendships, family roles, problem solving, social behaviors, success in school, expressing emotions, and self-esteem.
- *Middle school students:* Middle school students are particularly embroiled in issues relating to body image, interpersonal relationships, social skills, conflict management, social roles, diversity issues, self-esteem, transitioning to a new school, and academic development.
- *High school students:* As students are preparing to transition to adulthood, topics that are most relevant include career exploration and planning, dating protocol, intimate relationships, self-identity, assertiveness training, stress management and time management.

Although many of these topics overlap between age groups, counselors need to be cognizant of the level of development present in the particular student group or population in the counseling group.

Screening

The primary considerations for selecting and screening students for group counseling are the willingness and capability of the student to participate in a therapeutic group setting. Students may be referred by parents, teachers, other students or self-referred. While the self-referred students may intrinsically be indicating their willingness to participate, the other types of referrals indicate the need for counselors to screen students to see if they are amenable to group counseling. All students should be screened for capability to participate in a group setting, and if a group counseling format would be beneficial for them. In general, the counselor should consider the parameters of the group setting, which include both speaking and listening, respecting confidentialities and differences among its members, as well as other components of the group format, when screening potential group members. Some counselors prefer to have individual meetings with potential members before the first meeting; others devote the first meeting to information and screening.

Role of demographics: While it is not always indicated for counselors to specifically focus on demographics when choosing group participants, it is nonetheless a good idea to be aware of the demographics vis-à-vis the topics being addressed. Sometimes the referral process might result in a default group of students that is primarily one gender or one ethnicity. Although there are no definitive rules about this, it is often a good idea to include a spectrum of cultures and mix of genders in a group setting, when working with all age groups, but more so with adolescent students. This often allows for students to address personal and social skills in a mixed group, within the controlled environment of the counseling session. Younger children may be more comfortable in a group of their own gender. Of course, if the topic relates to culturally- or gender-specific topics, then the group would be comprised of student falling within the specified category.

Role of topics: Selecting group members based on topic can be approached somewhat holistically, in that some topics may be interrelated, however the group members will want to experience similarities and empathy among themselves. For instance, if the topic being addressed is dealing with authority, which may include students who stay out after curfew, as well as students who are perpetually late to class. Students whose parents are divorced may relate with students who recently moved from their home town, both of them dealing with separation issues and disenfranchisement. Nonetheless, if students are in fact dealing with the same issue, there may be enough diversity in personality in coping skills to comprise a dynamic group. In terms of age similarities, it is a good idea to have students in a group who are within the same age group or developmental level, although a small spectrum of emotional maturity can provide the interactive component that is valuable in a group setting.

Soliciting participation : Finding appropriate members for a counseling group can be a combined endeavor of advertising and referrals. Of course, counselors should have a profile of the types of groups that would be relevant and beneficial for a particular student body, which would arise out of conversations and other input from students and school staff. Often, this input will include referral of specific students and the need for group sessions focusing on particular topics. Counselors may otherwise know of students who would benefit from certain types of groups. Once the need for a group has been indicated, counselors can interest others in the group with notices in newsletters, flyers, word of mouth, or talking with students, groups of parents or school personnel. The counselor should specify the topic to be addressed, the philosophy and general format of group counseling, and the proposed times for the sessions.

Particular components and format ot screening: A good way to begin the screening process is for the counselor to give the student an overview of the group counseling format. This overview should include the purpose of the group, the role and expectations of the members, and the role and expectations of the counselor. The counselor should provide an opportunity for the student to ask questions, and express any concerns or anxieties s/he has about the group format. In the

- 93 -

context of this conversation, the counselor should look for indications that the student is either likely or unlikely to be able to participate in a group setting. Some of these indications relate to the student's ability to follow the rules of the group, his or her ability to commit to attend, participate and contribute in the group setting, his or her emotional capability to participate, and lastly his or her willingness to participate.

<u>Making referrals:</u> Students who are indicated as not suitable for the group counseling format may be referred to individual counseling. Although some students referred to individual counseling may never participate in group counseling, others may transition from individual to group counseling. For these students, the counselors will want to make a determination of readiness based on specific criteria. S/he then should communicate to parents the recommendation, and the criteria met, specifically improvements or maturity in particular areas that indicate the student's readiness for group counseling. The intent, format, and expectations of the group setting distinguished from individual counseling should be included. Counselors should refer to school policy regarding additional procedures to follow when transitioning a student in this manner. Also, students referred into group counseling from individual counseling should sign a consent form indicating his/her understanding, readiness and commitment to the group setting.

Guidelines and rules

Once the members of a group are selected and brought together, either at the first meeting or a pre-meeting, the counselor should give an overview of the guidelines and expectations of group counseling. This first meeting or pre-meeting will define the individual members as a group brought together for a purpose. As a collaborative group, students can be given a presentation of the ground rules in group counseling, and then individually sign forms of understanding and consent. These ground rules can include the importance of commitment, issues of conduct, and the importance of respect and confidentiality. It is significant that they agree to these ground rules as a group, since they will be implementing them as a group, with the counselor as facilitator. The counselor can also talk about group expectations, and allow members to voice their concerns and expectations.

Ground rules in a group counseling setting serve to cohere its members in unity of conduct and purpose. When reviewing ground rules, it is helpful to solicit input from the members, allowing them to participate in the establishment of the ground rules. Rules also contribute to a healthy and productive dynamic in a group setting. Lastly, rules can provide and ensure a sense of safety and trust in the counseling environment. Some typical rules which address these issues include, but are not limited to:
- Give respect to the counselor and other members by listening attentively and without interruption.
- Be willing to participate and contribute by sharing feelings and experiences.
- Respect the experiences, perspectives and backgrounds of the other members.
- Although confidentiality cannot be legally mandated for group members as it is for counselors, it is nonetheless effective to have members include a commitment to confidentiality in their overall consent to the ground rules.

Group counselor

The counselor in a group setting has the overall role of balancing and maintaining healthy and productive group dynamics. This includes attending to both the group as a whole and to the individual members. The counselor needs to be sensitive to the levels of participation within the group, observing fairness and contribution from all members. S/he should be available for consultation regarding any concerns, and act as the overseer and reminder of the ground rules. Counselors should facilitate the interaction of the members toward the benefit of each of the members. This may involve working with a resistant student, or intervening when there is negative, unproductive behavior. The counselor in a group setting can encourage group dynamics, while working with individual vicissitudes of exploration as appropriate. S/he should also strive toward a more integrated and self-regulating group by encouragement and guidance.

Particularly in a group counseling setting, counselors need to be sensitive to the possibility of the group becoming distracted and losing focus of the topic and goal(s) of the group. Although there will be a modicum of flexibility to incorporate the individual needs of the participants, it is the role of the counselor to maintain the focus and progress of the group. One of the early safeguards against this possibility is clear communication to the members, parents and school staff as appropriate, about the a) purpose and goal(s) of the group, as well as b) an overview of the therapeutic format and c) the process of resolution in a group setting. Defining and reviewing the goals and parameters of the group with participants is also helpful. It is important for counselors to be well-versed of the basic tenets of group dynamics in a therapeutic setting.

Since school counselors are working with students of different ages and developmental levels, they need to be sensitive to any developmental issues present as well as the overt topic. In the context of implementing strategies targeting the whole of the group, counselors may need to refine or revise their methodology in relation to the age group, or to the developmental level of its members. Within each age group are often inherent developmental crises such as separation anxiety, individuation, or self-worth, and counselors need to incorporate sensitivity to these crises in their topic-based strategies. A six-year-old will have different coping strategies than a fifteen-year-old, even though the topic for both may be divorce. However, these age-based sensitivities should not mitigate counseling strategies, but rather serve to make them more effective and more readily received. Some therapeutic strategies that have been successful in the school setting include cognitive therapy, reality therapy, Adlerian therapy and SFBC.

Knowledgeable about the group topic: Although no one can, or would want to, experience every difficult situation, it is nonetheless important for anyone in a therapeutic relationship to feel a sense of empathy and recognition from the counselor. This allows students to feel safe, understood, and not isolated in his or her situation. Therefore, it is important for counselors to have a basic knowledge of topics that will be addressed in group counseling. They should be able to discuss the processes and effects of such situations as divorce, teen parenting, stress management, poor academic performance, and peer pressure. It is also valuable to develop a cache of information and resources about particular topics that can be shared with students. Counselors can also recommend activities or anecdotes that relate to the student's situation.

Combined, these not only provide the empathy of knowledge, but also can serve to assist and empower students toward resolution.

Multisensory stimulation: Students exposed to multisensory stimulation are found to be more engaged, more responsive, and more attentive. This is particularly valuable in a group setting, since one of the inherent weaknesses is the ease with which its members can become distracted. Multisensory stimuli involve the mind and senses of children and adolescents, and target multiple intelligences. This is particularly valuable in a group setting, comprised of unique individuals with unique coping and learning styles. These stimuli provide the group with a comprehensive, experiential mode for addressing issues. Through the use of such creative and multisensory stimuli as puppets, music, drama, and movies, counselors can generate response and participation when broaching difficult topics. An added benefit is that of students forging positive associations between the topic and creative stimuli. Various media such as film, or puppets for younger audiences, can serve to present a problem in a manner that may be more palatable than a lecture format.

Cultural differences: Particularly in a school setting, counselors will often work with students from varied cultural and ethnic backgrounds. Knowledge of the belief systems, perspectives, and sensitivities of an array of cultures and ethnicities is invaluable when working with students from varied backgrounds, particularly in a group setting. The foundation of this knowledge lies in a recognition of the far-reaching influence of culture, as well as personal biases and perceptions that the counselor might have. Counselors should also be aware of misunderstandings and miscommunications within the group that might be culturally based, and work with the group to resolve these misunderstandings. In this context, students in the group can also gain an appreciation for different cultures, and an acceptance of the practices and belief systems within those cultures. A group counselor who possesses a knowledge and sensitivity of diverse cultures is a valuable resource in the school community.

Planning: It is the counselor's role to maintain focus on the topic, goals, and strategies to employ in each group and session. Therefore, it is important to approach each session with enough preparation beforehand to be able to facilitate the session effectively. This preparation should include discussion topics, planned activities and an informal agenda. Within the grid of this agenda, counselors will often allow time and flexibility for longer group discussion, particular concerns that might arise in the session, or individual responses or behaviors that may require extra time and attention. However, because of the preplanning and the agenda, counselors can redirect the group toward activities, specific discussion topics and the goals of that particular session, to maintain the focus and progress of the group. The activities and discussion topics in each session are understood as part of a larger agenda outlining the long-term goals of the group.

Beginning sessions: Before tackling the topic(s) and goal(s) of a counseling group, facilitators should first establish the environment and tenor of the group. In the first session or sessions, participants can become acquainted and possibly share a bit about themselves. The counselor's role is to assist in establishing an environment that is understood as safe. It is important that participants experience a sense of camaraderie with the other group members. Throughout the remainder of the sessions, they will be sharing personal insights and experiences as well as addressing possibly difficult topics. Therefore, this initial introductory period is vital in developing a close and collaborative group. During these first sessions, the counselor can review the purpose of the group, ground rules for participation, and the importance of confidentiality, all of which will serve to establish a safe and controlled environment for sharing experiences.

Middle sessions: Although particular activities will vary between groups, and particularly between different age groups, there are similarities that all will share. Counselors should establish a relatively standard routine for the middle sessions during which the group will be most heavily pursuing their goals. A good idea for each session is to always include an initial time of greeting the members, to reinforce each member's importance and contributions. Counselors can briefly review the ground rules and guidelines during the early part of the session. A review of the previous session's events, activities and accomplishments is recommended. Counselors can then focus the group's attention on the current topic and direct them to a preplanned activity or discussion designed for that session. As the session draws to a close, counselors can briefly review the session's activities and insights, and establish a regular routine for ending the session.

Ending sessions: Developing a structure for the closing session(s) of group counseling incorporates a different focus than the beginning or middle sessions. The closing sessions are those meetings that review accomplishments as a group and anticipate individual futures. There will necessarily be a refocus and possibly some apprehension. Counselors should announce the upcoming final session at least 3 meetings in advance. An important component in the final session or sessions is a review of the initial goals, and the reminder of the achievement of those goals. Counselors should take this time to empower and encourage participants to remember their newly discovered skills and insights, and to apply them to future situations, as well as to a continuum of changed behavior. Time should be allowed for participants to express feelings, and for leaders or other group members to respond to those feelings.

Particularly in the closing session(s), counselors should refer to a defined listing of topics and issues to be addressed, toward a healthy transition. Although the particular modes and media may differ between age groups and topic groups, the following are key components to consider when structuring a closing session:
- Review of the initial goals from the first meeting(s).
- Review of the accomplishment of those goals in subsequent meetings.
- Review of strategies, resources and activities experienced in the sessions.
- Validation of growth and new insights of the participants throughout the sessions.
- Direction for incorporating this growth and insight in future activities and behaviors.
- An opportunity to address any unfinished business or lingering concerns.
- An opportunity for the group to respond to unfinished business or lingering concerns.
- Allow substantial time for personal goodbyes.

Counselors may also want to schedule a post-meeting for evaluation purposes.

Group meeting evaluations: In order to assess the effectiveness of the group sessions, counselors should complete an evaluation at the end of each meeting. The format of these evaluations will in large part determine the kind of information that will be returned. If counselors are looking for the group response to particular components of the sessions, such as the scheduling or the structure of the sessions, a multiple choice or graded response format can be used. The results of these surveys will be more quantitative and focused. Another model is that of questions or open-ended sentences that ask participants how they felt about a session, such as "my favorite part of the session was . . ..". These types of survey instruments can provide more qualitative information, as well as provide an ongoing profile of participant satisfaction and involvement. Counselors may also provide pre- and post-surveys to parents and school staff, as wall as post-surveys to participants several weeks after the last session.

Assessment

Types of Assessments

Formative assessment

Formative assessment is the testing carried out by the teacher during the course of the school term. Its aim is to ensure that students understand the material, as well as to diagnose any gaps in their understanding. It should provide a clear view of the varying ability levels of the members of the class, and it should indicate some ways in which the teacher needs to improve his or her instruction. Formative assessment should often result in a different means of presenting information, or more time spent with troublesome material. It is a good idea to include self-assessment and peer-assessment, so that students can indicate how they feel about their progress in the course and alert the teacher to any problems in morale.

Summative assessment

Summative assessment is carried out less frequently by the teacher; it is appropriate for checking knowledge at the end of a unit of study or at the end of the course. Whereas formative assessment is an assessment for learning, in that it helps the teacher to make positive adjustments to the course, summative assessment is an assessment of learning. It is likely that the means of summative assessment will be affected by the performance of students on formative assessments. It is important that summative assessments provide a comprehensive evaluation of students' mastery of the material, such that every area of knowledge is questioned and every skill is tested. Also, summative assessment should include questions of varying difficulty, so that students can distinguish themselves.

Written comments on class assignments

Perhaps the most important kind of formative assessment a teacher can provide is helpful written comments on student papers. This is the place for teachers to clarify the strengths and weaknesses of the student's work, as well as to generally assess the student's progress in the class. Moreover, this is the perfect venue in which to differentiate between students; in order to keep all of the students motivated, teachers must set different standards for them, and indicate these standards in their comments. Comments should always be positive and supportive, but not at the expense of being constructive: simply assigning a letter grade is inadequate. The important thing when commenting on student work is to indicate areas for improvement without alienating or embarrassing the student.

Assessments of student achievement

One way to determine instructional strategies and priorities is to examine the assessments of student achievement. Student assessments give administrators and instructors a chance to see on what level the students are achieving or struggling. If students are struggling in a certain area then it is time to decide if a certain teaching method needs to be changed or adjusted in some way. Priorities also need to be set in regards to deciding what teaching methods need to be changed and which ones work best with what student. If the assessments show students are achieving in certain areas, then administrators will know certain methods are successful.

Priorities should be set on how to decide continuing with this achievement. The instructors should be asked if they need any additional materials to continue on this road to success.

Self-assessment and peer assessment

It is always a good idea to incorporate some self-assessment and peer assessment into a class, so that students will be encouraged to think about their own progress relative to the progress of the class, as well as to stay focused on the goals of the course. Interestingly, students are usually much harder on themselves in their evaluations that they are on their fellow students. In order for self-assessment to be successful, the teacher must have clearly outlined the learning objectives of each activity. Furthermore, the teacher must have provided adequate constructive criticism, so that students will have a clear idea of where they stand. Sometimes, it may be useful to design a specific assessment checklist so that students will not resort to vague praise or criticism.

Program assessments

Needs assessment

Needs assessment serves to analyze and identify needs of the school, the student body, and the community. An effective needs assessment will identify the particular needs of specific subgroups, and whether or not the needs of all groups and subgroups are being met. Comprehensive needs assessment will reveal areas to be addressed in the student body and its respective demographic subgroups, also in school community including parents, staff, administrators, local business, community organizations and community members. Counselors can analyze the results of needs assessment toward recognizing those students who are not reaping the benefits of various academic and personal programs in place on the school campus. Counselors can create effective, comprehensive counseling programs that will enable students to realize improvements in their personal and academic performance. Needs assessment can also assist counselors in better understanding the distinguishing needs of different subgroups, and to better address the significant issues of the school community.

Program evaluation

The purpose of process evaluation, or program audit, is to determine if the program is appropriately implemented in all areas, and if that implementation is properly documented. The evaluation reviews whether or not there is implementation and sufficient documentation of all relevant facets of a comprehensive school counseling program. By providing an analysis of each component of the program, the audit identifies areas of strength and weakness within the program, and indicates how these areas compare with district or state mission statements. The following terms are used to evaluate areas of the program:
- *None:* Not in place
- *In progress:* Started but not completed
- *Completed:* Possibly not implemented
- *Implemented:* Fully in place
- *Not applicable:* Areas where the criteria do not apply

Service assessment

Counselors may be required to provide service assessment reports to guidance supervisors as well as superintendents and/or school boards. Although guidance supervisors may request general service assessments, school boards and superintendents may ask for more specific event-topic counts. These counts refer to specifically how a counselor spends his/her school time and in what capacity. Counselors are asked to document each time a student is contacted, receives any type of counseling service, and/or interacts with the counselor in any capacity. Reporting these counts may be in the form of a log or a simple count, and requires the counselor to maintain a weekly or monthly recording of how many students receive general counseling as well as those individual sessions to treat depression, behaviors, anxiety, social skills, anger management, family changes, or conflict resolution. Administrators and school boards can appreciate the contributions of the counselor evidenced by quantified event-time counts.

The purpose of time logs is generally determined by the school, the district or other oversight entities. Time logs can provide valuable compliance documentation to administrators and school boards for funding purposes. Certain states and school counseling programs require the use of time logs in order to quantify the type of work being done in the school community and surrounding areas. Some school programs may require the counselor to spend a certain percentage of their time in meetings with students individually, in groups, or for guidance purposes. Counselors should set up the time log format in a manner that will best document the time spent in which capacity, and be categorized in a manner that will be most useful to the entity requesting the time log. The amount of time spent on any counseling-related activity should be documented and categorized as accurately as possible. Counselors may want to maintain daily time logs to effectively capture data regarding time spent.

Outcome assessment

In contrast to service assessment which quantifies time spent, a well defined outcome assessment can provide a profile of the effectiveness of particular aspects of the program. Counselors should recognize that it is not intended as an evaluation of his or her performance, but rather a useful assessment of the program itself. Counselors can focus on the two key features of outcome assessment:

- It is not a professional evaluation of the counselor, a limit to his/her ability to perform the job, a requirement for standardized tests or curricula, or a prescribed process with no capacity for expansion.
- The assessment is
- a vehicle for garnering information on program-related questions.
- the responsibility of an accountable counselor.
- an ongoing and evolving process.
- a cooperative outreach to other SCPAC members and stakeholders.
- a path toward better education for all students.

Assessment terms

The following are assessment-related terms and their definitions:

- 101 -

- Evaluation implies a measurement of worth, indicating that the effectiveness will be judged.
- Evidence refers to all data that can be used to judge or determine effectiveness. It is either quantitatively or qualitatively derived.
- Formative evaluation describes specific feedback received during a program implementation.
- Summative evaluation refers to anecdotal feedback received during the evaluation process.
- Stakeholder refers to any person or persons who are involved in or benefit from the school counseling program.
- *Baseline* refers to data gathered at the onset of evaluation, to define a starting point.
- *Pretest* describes an administered measure given before an intervention.
- *Posttest* describes an administered measure given after the intervention has been completed.
- *Value-added assessment* refers to the timing and final result of the intervention.

Planning for outcome assessment in research design

When designing research or implementing new intervention strategies, counselors should consider outcome assessment in the initial stages of planning, and definitely before beginning an intervention. Otherwise, they are reliant upon pre-prescribed case studies, non-experimental design paradigms, or static-group comparison studies to analyze the effectiveness of the intervention. By planning for outcome assessment, counselors can tailor the assessment to the intervention. The optimal format for research design is random assignment of participants to treatment conditions. This will allow the counselor to implement true experimental designs. Otherwise, with little or no control over assignments, counselors must rely on the results of a quasi-experimental or non-experimental design. The completion of pretests and posttests is also optimal, although not all counselors are able or need the dependent variable.

Implementing an original outcome assessment

There may be occasion when a counselor may choose to develop an original outcome measure that directly addresses the application, or is most appropriate for the group. When posing questions to the group for responses to be used in the assessment, the following considerations should be incorporated:
- Use simple language and question the group members only on events or circumstances with which they are familiar.
- Each question should be specific, and any unclear terms should be specifically defined in the appropriate context.
- Counselors should always avoid yes-no questions since this limits the responses.
- Counselors should always avoid double negatives since this can confuse the response group.
- Questions should be posed individually, and not in combination with another question.
- Topic-specific wording should be consistent with the wording used in the discipline.
- Counselors should be sensitive to cultural differences.
- Learn to handle difficult response groups effectively.

- Second-hand opinions should only be acceptable if firsthand information is unavailable.
- Background information can be provided to remind the group members of a specific event or reaction.

Data collection methods
Counselors can collect data through the following methods:
- Interviewing counselors, educators or members of stakeholder groups in a structured, semi-structured, or unstructured manner.
- Observing students informally and formally.
- Distributing written questions, rating scales and surveys containing open- and closed-ended questions requesting factual responses or anecdotal perceptions. This method may prove problematic for participants to complete in its entirety.
- Reviewing program records or schedules usually kept in a database format for easy retrieval and archival use.
- Quantitatively comparing the results of standardized tests with educator-generated tests to measure student performance.
- Analyzing performance indicators such as grade point average, classroom grade, attendance, and daily behavior.
- Studying products and portfolios of student performance in the classroom.

Appropriate assessment methods
The following considerations should be incorporated in a choosing an assessment method:
- How the test developer defines that construct that will be used, e.g. aptitude, achievement, etc. The counselor should not utilize the assessment in another context than the original one, since the results could be misrepresentative. The technical manual should also be studies, in order to value the utility of the test as well as the reliability and validity of the scores.
- How other organizations reviewed the test. Professional literature is available to counselors that will provide reviews from other counselors and similar organizations.
- What key factors should be considered. Counselors consider a quantitative or qualitative assessment should analyze if the baseline and original population are appropriate for the student and whether the instrument can indicate a direction for intervention.

Collaboration, Consultation, and Professionalism

Overall importance

Because the average student to counselor ratio can range from 100:1 to 300:1, the accessibility of counselors is sometimes well below optimum. The moderate needs of many students can be eclipsed by attention paid to the more severe needs of a few. Therefore, it is advisable for counselors to consult with parents and school personnel in the design of effective prevention and intervention programs. Parents and school personnel experience day-to-day contact with students, and are able to observe them in the classroom and home environments. The combined student contact that parents, teachers and school administrators have can provide valuable feedback to counselors for designing programs and intervention strategies that will benefit the most students most effectively, augmented by individual sessions as indicated. Counselors who meet with the larger school community are able to maximize their efforts and therefore the efficacy of the school counseling program.

Goals

Goal-setting is important because it allows an individual or organization to identify what they wish to accomplish and determine the best way to accomplish those objectives. Goal-setting also usually implies setting a particular timeframe in which the goal should be achieved. The combination of the individual or organization knowing what goals they are striving for and that those goals need to be completed in a set amount of time aids in motivating the efforts of each individual involved towards that ultimate objective. Goals also give the individual or organization a means of measuring the amount of effort, or the lack thereof, that each individual puts into obtaining those goals. In a family or corporate setting, goals can give the organization a means of measuring its success as well, which can be important when attempting to determine what actions the organization needs to take in the future.

Creating a valid goal
An individual or organization that is attempting to set a goal can follow the common management mnemonic SMART to make sure that their goal is well-defined, valid, and useful when attempting to measure success and motivate the organization as a whole. SMART, when relating to goals, usually refers to specific, measurable, achievable, relevant, and time-related. Goals need to be specific and well-defined, have some way of being measured in an accurate fashion, be achievable rather than unattainable and ridiculous, and relevant to the tasks that need to be completed for the success of the organization. The individual or organization should also decide upon a set amount of time that the goal should be completed in to make sure that it is achieved in a timely fashion and that it can be compared to other goals in the future.

Examples: *A manager of a local retailer, that usually does somewhere between $35,000 and $60,000 a week, decided that his or her store should set a goal of making $50,000 in sales a week each week for the month of November.* This is a completely valid goal as the goal is very well-defined, it can be measured by examining the amount of sales the store has done each week, and the goal is achievable as $50,000 is within the store's normal sales range. The goal is also relevant to the store's ability to make a profit and there is a set amount of time that the goal must be achieved in.

A mother with a son who is having difficulty in school has decided that her son needs to improve his grades. This is not a valid goal as the goal is not well-defined, there is a manner of measuring the goal, but there is no mention of what is a satisfactory improvement in the son's grades, and there is no set timeframe for the goal to be completed in. The goal may be achievable and is certainly relevant to the success of the child, but it is not well-defined enough to be an effective goal.

Goal achievement
Many internal and external factors can have an effect on whether or not an individual or organization is able to achieve a particular goal. However, the most important thing for an individual or organization to keep in mind, regardless of the situation, is that there is a strong need to remain focused on the goal and the appropriate way to achieve that goal. This means that if a goal is important to the success of the individual, or the organization as a whole, it is important that every possible effort is placed into achieving that goal. Any other goals that might be less important or irrelevant should not be allowed to distract the individual or the organization from the primary goal and these secondary goals should ultimately be ignored until the primary goal is achieved. It is also necessary that the individual or each individual within the organization can continue to recognize that the goal is achievable so no one gives up before the goal is actually reached.

Decision-making

The primary reason that the decision-making process is important is because understanding the process can aid in the discovery of a future rational and reasonable course of action when presented with a decision that needs to be made. Each individual has a different perspective and therefore a different way of coming to a particular decision, but through a combination of intuition, knowledge, and an understanding of how the process works, a decision that is more suited for the goals of a particular individual or group can be made. A well thought out method of decision-making consists of identifying the decision that needs to be made, identifying the benefits of each choice relating to that decision, identifying the potential drawbacks of making each choice relating to that decision, and finally actually making a choice. An individual or organization by understanding what needs to be identified at each stage of the decision-making process will be able to make a more informed decision that will be more likely to lead towards a particular goal.

Actions to avoid
Some of the most common pitfalls that need to be avoided when attempting to make a well-informed decision are entering the decision-making process with a preconceived notion that the individual is unwilling to abandon, allowing peer pressure to influence a decision, and over-generalizing. Entering the decision-making process with a prejudice against a particular idea or source of information or with an inappropriate bias towards a particular choice will often lead to the individual or group choosing an option that is not the best or most logical of the choices

available. Outside sources should be used to gather information about the decision that needs to be made, but no single source should be allowed to force or pressure the individuals involved in making the decision into choosing a particular choice. Finally, the overuse of generalizations, stereotypes, and attempts to attribute effects to causes that may not have any logical link will often lead to a decision being made that may not be the best course of action.

Techniques

An individual that is attempting to make a well-informed decision will often attempt to gather as much information as possible from as many reliable sources as possible, list the advantages and disadvantages of each choice, and then compare each choice with each other. In an employment or business situation where finances are involved, an individual may use a mathematical approach and calculate exactly how much money each job choice or each potential new product could offer and how much it might cost the individual if something goes wrong. A mathematical approach, when it is possible to use one, can be an extremely sound strategy when attempting to determine which choice is more appropriate. However, many individuals do not make well-informed decisions and they may rely on random chance such as flipping a coin, on the opinions or pressure of the individual's peers, or rely heavily on information from unreliable sources such as a high school student's web page.

Strategies

Some of the most common decision-making strategies that a business or other organization might use when attempting to make a decision are the Pareto analysis system, a cost/benefit analysis strategy, a force field analysis strategy, a grid analysis strategy, and a scenario analysis strategy. Each business or other type of organization will usually choose the system that best suits the kind of decision that they are attempting to make as each strategy has its own advantages and disadvantages. For example, a Pareto analysis system can be useful when an organization is attempting to handle a particular group of problems and it is obvious that a particular small group of causes is responsible for most of the problems that the organization is having. However, a Paerto analysis system will not work as well, if at all, in situations where there are a large number of problems caused by completely unrelated factors.

- *The Pareto analysis system:* Basically, the Pareto analysis system is a decision-making model that assumes that approximately 80% of the benefits that an organization receives from a particular task are a result of 20% of the effort that the various individuals within the organization put into the task. It also assumes that 80% of the problems that the organization is faced with are produced by approximately 20% of the factors that may be causing them. The first step necessary for the Pareto analysis system is to list all of the problems that need to be addressed or the choices that are available. Next, each of those problems or choices needs to be grouped so that the choices that offer similar benefits or are factors that are leading to larger similar problems are grouped together. Each group is then given a score based on how much that group affects the overall benefit that the organization is attempting to achieve or the overall problem that the organization is attempting to solve.
- *The cost/benefit analysis strategy:* Cost/benefit analysis is a decision-making strategy that examines the total estimated cost of each option that is available, the total estimated benefit of each option available, and then compares the cost with the benefit to see if the benefits of the option outweigh the cost. Usually, a cost/benefit analysis refers to the financial cost and

benefit of a particular decision, but it can actually be used in any situation where the use of resources is involved. For example, if a corporation has two clothing materials, A and B, that both cost the same, but material B can be used more efficiently, the cost/benefit analysis would show that material B is the best choice as it offers the most clothing for the least amount of material. Cost/benefit analysis can be extremely useful when attempting to decide which option will have the greatest benefit. However, this method also relies heavily on estimation so there may be instances where it is not as accurate as other methods.

- *The force field analysis strategy:* Force field analysis is a decision-making strategy that attempts to examine all of the factors that affect a particular situation and identify those factors as either aiding the organization in achieving a goal or ultimately causing the organization to fail. Basically, it is the process of identifying and listing which factors involved with each option are helping the organization and which ones are actually hurting the organization. The first step of the force field analysis strategy is to make a list of all of the factors involved with a particular option and identify them as either aiding the organization in moving towards a particular goal or hindering the organization's movement towards that goal. Each factor is then given a rating on a scale of 1 to 5 with 1 being the weakest and 5 being the strongest. If the forces that hinder the organization are stronger overall, the option is probably not realistic, however if the forces that aid the organization are stronger, then the option may prove beneficial.

- *The grid analysis strategy:* Grid analysis is a decision-making strategy that takes all of the factors involved with each option, rates each factor, and then weights each factor based on their importance to the decision as a whole. For example, if the owner of a clothing factory had three materials and was attempting to decide which material would provide the most profit, the owner might consider each material's cost, how much material is wasted, and how difficult each material is to use. The owner would then use a set scale, such as from 0 to 5 with 0 being the most expensive or wasteful and 5 being the least, and rate the cost, waste, and difficulty of use for each material. The owner would then assign each factor a weight based on the effect the factor has on the overall profit, using a similar scale, and then get a weighted score by multiplying the weight by the rating that each factor received. The material with the highest total score would be the best option.

- *The scenario analysis strategy:* The scenario analysis strategy is a decision-making method where an individual or organization attempts to use their experience, knowledge, and intuition to predict what kind of situations may arise from each option if that option were chosen. In other words, the scenario analysis strategy is where the decision-maker attempts to determine all of the possible outcomes of a particular choice and what effect each outcome might have on the organization or individual as a whole if that choice was made. In some instances, especially in a business setting, each of these potential outcomes might be assigned a score based on how likely it is that that scenario will actually occur. However, regardless of whether the potential outcomes receive a score or not, it is impossible for an individual or organization to arrive at every possible outcome that might occur and accurately predicting what events are most likely to occur in the future can be extremely difficult.

Resources

A resource is simply anything that can be used to aid an individual or organization in either the daily functioning of the individual or organization or aid in the achievement of a particular goal. The four primary types of resources are land and natural resources, labor resources, capital and capital goods, and information resources. Land and natural resources include anything that comes from the environment such as water, oil, the land itself, soil, etc... Labor resources are the actual effort that various people involved in an organization put into a particular project towards the goal of completing that project. Capital and capital goods are any financial and human-made resources such as money, tools and equipment, buildings and houses, or anything else that is man-made. Information resources are any resources that allow an individual or organization to find and put to use knowledge that might help in achieving a particular goal.

An individual or organization that is attempting to assess if there are enough resources available for a particular project may want to start by determining exactly what the project consists of and attempt to research how much the project will cost in time and money. After the individual or organization has developed a basic outline of what the project needs, an inventory of which resources are readily available should be conducted. This inventory would include noting resources such as how much money is available, how many people are available to work on the project, what kind of equipment is available to complete the project, and is there enough information regarding the project available for the workers to complete the project. If the individual or organization determines that the resources necessary to complete the project are not available then the project is not realistic based on the resources that the individual or organization currently has.

A family that is attempting to determine the status of its financial resources should start by collecting all of the financial records that the family has available from each source of income. The family should then attempt to determine and list all of its assets including the amount of cash the family has on hand and the amount of cash the family could get if they sold off any stocks, bonds, mutual funds, property that the family owns, etc... After adding up all of the on-hand assets and potential assets that the family has available, the family should then list all of the loans, unpaid bills, balances due, and other liabilities the family needs to pay and add them together to get the family's total amount of liability. The family can then get an idea of their financial standing by subtracting their estimated total liability from their estimated total assets giving them a good estimation of their net worth.

Types of resources

Land resources can be used as locations for homes, businesses, or even searching for other natural resources located on that land such as oil, minerals, soil that can be used for planting, water for drinking and fishing, etc... Examples of people who might be considered as labor resources are marketers who determine the best way to sell a particular product, salespeople who sell a particular product to the consumer, the factory workers who actually assemble that product, and anyone else who actually aids in achieving the end goal. Capital refers specifically to money, but capital goods, such as in a factory setting, can be the machinery that turns the raw goods into the end product. Information resources may be books or online sites that can be used to learn how to construct a better product or how to better manage a particular organization. All of these resources can be used in a variety of ways and most projects actually require a combination of different types of resources.

Non-financial resources
Non-financial resources, or resources that are not cash or can not be sold outright and turned into cash, can be extremely useful to a family that is experiencing financial problems. Even though non-financial resources are not actually cash or property that can be sold, they can often be used to produce income or reduce costs that the family is experiencing. For example, even though a family may not want to sell their house outright, and they obviously can't logistically sell just one room in their home, they can still rent out a room to make additional money. A family who has a seamstress or a carpenter as a member of the family might also be able to lower the family's costs by mending the family's clothing instead of throwing it away or making necessary repairs to the family home without paying for labor. Any skill that a family member possesses can cut the family's costs and any service the family can offer can act as a way of gathering additional income.

Change management

Change management is the process by which an organization attempts to modify a particular aspect of how the organization operates with as little harm to the organization as possible. In most cases, an organization makes these operational changes either to adapt to changes in society or to improve the manner in which the organization operates overall. Change management is important as almost everything around us is constantly changing, but many individuals have difficulty adapting to social, economic, or other changes despite how important making these changes might be. Organizations that want to continue functioning need to change in order to continue working with the world around them as it continues to change. Change management is simply the process that each organization uses to implement the changes that are necessary without putting too much unnecessary stress upon the members of the organization.

Organizational changes
There are three major types of strategies that an organization might use when attempting to make changes in the way an organization functions overall. The three types of strategies are the empirical-rational strategy, the normative-reeducative strategy, and the power-coercive strategy. Each strategy has its own advantages and disadvantages and which strategy an organization chooses is usually based on how much the organization needs to change and what resources are available to relieve problems that may be caused by particular changes. Which strategy an organization uses may also be based heavily on how much time is available to make the changes and how great a risk there is of members of the organization rejecting the change and refusing to adapt.

Empirical-rational strategy
The empirical-rational strategy of managing change assumes that people are ultimately interested in their own well being and will more quickly accept changes if they understand that those changes offer some sort of benefit. In other words, this strategy of managing change relies

on either offering an incentive to the members of the organization to take part in some sort of change or convincing the members of the organization that the change will benefit them in some fashion. For example, if the board of directors of a particular company realized that the company's competitors had employees that were performing more effectively, because their employees had more education, the board might decide to use an empirical-rational strategy to encourage employees to go back to school. The company, by offering perhaps to pay for additional schooling and/or offering promotions, raises, or other incentives might be able to get some or most of their employees to seek out further education and return to the company better trained.

Normative-reeducative strategy
The normative-reeducative strategy of managing change relies heavily on peer pressure to bring about the changes that an organization needs. Basically, this strategy assumes that people rely heavily on social interaction and therefore will normally behave according to the expectations of the rest of society. Using this assumption, an organization can institute new changes by slowly redefining aspects of the organization's culture and each individual will then begin to accept the changes as social norms. For example, if the board of directors of a retail chain begins to realize that customer service is becoming a more important marketing point than price, the directors may attempt to use a normative-reeducative strategy. The company can slowly begin altering the behavior that is deemed socially acceptable by the employees by placing posters in the break room suggesting the importance of customer service, addressing the appropriate way to treat customers at meetings and performance reviews, and training new employees in good customer service tactics.

Power-coercive strategy
The power-coercive strategy of managing change assumes that people will usually listen to authority figures and do as they are told. This strategy works simply by preventing the members of the organization from choosing any option other than the path that the manager wants them to follow because it is made clear that there are no other options available to them. If an individual still refuses to accept the changes that the organization has decided upon, the organization might punish the individual for not complying. For example, if a child is doing poorly in school because he is spending too much time watching television, the child's mother might simply turn off the TV and tell her child to do his homework. If the child then turns the television back on, his mother might send him to his room and ground him for a week as punishment for disobeying.

Advantages and disadvantages
The empirical-rational strategy is very effective when an organization has the resources available to offer the incentives necessary to make the changes more palatable or if the changes have an obvious benefit to the individuals who need to implement the change. However, it is much less effective when the organization lacks the resources to give incentives substantial enough to sway the members of the organization or the changes do not seem beneficial on the surface. The normative-reeducative strategy is useful when the managers and workers of the organization have a strong relationship and there is a lot of time available to implement the changes, however, this strategy is much less effective when there is limited time available or

relations between management and staff are strained. The power-coercive strategy is particularly useful in situations where time is limited and the threat to the organization or individual is more serious, however, it often can promote unrest amongst members of the organization especially in organizations that allow more individual freedoms.

Consultation

Counselor and school system

Developing strategies
Particularly in a school counseling environment, any kind of intervention or therapy must be considered and delivered within the context of the larger school system and community. The primary purpose behind this is efficacy of treatment. Counselors who are working with at-risk students or students who are facing personal problems will gain benefit for the student and for the counseling program by collaborating with school personnel. This may include a collaborative consultation, or may just be a matter of available resources. Counselors may also want to serve as a liaison in suggesting student-orientated changes to the school system. Counselors can also adopt a holistic approach to therapy, within the context of the school community. It is important to remember that students are classmates and have classmates, take course work within a prescribed curriculum, and operate within the mandates of the school system. Therefore, when working with students, counselors should be cognizant of a student's daily routines and environment.

It is important for school counselors to remember that they are one member of the school personnel community. Their role is to provide individual or group therapy to student members of the community who are at risk for self-destructive behaviors which usually include academic failure. It is the intervention focusing on the dangers of academic failure that serves as the linchpin of the collaborative goals of the entire school community including the school counselor. For school counselors to be most effective and of value to their student clients, it is important to remember that the school counselor in serving his/her students, is also serving the greater good of the school community. This greater good includes the safety of the student body, and the academic goals of the school and the district. Those academic goals can be reflected in test scores, retention, and other quantifiable data.

When becoming a part of a school community, a school counselor can take proactive steps toward developing a collaborative relationship with other members of the community. These steps include:
- Recognize that the school staff are in a fiduciary role of implementing the academic goals of the school and the district.
- Be open to the evolution of your role within the school community, as opposed to imposing preconceived ideas about your role on the school staff.
- Become familiar with the rules and expectations of the school community.
- Recognize that any operational entity will have both explicit and implicit hierarchies, and become aware of those levels of authority and power.

- Cultivate alliances and friendships through shared agendas and recognition of individual strengths.
- Develop effective and collaborative vehicles of communication with members of the school and the larger community.
- Maintain objectivity when working with any educator or family member.
- Refrain from provocatively challenging the authority of an educator or community member.

Each school system will have particular nuances and interpretations with respect to issues of confidentiality and parental rights. Counselors should be cognizant of these policies/procedures when working with students in order to know:
- When and how to notify parents of student participation in counseling.
- How to respond to suspicion of child abuse.
- Issues of confidentiality in the therapeutic environment, e.g. when and how to report severely at risk behavior, when and how to recognize and report students who may be at risk of harming others.
- When and how to open up the counseling strategies to include collaborative consultation.
- When to involve teachers and other school staff in intervention strategies.
- Understanding the policies and procedures includes not only reading them, but understanding how these policies are implemented in a particular school environment.
- Open communication and cultivating relationships with school staff will be beneficial to the counselor in developing an understanding of school policies and procedures.

Policy interpretation
Although most school policies and procedures are clearly delineated in written form, their interpretation can be less clear-cut, and can even vary between teachers and classrooms. One policy area that can easily vary between educators is that of allowing students to participate in counseling during time normally set aside for classroom instruction. Some teachers may be in support of students receiving counseling, and may be willing to let that student leave his/her classroom to do so. Others may also be in support of students receiving counseling, but may feel that it should not be done at the expense of classroom time, but rather after or before school. Teachers may also have differing opinions about collaborating with school counselors by implementing behavior modification strategies in the classroom. Counselors should be sensitive to these differences in opinion, and the spectrum of teachers' responses to the need for and implementation of a counseling program.

Deferring to the authority of the principal
The principal of a school administrates the allocation of both monetary and personnel resources. For a school counselor to successfully plan and implement a counseling program at a school, the support and endorsement of the principal is pivotal. In deference to the principal's responsibilities, counselors should keep him/her apprised of the scope of the current counseling program, as well as revisions or plans for future revisions to the program. Not only is this respectful of the principal's/school's agenda; it is also good practice in order to retain the support and endorsement of administration. It is also recommended that counselors meet with

principals on a regular basis, at the principal's convenience, and s/he will most likely determine how often these meetings need to occur. Counselors should allow sufficient time to apprise the principal of updates and for discussion as appropriate. Principals may also make suggestions and recommendations for the counseling program, which should be taken into account by the counselor.

Recognizing influencers
When a counselor recognizes that s/he is just one member of a school community, s/he should also recognize that a community contains both formal and informal power structures. Although it is necessary for a counselor to keep open communication with the principal, that line of communication may depend on the counselor's interactions with the principal's secretary or other assistant administrator. School counselors should also be cognizant of the network of communication and influence that exists within the school system, as it does within most communities. Counselors can cultivate relationships with teachers, parents, other administrators, etc. in order to gain an understanding of underlying concerns and agendas within the larger school agenda. These relationships can also provide a vehicle for counselors to inform the school community of his/her concerns for the students and plans for an appropriate counseling program to address those concerns. A healthy environment for a school counseling program includes shared agendas and collaboration.

When counselors are able to communicate and collaborate with influential and interested members of the school community regarding the counseling program, there are positive far-reaching effects. By recognizing and incorporating the interplay of agendas and concerns in a school community, counselors are able to gain the respect, endorsement, and also the contributions of those individuals. When counselors can recognize and utilize the strengths and contributions of individuals working in the school community, the counseling program is able to thrive and grow within the context of the school system. The added benefit is that when the program is working within this context, peripheral individuals and programs will associate the counseling program with the larger agenda(s) of the school community and more readily accept and endorse the program. As these working relationships evolve, the counselor can develop rich alliances and friendships within the school community to the benefit of all the members.

As with any group dynamic, the interplay of agendas and concerns within a school community may be organic and healthy, may be dysfunctional and conflicting, or may be somewhere in the spectrum between these two extremes. Although it is not necessarily the counselor's role to analyze the dynamics at play in the school setting, s/he nonetheless needs to be cognizant of conflicts between individuals and agendas, particularly if individuals or groups are in opposition to the principal's goals and overall agenda. Counselors should exercise some caution when forming alliances to the benefit of the counseling program which may be in opposition to other groups or the overall agenda of the school principal. It would be better to cultivate relationships with a measure of caution, until a counselor understands the overall interplay of agendas within the school community. Counselors can also strive to facilitate cooperation and collaboration between the parties involved.

Working with members of subsystems

The larger school community is comprised of many subsystems, including but not limited to parents, service staff, librarians, community groups, etc. Even within the teaching staff, there are subsystems comprised of education specialists, resource teachers, etc. Although not necessarily in conflict with each other, often these groups operate quasi-autonomously and are not aware of their contributions to and impact on the totality of the larger school community. This is best illustrated within the experiences of the students, who interact with and depend on most or many of these subsystems. Counselors working with students who have complex needs may need to involve several subsystems in order to provide effective treatment for students. It might be beneficial for counselors to form acquaintances with members of the larger school community, in order to better understand the complexities of subsystems in the school, and possibly to facilitate communication between these entities.

Emotional objectivity

When counselors join a school community, they may encounter resistance to their contributions from certain members of that community. Although the school community/system as a whole may endorse and support the counseling program and its inclusion in the larger efforts of the school, the resistance of a few may manifest in covert or overt actions that undermine or impede the counseling program. Counselors need to maintain objectivity when facing these kinds of challenges, and recognize them as symptoms of systemic change. Recognizing this objectively, the counselor can then approach the challenge(s) professionally. Relying on their knowledge of systems change analysis, counselors can objectively isolate and identify the resistance, and openly approach the individuals or entities involved toward a mutual resolution. It is important to remember that, without this objectivity, counselors can become mired in conflict and programs can be rendered ineffectual.

Working with other educators and mental health professionals

School districts may employ or call upon numerous professionals in the endeavor to provide mental health services to students. These may include psychologists, school nurses, social workers, crisis intervention counselors, as well as staff educators and administrators. School counselors often form a part of this larger network of mental health professionals on the school campus, working with the same population of students. It is in the counselor's and program's best interest that school counselors develop and maintain a spirit of cooperation when working with these diverse groups of mental health professionals. It is not advisable, nor is it generally successful, to generate an attitude of superiority or a hierarchical stance when working with other professionals. Remember that all of the groups and individuals involved are striving for the same goal: the mental health of the students. By working cooperatively and inclusively, counselors can benefit from the support and expertise of those in peripheral professional positions.

Authority

A business organization is centralized when there is little delegation of authority, and decisions are mostly made by the top executives. Obviously, the most extreme version of centralization is when one owner makes all the decisions in a business. Decentralization, conversely, is exhibited in a business where authority is dispersed widely throughout. Most businesses operate in degrees of centralization and decentralization. Important decisions, particularly those regarding large amounts of capital, will probably be reserved for top executives; more trifling decisions are likely to be left to lower managers. Business analysts have noted that most businesses tend to be too centralized in their early years, but can become too decentralized once they have had some success and established a company policy.

Collaboration

Problem-solving

Once a consultant is in the school system, s/he is in a position to initiate problem solving. Regardless of the problem, or the complexity of the problem, the initial stage of problem-solving is generally that of identifying the problem to be addressed. This involves collecting information necessary to comprehensively assess the issue at hand. If the difficulty relates to a student, the information collecting may involve parents, teachers, and/or the student directly. The problem-solving process can also engage other educators or family members to form a collaborative problem-solving team. Problems to be addressed might also be more macrocosmic, involving several students with violent behavior, or possibly system-wide issues affecting the entire school. Counselors can be most successful in tackling large or small issues by first identifying the problem to be addressed. Once the problem has been comprehensively isolated, counselors can then progress to determining the most appropriate consultation model for working toward resolution.

School teams brought together to resolve an issue are often task-oriented, and generally not focused on process. Without some attention paid to process, the collaborative effect of the team can be much diffused and the efficacy of the group diminished. The counselor as consultant can contribute to the group discussion with not only knowledge about a particular issue, but also specific expertise in group dynamics. As facilitator, s/he can encourage the group process necessary for completing the problem-solving task. As with any interaction with other professionals, counselors will do well to remember they are a part of a larger whole, and maintain an openness to the strengths of the group and the individual members. If approached well, a successful collaborative process will significantly contribute to the overall success of the task team, as well as establish the counselor as a valuable member of the school community.

Collaborative group dynamic

After the counselor as consultant has been assigned a role in the group, s/he may have the opportunity to facilitate the process of collaboration. When working within the context of a problem-solving team, counselors can initiate specific practices and procedures toward a collaborative group dynamic. These practices include:
- Noting and encouraging behaviors among the group that contribute to collaboration and cooperation
- Noting and discouraging competitive remarks and behaviors

- Working with the group to establish a collaborative group norm
- Creating an open communication policy which allows the input of all participants to the problem-solving process
- Recognizing and respecting the expertise and contributions of all members of the group

These practices can lay the foundation for collaborative group process. Facilitating a collaborative group dynamic may also occasionally include soliciting the support and endorsement of a school administrator by explaining the value of the collaborative process in a problem-solving group.

Framing objectives

The counselor as facilitator can work with members of the group to set goals and create a viable action plan. It is important that the parameters of this action plan fall within the capabilities and contributions of the group members. Individuals in the group should be able to recognize and embrace their role in facilitating change in the student(s). Specific steps in the process of developing an action plan include:
- The goal and the action plan for achieving it.
- Determine an appropriate and reasonable measurement of outcome.
- Empower group members to act as change agents.The individual and group strengths applicable to the action plan.
- Encourage flexibility of roles and expanded boundaries as appropriate.
- Encourage collaboration within the group and with other entities as appropriate.
- Develop a plan to implement and retain the changes.

Identifying goals and outcomes

It is important to remember the initial process of problem solving is that of comprehensive problem identification. This identification should include the scope of the problem, specifically if it is isolated to a particular student and/or the student's family dynamic, or more generalized within a group of students, or throughout the school system as a whole. Once the problem is identified, the problem-solving team should clearly identify goals for the student or the particular group, as well as anticipated outcomes. Academic goals for students should fall within the academic parameters and mission of the school. Inherent in the process is the need for developing viable outcome assessment measures, which will be made easier with clearly stated objectives. When the group can articulate the objectives, as well as measurements of outcome, they can best formulate goals that are reasonable and achievable.

Framing issues inclusively

When a student's behaviors or problems become such that intervention is necessary, it often provides fertile ground for blaming others for the problems. Parents may harbor blame toward the school for his/her child's problems, and schools may hold parents accountable for student behavior. As consultants, counselors can stress that the student's situation should be viewed as a catalyst for change which will involve the student, the school and the parents/family. Viewed in this way, intervention becomes a collaborative goal rather than an exercise in finding evidence to support blame. Counselors can encourage participants to feel committed to resolution, and to each embrace his/her respective role in its achievement. The strengths of the teachers and family members should be affirmed and used to bring about the desired objectives. Counselors should remind and encourage participants that change is a process that will take time and the commitment of those involved in the student's life.

Identifying systemic change need

When student intervention necessitates a group effort, this usually correlates with a multiplicity and complexity of issues. Consequently, resolution is usually correspondingly complex, and may involve many entities. Sometimes, any change anticipated in the student relies at least in part on changes in family dynamics and/or school systems. Counselors will be well served to remember that student behaviors point to need for change, and to refrain from blatantly identifying any system or individual as a cause for the problem(s). Rather, counselors should use diplomacy in suggesting changes in family or school dynamics, particularly if the respective parties are operating under the assumption that the student's behavioral problems are not connected to other influences in his/her life. This is a situation in which the trust and alliances gained from members of the school community are particularly valuable. Counselors can work separately with a teacher or family member to encourage change as applicable.

Flexible roles and boundaries

The optimum consulting group is one in which the whole is greater than the sum of its parts. Practically speaking, each of the participants comes to the task at hand with particular expertise, a specific set of skills, and a paradigm or perspective regarding the problem and an anticipated resolution. Each member sees himself/herself in a predetermined role. Educators generally approach student problems from an academic perspective; psychologists will tend to be most concerned about the student's mental health. However, in a group setting, with good facilitation, the participants can be encouraged to step beyond their prescribed roles and expectations toward a comprehensive intervention strategy that will bring their collective expertise to a cohesive front. In this setting, counselors may ask a teacher to co-lead the group, or a psychologist to facilitate a discussion about academic goals. This shared crossing over can be most beneficial in a consulting group.

Strategies for protecting change

Counselors understand that any kind of behavioral change is an ongoing process and will often include backsliding or digression. When facilitating a consulting group, counselors can first remind the group that any intervention strategy needs to include plans for protecting the anticipated change. Knowing this initially will enhance the long-term success of intervention strategies. Consultants can assist the group in developing a post-plan for this purpose. This post-plan should include delineation of responsibilities and benchmarks to be used in evaluating progress. It may also include mechanisms that will allow for ongoing communication among the members, as well as support resources. In a school setting, student progress is generally associated with academic achievement, which can provide a clear marker for determining strategy success. Behavioral changes can also be monitored by noting clearly identified actions.

Evaluating implementation

When an action plan has been developed and implemented, the evaluation process should begin. A component of the action plan should be strategies for evaluation and outcome measurement. It may be appropriate for each member of the consultant group to also participate in the evaluation process by monitoring such successes as academic progress, changed behaviors, etc. The evaluation should focus on whether any change has occurred, and to what degree that change can be measured. Participants can develop vehicles for collecting as well as presenting the relevant data. Counselors should provide oversight for this phase of the action plan. They should be attentive to the degree of change, and determine if it is sufficient to be considered successful. They should also be attentive to any changes that constitute digression, or negative change. If this is the case, they might want to assess possible factors, and meet with the group to develop alternate strategies.

Ad hoc consultation closure

If the consultant is not a regular member of the school community, closure may be more definitive than if the counselor as consultant is a part of the school staff. In that situation, counselors can maintain communication with the participants and provide validation of successful completion. The counselor can also conduct debriefings with the participants to reflect on the process, the success(es), and the value of collaboration. Counselors can also maintain communication with school administrators and peripheral professionals as a follow-up to a successful intervention, as appropriate. If, on the other hand, the counselor as consultant is a regular member of the school staff, it is important to be attentive to sensitivities that the student might have regarding regular proximity to the participants of the consulting group, including the counselor. In that event, formal follow-up might be less appropriate than if the consultant is regularly not on campus.

Cross-cultural consultation

When working with consultees from diverse cultural backgrounds, counselors should refer to their knowledge of cross-cultural counseling in order to facilitate the group with confidence and skill. Multicultural participants in a consulting group will inherently present certain considerations regarding diversity of culture:
- *Impact of culture:* How do diverse cultural paradigms impact the consultation process?
- *Recognition of culture:* Understand the richness of contributions from diversity of culture.
- Be sensitive to cultural differences when developing rapport within the group.
- Be cognizant of cultural factors within the group as well as between the group and the student.
- Develop appropriate interventions with these cultural considerations in mind, if indicated.

- Respond objectively to diverse circumstances. And emphasize similarities between the represented cultures, as appropriate.
- Address balance of power issues.
- Endorse success of student and consultees.

Broadening collaborative consultation

It may be the case that a student is already interacting with other professionals/professional groups outside of the school community. Often this is the case if students present a complexity of issues. In order to approach the student holistically, counselors may want to include these individuals in a consulting group, or as part of the school-based consulting group. Through collaborative consultation, the individual members should endeavor to adopt an integrative approach that will result in shared input and shared responsibility. It is generally recommended that each member's interaction with the student should be suspended or altered in deference to the participant's involvement in the collaborative consultation model. Counselors as consultants should become familiar with the expertise and scope of each professional/group, and possibly involve the parents in the consultation. Overall, the collaborative consultation model can prove much more effective than if counselors were to meet individually with respective professionals/groups.

Including parents
Counselors as consultants are in a position to recognize when a student issue could be best addressed by generating dialogue between parents and members of the school community. The initial process should involve bringing the parents together with educators or other school members as appropriate, to discuss and come to an agreed understanding regarding the needs of the student. Through collaboration, parents and school members can recognize that each of their efforts as individual entities would likely not be as effective as the collaborative efforts of the group members, including the parents. Counselors can facilitate the process by helping members to understand each others' roles and prospective contributions. Counselors can guide the group discussions by allowing each of the participants, which may just be a teacher and a parent, to understand their mutual goal of academic success for the student, and to encourage trust in the collaborative process.

Increased parental involvement and awareness strongly correlates with increased academic success in students. There is also a significant benefit to students who are able to dovetail their school experience with their home experience, by parents becoming more involved in and aware of students' academic requirements. When parents are able to supplement classroom instruction with additional teaching at home, their children generally perform better and are more engaged at school. Counselors and other members of the school staff can cultivate parental involvement through a number of vehicles. Open house events and parent-teacher conferences are common modes for increasing parental involvement. Other recommendations are parent resource centers, phone calls or even visits to the home as appropriate. If the school community as a whole recognizes the value of parental involvement and endeavors to forge a partnership with parents on a regular basis, the overall student achievement can be expected to improve.

There are numerous arenas in which counselors can encourage and recognize the importance of parental involvement in students' academic achievement. Augmenting those events in which parents are invited to visit the campus, counselors can build on this involvement by including parents in planning and decision making programs as appropriate. Another suggestion is to research the talents and skills of parents, and develop a volunteer pool. Educators and counselors will need to give specific directions for participation, and can diversify the selection of areas in which parents can contribute their time and expertise. Counselors can also acknowledge parental involvement through written newsletters, or at school events. Counselors should focus on the mutual goal of academic success, and recognize the parents' contributions. Counselors can distribute additional academic resources to parents. The school should be portrayed as welcoming to families. Counselors may want to even coordinate transportation and baby-sitting for parent visits.

Communicating with parents

Counselors can set a welcoming tone each year, by proactively welcoming parents and encouraging participation in their students' academic lives. The following are some effective modes for setting this tone:

- Send a welcome letter at the beginning of the year which includes a calendar of events, and invites parents to participate.
- Provide a resource brochure or informational handout with general school policies and the counselor's role in the students' lives.
- Distribute informational resources explaining the counselor's role, the counseling program(s), community resources and pertinent contact information.
- Send event and meeting calendars on a regular basis, which could include contact information for support resources, including that of the counselor.
- Generate a school newsletter that will give parents and the surrounding community information with information about school resources and possibly include peripheral articles or notes of interest.
- Schedule new-family meetings right before school starts.

Promoting social justice

A campus that endorses and supports social justice does not differentiate between members of diverse cultures, races, economic status, special needs, sexual orientation or gender, religious background, appearance, or second language speakers. Counselors can facilitate this kind of campus through their work with individual students, and by working with the particularities of the data system. All members of the community will expand their commitment to social justice and educational equity when the systemic data-driven approach is initiated at the school, which will increase the probability of all students having equal opportunities within the school counseling program. The counseling program in particular is a prime area in which to model equal access to resources by advocating and affirming all students with no attention to personal characteristics that define each student. By promoting social justice, campuses provide a model for the surrounding community.

Data-driven counseling program

Counselors may find that an existing counseling program or other student services model may be data driven, meaning that statistics are routinely collected and presented, from which curricular and student services decisions are often made. Counselors may discover that either the data being generated is incomplete, or it is being organized and presented in a manner that does not reveal pertinent information about particular student issues. Data may reveal information about the entire student body without focusing on groups of students in need. Counselors can apply system analysis to the data system toward the goal of redirecting either the data collection or data presentation in a manner that will isolate student needs that can be addressed in the counseling program. By placing the student at the center of the system, data regarding school, family and community becomes more relevant. School counselors can also view the entire system, including subsystems, and the interconnectedness of those systems.

Holistic counseling

It is understood that the benefits of a data-driven counseling program include quantifiable accountability and assessment of professional review organizations. The ASCA views it as being clearly defined and sequential. This can also offer a holistic, comprehensive assessment of individual students. Counselors can provide the bridge between the systemic overview and the needs of individual students by working with the design of the data collection system toward one that promotes holistic development in students. This includes nurturing individual qualities in students, and cultivating the particular goals and skills identified in the data. Using the data-driven system for the planning of implementation of the program, counselors can partner with school members to develop a comprehensive program that identifies the needs of individual students as well as the student body as a whole. This type of program will benefit the students by giving them the confidence and leadership to pursue their dreams.

School mission statement

Counselors will be well served to refer to a school's mission statement when developing or revising programs or data system. A mission statement represents the basic tenets, philosophies and goals of the school as a whole, which should be represented appropriately in its programs and practices. The mission statement can assist counselors when proposing programs or outreach efforts, so that the overall direction and mission of the school can be incorporated in the rationale for the proposal(s). Counselors may also be in a position to collaborate with school officials in developing or revising a mission statement, possibly to better serve a diverse population and/or the surrounding community. The statement should embody a collective result for all students, and provide a clear and concise focus that will frame future program development and evaluation as well as data collection systems.

Assessment component

When developing assessment methods for a systemic approach, counselors may first want to refer to existing data from school and district databases as well as adequate yearly progress (AYP) reports for a baseline representation of academic achievement or other pertinent information. Qualitative assessment from focus groups, interviews and observations can provide a profile of key areas to be addressed. Counselors can then glean a basic understanding of what influences the access, attainment and achievement of students. Counselors may then want to choose the best format for assessment, incorporating best methods for garnering information, most comprehensive participation, and best feedback. They will want to look at those specific areas that will provide the clearest and most comprehensive picture of assessment of the program. Once the data is synthesized into a rubric, or other assessment vehicle, counselors can identify the students' needs more clearly and the areas that need to be addressed within the school community.

Goals to be addressed

Counselors developing a systemic approach to counseling and assessment can first refer to those identified goals at the school, district, state and federal levels, in order to tailor the quantitative data in accordance with recognized goals for which the school is accountable. Some of the identified goals are as follows:

- *National goals:* Reduction of attainment and achievement gaps, attendance improvement, likelihood of a drug-free school environment.
- *State goals:* National goals, some of which are identified above, as well as state-specific goals such as improving the rate of literacy, post-secondary matriculation, etc.
- *District goals:* At the district level, there may be additional goals to state and national that address key areas identified at the district level.
- *Local goals:* Further focus on the needs of students and how those goals can be realized in students' lives.

Program integration

The effective data-driven approach to improving student achievement is a collaborative endeavor shared by educators, counselors and other school personnel. Recognizing that each program strives for equal access, attainment, and achievement for the students, counselors can work with educators and other school staff toward a comprehensive data assessment system, and ongoing oversight and revision as needed. A holistic systemic approach utilizes inherent connections between programs. Education and counseling programs are connected by a related structure that allows for the alignment of content, delivery, and the reporting of results. The systemic data-driven counseling program is further connected to the school mission, inherently aligning it with the program goals, development, and evaluation of educational goals. All school-based programs are aligned with federal and state goals, and any counseling goals are aligned with ASCA standards that address goals and strategies to best target student needs. Through these combined efforts, students are supported toward their academic and career goals.

Programs and participants

Schools that are regulated and data driven nonetheless recognize that targeting the whole student can include not only classroom delivery, but also extracurricular activities. Since the school is also a social system, it includes a hierarchy of activities and relationships that incorporate the entire school community. Standards-based educational programs can generate standards and competencies for classroom delivery, tutoring programs, extracurricular clubs, peer programs, mentoring programs, school sports, service learning projects, honor societies, and arts-music groups. The comprehensive education program can also include the contributions and considerations of parents, business collaborators, and pertinent outreach programs. The presence of absence of this kind of holistic inclusion can define a school culture in a way that either supports or hinders students' achievement. When developing a counseling program, counselors should endeavor to support and enhance existing educational program approaches, to the maximum benefit for students.

<u>Implementation</u>
Implementation of a data-driven program is uniquely delivered at each of the following levels within the school community:

- Individual levels focus on particular students, including crisis situations and student-specific situations, and can provide insight into issues experienced by the entire student body.
- Grade levels focus on age-specific experiences and may be best implemented by long-term planning.
- Classroom levels align the counseling program with the academic curriculum.
- School-wide levels call for coordination of interventions, toward benefiting the entire school.
- Family levels involve parents and/or guardians as equal partners in the promotion of student achievement.
- Community levels involve members of the surrounding area to form partnerships toward the promotion of student achievement.

<u>Program value</u>
Counselors and other interested parties can view firsthand the effectiveness that data-driven accountability can add to the contributions of counselors toward student achievement. Data-based assessment that is designed around standardized categories can also assist state and national data management in evaluating their goals for equity in academic achievement. Information gleaned can assist counselors in identifying which programs were successful, and which programs could be improved. Data revealed in well-designed systemic programs can isolate particular academic areas, student issues or student populations that are not being well served. Counselors can implement strategies for program improvement, incorporating its assessment in the data system. As counselors are regularly able to evaluate and revise the process of setting goals and assessing their achievement, they can tailor the school counseling program to effectively and comprehensively serve the needs of the students, the school, and the community.

<u>Counselor's responsibility in development</u>
Counselors who do not adopt the data-driven model of program development inherently place themselves out of the accountability sphere that includes the school and district. They may place the program at risk by not aligning it with the accountability paradigm. Counselors who are ethically responsible should garner the benefits of a data-driven system of planning and accountability. Counselors can embrace the systemic approach by utilizing the expertise of school administrators and district counseling resources. They can then serve as mentors for emerging school counselors. Counselors should take the time to research available information about data-driven programs, and how they can best benefit the students and the counseling

program. This includes learning how to analyze the data, apply it to existing strategies and programs, and revise intervention strategies accordingly. Although data-driven counseling does not replace individual counseling, it can provide valuable empirical oversight to assist the counselor in maintaining an effective and relevant program.

<u>Utilization steps</u>
Counselors can apply the following steps to realize a program that embodies social justice with a mission of access and equity:
- *Analyze data to identify need.* Example: Graduation rates may identify inequity between demographic groups.
- *Develop goals.* Example: Graduation for all students.
- *Align goals with school mission:* Sequential year plans for graduation involve all stakeholders.
- *Integrate interventions.* Example: Utilize existing educational programs toward the goal of graduation for all students.
- *Implement interventions at different levels:* Incorporate interrelated and interdependent interventions at various levels.
- *Collect data results:* All levels of program intervention should be collected.
- *Analyze data and present for evaluation:* Include goals met, goals not met, and discuss strategies.
- *Revise programs if needed:* Make changes to program strategies in accordance with new data.

Counselor as ambassador

Data-driven accountability of a school counseling program can provide counselors with ordered data and methodical strategies for strengthening appreciation for the program by the school community. Counselors can provide the following accountability information:
- Program evaluations or audits when asked about the comprehensive, standard-based program in place.
- Needs assessment results when asked about the specific needs of the student population based on the results of evaluations.
- Service assessment results when asked to provide examples of implementations that address student needs.
- Results or outcomes of studies when asked about the results of interventions.
- Performance evaluations when asked about counselor performance.

The school counselor must perform the tasks of needs assessment, program evaluation, test program management and interpretation of assessment results, in order to effectively address the accountability of the counseling program to school boards, parents or other members of the community who may be concerned about the value of the program.

Accountability model

A proactive approach to school counseling accountability includes clearly articulated parameters for responsibilities and duties, well-defined evaluation and assessment vehicles, and reporting the results of the evaluation to stakeholders. The following components contribute to a dynamic accountability model:

- Collaborate with stakeholder groups. Take a proactive, collaborative stance.
- Collect data and assess the needs of students, educators and community.
- Set goals and establish outcomes as revealed by data.
- Implement effective interventions that address the goals and objectives.
- Design and implement effective outcome assessment for the interventions.
- Utilize the results to improve the counseling program.
- Share the results with students, parents, educators, school administrators, school boards, school counselors and supervisors, and community leaders.

Reporting outcome assessment

As a member of the school community, counselors can report outcome assessment in a way that will be best understood and accessible by the other members of that community. One of the ways that this can be achieved is by categorizing outcome results in alignment with the groupings established by the school. By presenting data that aligns with educational outcomes, the connection between the counseling and educational programs will be more clearly understood. Counselors may also want to provide access to outcome assessment to the larger school community. Results can be disaggregated to profile outcomes for grade levels, individuals or subgroups on the school campus. Some counselors may also provide online access to outcome results for students, families, or community, in a report card or other user-friendly format. By providing reasonable access to easily understood data, counselors can further cultivate the integration of both educational and counseling goals achievement.

Counselor's transformed role

The role of the school counselor has broadened and integrated, so that the goals and delivery of the counseling program dovetail with those of the school as a whole. School counselors as educators recognize that school curriculum delivery and achievement standards are quantifiable media to address the access, attainment, and achievement goals of each individual student as well as the student body as a whole. Counselors also frame their approach with a basic premise that students who are given rigorous curriculum and good support are capable of realizing their potential. Augmenting individual sessions and group workshops, counselors can participate in academic program planning. By integrating educational and counseling goals, counselors can provide the bridge between personal success and academic achievement. The counseling program can provide finger-on-the-pulse assessment that profiles holistic achievement of the students, by operating within the accountability paradigm of the school.

Equity in policies

Well documented assessment provides accountability for the success of the program in addressing student needs. Assessment reporting and documentation can also isolate and identify student groups that are not being served by current programs and policies. By disaggregating data, school counselors can reveal portions of the student demographic – such as those identified by race, ethnicity, socioeconomic status, and other defining categories – that are not being met. Counselors may also want to conduct longitudinal studies that will reveal success or failures of strategies within these subgroups. This kind of focused, delineated data can clearly point to underserved students, and the need for revisions in policy or program development to incorporate the identified students. The contemporary school counselor can serve as a leader in the creation and refinement of school programs that equally address the needs of all students. Documented assessment can provide the kind of tangible evidence that may be needed to garner school support for policy changes.

Integration of goals

Counselors can best serve their students and the school system as a whole by continually integrating developmental goals with academic goals. Since students mature and move through the graded school system simultaneously, counselors should maintain a conscientious awareness of achievement standards in the areas of academic development, personal-social development, and career-focused development. These areas are inherently interdependent, and an effective counselor will consciously integrate them toward the holistic development of his/her students. The ASCA identifies three key strategies for this integration:
- Counselors should be cognizant of the academic content in classes, and when those classes are being taught, tailoring his/her counseling sessions around the academic needs of the students.
- Counselors should refer to the school documents and personnel for explicit and implicit goals and competency standards for the students.
- Counselors can be proactive in enriching certain academic areas for students.

Accountability studies

Accountability studies can enhance counselors' overall knowledge and awareness about the effectiveness of strategies or programs, so that they can provide valuable input to the decision-making process involved in new programs or practices. Based on the results of these studies, counselors may become aware of professional development or staffing needs. The quantitative data from the studies can provide the tangible rationale for these requests. Counselors who are well versed on the assessment results of their program are better able to network with other counseling professionals to share program results and increase their awareness of new intervention strategies. Accountability studies can be a valuable public relations vehicle for informing educators and the larger community about the accomplishments of the school counseling program and the focus of the school system for its students. Counselors who engage in accountability studies demonstrate a personal and professional commitment to ongoing standards of quality and success.

Although accountability studies can provide valuable information for the school counselor as well as the school community as a whole, there are inherent disadvantages and cautions associated with the studies. An obvious disadvantage is that the studies take time away from individual or group counseling, in order for the counselor to implement and assess the accountability model of evaluation. Although this time could be well justified by the overall benefits to the program and to the student body, these benefits can only be realized if the counselor is trained in utilizing the data, and spends the time on research and evaluation to garner any useful results. Counselors may have misgivings about utilizing accountability studies because they may produce results that are counterintuitive to implementation strategies that have proved successful in individual and/or group counseling. Some counselors may also be hesitant to perform accountability studies because of a perception of being micro-managed by the stakeholders requesting the data from the studies.

SCPAC

The school counseling advisory committee (SCPAC) is generally comprised of counselors, parents, educators, and other members of the community, all of whom have a stake and influence in the school's decision making. The school principal should always be included, particularly since s/he will need to be included in the discussion about proposed program improvements or recommendations, and will be instrumental in approving funding for these proposals. The SCPAC can serve as a backboard for decision making and can assist the counselor in introducing needed program changes or requesting resources. The SCPAC can serve as a liaison committee with the larger community, and can include parent-teacher organizations by invitation or at least by communicating with them regarding relevant impending decisions. By including community input through the liaison SCPAC committee, counselors demonstrate their willingness to consider outside perspectives and additional sources for funding.

Assuming that the SCPAC is active, ongoing and not undergoing significant changes, it is customary for the group to meet once each semester to discuss the needs and available resources of the counseling program., and to provide recommendations and endorsement for proposed improvements. The group can analyze assessment results, propose program modifications, and consider recommendations from staff members. Program proposals are generally based on the results of assessments. The group can identify potential funding sources, but the school principal should always be included in any funding discussions. The group can serve as a valuable resource for demonstrating support among the school community for program enhancement, and potentially for influencing the principal in funding and approval decisions. Counselors should consider the benefits and the potential impact of the SCPAC and focus their attention and time to the group as needed.

Legal and ethical obligations

Counselors are obligated both explicitly and implicitly to treat each of their clients ethically and within legal boundaries. Counselors need to be aware of all federal, state, district and other institutional laws and mandates regarding school counseling. Counselors also should recognize the ethical obligation to be cognizant of current research and resources pertaining to issues that students will be dealing with in the counseling sessions. Although it is understandable that no one can know resources for all the possible situations facing students, it is nonetheless ethically required of counselors to endeavor to add to his/her knowledge as is reasonable, to best serve the students. Counselors who are beginning their careers may spend more time researching specific issues, but will become more increasingly more knowledgeable about issues impacting students. Professional associations provide guidelines and sources for counselors regarding this aspect.

American Counseling Association

The American Counseling Association (ACA) is a professional organization which purposes to promote the development of counselors, advance the counseling profession, and promote social justice within the profession. Their scope is all professional counselors. The ACA seeks to apply the profession and practice of counseling to the purpose of promoting and respecting cultural diversity, while enhancing the overall quality of life in society. The ACA includes 18 divisions that focus on particular areas or work settings within the counseling profession, four geographic regions and 56 affiliate branches. It actually is comprised of a partnership of associations. The Association influences many aspects of professional counseling including credentialing of counselors, accreditation of counselor education programs, public policy and legislation, and professional resources and services. The Association operates in part through committees, holds functions, and has developed specific programs for the advancement of the profession.

Standing committees

The following are the 15 standing committees of the ACA, identified by the professional issues addressed by each: Ethics, Awards, By-laws and Policies, Cyber-Technology, Financial Affairs, Human Rights, International, Interprofessional, Nominations and Elections, Professional Standards, Public Awareness and Support, Public Policy and Legislation, Publications, Research and Knowledge, Strategic Planning.

Ad hoc and task forces

Ad hoc task forces are created annually to address current concerns and relevant business issues. Most task forces are brought together for a year only, but can stay together if additional time is needed for the purposes at hand. In that case, members must be re-appointed. The ACA, with its affiliates, offers training workshops, professional development conferences, and learning institutes. ACA publications address current research and other relevant information. Many ACA books are used as textbooks in counseling courses.

ASCA, NBCC and ACA

A subgroup of the ACA, the American School Counselor Association (ASCA) addresses those issues in professional counseling that pertain to students, with a focus on academic, personal-social, and career development issues. School counselors are particularly pivotal in the lives of students in that long-term life success patterns are often closely tied to academic success and a positive school experience. The ASCA provides additional information to school counselors through professional development, research and advocacy.

The NBCC, the National Board for Certified Counselors, is the only national credentialing organization for counselors. The Board also has established several specialty-area certifications requiring passage of the National Counselor Exam (NCE).

A corporate partner the ACA, the CACREP, the Council for Accreditation of Counseling and Related Educational Programs, establishes state-of-the-art standards for counselor education programs which address curriculum, program objectives, program evaluation, faculty and staff criteria and other requirements.

Providing optimum competence

In addition to keeping abreast of laws and guidelines, counselors should include the following practices in order to provide current, optimum competence to their clients:

- Pursue opportunities for professional development. Most national and state credentials even require counselors to complete continuing educations training in order to stay current on theories, trends, and new data in the field.
- Remain current within the counselor's area of responsibility by reading, consulting, networking, and otherwise bringing new research, trends, and information as added resources for serving the clients.
- Represent credentials accurately. Only earned and applicable credentials should be listed.
- Provide only those services for which the counselor is trained and qualified. Counselors should have training in a particular technique before they practice it and should not try to work with students who have conditions beyond the counselor's realm of knowledge.

Ethical standards

Ethical standards are developed by most professional organizations, and are designed to direct the behavior of its members. The ethical standards for school counselors are frequently updated to reflect changes in the school system, usually at the federal level. These updated standards are revised in order to be relevant and appropriate for the school counseling profession. Ethical standards generally address the following three purposes:

- To educate members about sound ethical conduct.
- To provide a mechanism for accountability.
- To provide a mechanism for improvement of professional practices.

The ACA's Code of Ethics is based on the following five moral principles:

- *Autonomy:* The ability to make independent decision.
- *Justice:* Treatment that is fair and appropriate.
- *Beneficence:* Services and actions that are in the students' best interests.
- *Fidelity:* Commitment to the student regarding honor, loyalty and faithfulness.

- 129 -

- *Nonmaleficence:* Avoidance of actions or services that would cause harm to others.

Discrepancies in ethics codes

There is some responsibility on the part of the school counselor to critically apply codes of ethics in his/her professional life. It is worth noting that there are minor differences in the codes of ethics published by different professional organizations, for instance between those published by the ACA for counselors in general, and by the ASCA for school counselors in particular. Counselors should be cognizant of the codes and any relevant disparities, and be prepared to apply the appropriate code based on both the counseling setting, and in what capacity the counselor is operating. There are also, on occasion, ethical codes regarding a particular situation or relationship that seem to conflict with laws governing the same relationship or situation. Counselors are, within reason, obligated to adhere to the applicable law. However, counselors are encouraged to participate in the dynamics of setting ethical standards by initiating changes to mandates as appropriate.

Scope of the ACA Code of Ethics

Codes of ethics for the counseling profession generally apply to, and are designed for, actions and behavior that are best for the student, the situation and the profession. These codes are reviewed and revised as appropriate. The most current revision in August 2005 addresses the following key areas:
- The Association asks for clarity regarding all ethical responsibilities for current members.
- The Association and its Codes support the mission of the membership.
- The Association endeavors to establish principles by which ethical behavior is identified, and the practices of its members are delineated.
- The Association assists its members in generating a course of action that will utilize counseling services and promote the overall values of the counseling profession.
- The Association establishes the manner in which ethical complaints should be processed, and inquiries against its members should be initiated.

Scope of the ASCA Code of Ethics for School Counselors

Since the ASCA falls under the organizational umbrella of the ACA, its Code of Ethics parallels that of the ACA in general scope of benefit to the student, the situation, and the profession. The ASCA Code is delineated more specifically through its eight major sections:
- Duties to Students
- Duties to Parents
- Duties to Colleagues and Professional Associates
- Duties to the School and Region
- Duties to Self
- Duties to the Profession
- Adherence to Standards
- Resource Materials

Counselors should treat each student with respect and consider the student's best interest. They should involve the parents when possible, and exhibit professional and ethical behavior. They should also maintain their expertise through continued learning and development. School counselors should be well versed on both the ACA Code of Ethics, and the ASCA Code of Ethics. They should endeavor to incorporate the tenets of both in their professional life, and carefully research both in the event of an ethical dilemma.

Determining if an ethical problem exists

There are prescribed steps to take in the process of identifying and addressing an ethical problem in the counseling profession. The ACA model is comprised of the following steps:

- Recognize the issue.
- Consult direction from the ACA Code of Ethics.The type of issue and its components.
- Consider possible courses of action.The potential consequences of each course, and choose the most appropriate action.
- Assess the results of the course of action.
- Implement the course of action.

The ASCA model specifies:

- The issue is addressed both realistically and philosophically.
- Consult direction from the law, the ACA Code of Ethics, and the ASCA Code of Ethics.
- Factor in the developmental and chronological age of the student.
- Assess the student rights, parental rights, and circumstances.
- Adhere to ethical and moral principles.The potential courses of action and consequences.
- Assess the results of the selected action.
- Consult
- Implement the action.

Laws

Although laws are based on generally accepted norms, customs, values and beliefs, they are more binding and carry more severe penalties than ethical standards. Laws are codified into written governing documents. Laws are more prescriptive and require that counselors comply or be penalized. Both laws and ethical standards are designed to ensure that professionals following appropriate behavior patterns and act in the best interests of the student(s). Laws and ethical standards should adhere to the same patterns and expectations, but if on occasion a law conflicts with an ethical standard, the counselor is encouraged to comply with the law. Counselors must advise the student if they encounter a situation where the laws and ethical standards are in conflict, and inform the student that they will follow the legal course of action, provided there is no harm to the student as a result.

Legal mandates for professional counseling behavior

There are numerous laws and levels of law governing the behaviors, expectations and limitations of school counselors. Counselors are obligated to follow the laws of their state, and those of the federal government. However, these laws may be further tempered by statutory laws, common laws and/or appellate decisions. Although counselors are not expected to be legal experts, they should nonetheless be cognizant of the federal and state laws governing their scope of responsibility. As needed, they should critically analyze relevant interpretations of the law, such as in common law . They should also refer to peripheral mandates and appellate decisions if a particular situation warrants the time and clarification of researching it to this extent. If counselors are researching appellate decisions, they should have a working knowledge of the appeal process in their particular state, and any relevant appeal procedures in other states, should the situation call for reference to precedent.

Parameters of statutory law governing school counseling

Generally speaking, federal law serves to enact the Constitution. Under this umbrella, state laws generally address education, health, and other comparable programs through mandates. These state mandates, the body of which is referred to as statutory law, are created through legislation passed by state legislatures and the U.S. Congress. State mandates generally are more specific and more prescribed than federal laws, although they cannot be more restrictive than federal law. State legislatures create state laws that implement federal legislation, as well as laws specific to the state. The federal government has also passed several laws, within the parameters of the Constitution, that affect professional school counselors and others in comparable fields. Because statutory law generally addresses issues related to health and education, school counselors should be well versed in relevant state law, but should also be aware of federal laws that can impact their profession.

Incorporating state laws into rulings and guidelines of district, regional, and state education governance agencies

In the broadest sense, governance is the interpretation and implementation of codified laws. Tailored to the school counseling profession, the state legislatures as a rule create legislation that addresses the field of education, from which state and local agencies interpret and implement rules and guidelines. The state boards of education generally enact regulations at the school district level that either address areas not specifically addressed in state legislation, or interpret it more specifically to that arena. These regulations, or guidelines, are not legally binding like legislation, but are representative of how agencies view certain circumstances. This interpretation is subject to the oversight of the state attorney general, particularly if a regulation is challenged. Local school systems may also develop guidelines and policies, tailoring state regulations to the local environs. Individual schools may further refine these policies addressing the professional behavior of school counselors.

Incorporating knowledge of the law into professional decisions

For school counselors to act professionally and ethically, a basic knowledge of the laws governing their profession is expected. Beyond that, counselors should avail themselves of information regarding updates or interpretations of relevant law, and other pertinent data. Sources for this information can include on-site supervisors, ACA newsletters, professional journals, commercially available newsletters, the internet, etc. Counselors should recognize that the law and its interpretation are not static, and knowledge of the law needs to be maintained on an ongoing basis. Counselors also have the responsibility to implement and interpret the law reasonably. If state mandates appear to be in conflict with other regulations or ethical standards, counselors should apply common sense and critical thinking to the interpretation or application of the ruling. If this should occur, any decisions or actions should be documented carefully, and counselors should bring the conflict to the attention of appropriate parties as soon as possible.

Responding to subpoenas

Counselors may be served with subpoenas, relating to allegations of child abuse, neglect, custody disputes, etc.. Counselors should recognize that subpoenas are legal documents, but should respond within the context of his/her obligation to the student and the school guidelines. Counselors should not violate a student's confidentiality beyond that mandated in the school guidelines. The subpoena should always be discussed with the student or the student's attorney, and in some cases the school attorney, before any information is provided to any legal entity. Once the appropriate counsel approve compliance with the subpoena, school counselors should then discuss how the release of information will affect all parties, and should obtain a signed informed-consent form in order to release necessary records. If, on the other hand, the attorneys do not approve the release of information, they should file a motion to quash, which will release the counselor from the obligation to respond. All actions should be clear and documented.

Legal and ethical parameters of confidentiality

Counselors are both legally and professionally committed to respect and protect students' confidentiality. The primary professional consideration relates to the establishment of trust with the student. Confidentiality essentially belongs to the student. It is his or her right and choice to disclose information. Counselors who respect this contribute to the cultivation of trust that is vital to the counselor-client relationship. However, if students who are under 18, this legal right expands to the students' parents. In the case of counselors working with students under the age of 18, they can request that parents respect the student's confidentiality, but parents of minors are allowed to be present during the session(s). Nonetheless, whether a student is a minor or over 18, counselors can communicate with the students regarding the rights and responsibilities relating to confidentiality, whether that means parents must be informed or if that is optional.

Including parents in sessions

The ideal situation regarding a minor student is if a student readily accepts and invites his/her parents to participate in the session(s). However, if this is not the case, there are steps counselors can take to ease the disclosure. Counselors should discuss confidentiality with students at the initial session, and let them know the legal parameters. Students may be hesitant to let parents know about their problems, for fear of the parents' reactions. Also, when broaching the subject of disclosure, counselors should be sensitive to the possibility of family secrets, sensitive information, cultural issues and other factors that could be problematic when including parents in counseling session. Counselors can work students to get them comfortable with the idea of including their parents, and can discuss reasonable boundaries before the parents are invited to participate. However, if minor students refuse to include their parents or to give permission to disclose information, counselors may still be obligated to report certain types of information to the parents.

Confidentiality exceptions

There are certain circumstances, as outlined in the ACA Code of Ethics, whereby a counselor may break, and in some cases is obligated to break, student confidentiality. Generally, counselors may break confidentiality if a student is in danger of harming his/herself or others, if there is indication of abuse, or if there is any other life-threatening situation. There are other circumstances for which confidentiality may be breached:

- Counselors may disclose confidential documents with subordinates in the regular course of business.
- Members of treatment teams, consultation groups, families, and third-party players may break confidentiality through regular verbal interaction.
- Parents may be legally informed of the counseling discussions held with their minor children.
- Parents or family members may be justifiably informed if they could contact a life-threatening disease through association with the student.
- Court-ordered disclosure by way of a subpoena may require the counselor to share information, although that information can be restricted to what is absolutely necessary.

Minor consent laws

Minor consent laws are mandated at the state level and define the circumstances under which counselors may protect the confidentiality of a minor student. These laws fall under the federal regulation that prohibits the breaking of confidentiality for patient recovery, regardless of the patient's minor status. Generally, minor consent laws allow confidentiality regarding issues such as substance abuse, mental health, and reproductive health areas, without releasing information to parents or guardians. There is some controversy regarding the interpretation of these laws, but a common implementation is a school-based student assistant program (SAP) comprised of teams that include an administrator, a counselor or a nurse, a teacher and possibly substance abuse assessors from local agencies. School staff can refer students to the SAP team who will collaboratively determine best action for the student. Counselors should be well informed about the state mandates and local interpretations of the minor consent law.

HIPAA and FERPA regulations

There are three key federal acts governing the disclosure of student records. The most significant is the Family Educational Rights and Privacy Act (FERPA) of 1974 which limits the disclosure of student records. The Privacy Rule of 2001 established national rights for privacy and security regarding health information, which rights were in concert with FERPA. The Health Insurance Portability and Accountability Act (HIPAA) of 1996 generated national standards regarding the privacy of individually identified health information, set criteria for health records, and delineated patients' rights. Any school records, including health records, that are protected under FERPA are not subject to HIPAA regulations, however educators in special education may be required to obtain the services of outside professionals whose services are governed by HIPAA. Counselors should be knowledgeable and aware of regulations regarding the exchange of student information, and when exceptions to FERPA are warranted by HIPAA or other law.

Child abuse

Counselors are required by federal mandate to report any cases of child abuse or neglect. This is mandated by the Keeping Children and Families Safe Act of 2003. If a counselor or other professional has reason to believe that abuse or neglect has occurred within 24 to 72 hours, s/he is obligated to call Child Protective Services (CPS) and report orally and in writing their suspicions with a time frame specified by the state. Note that if a report proves false, the counselor/professional is not liable unless the report was made with malicious intent. Child abuse can include physical abuse, mental injury, sexual abuse or exploitation, maltreatment of a child under 18 or the age specified by the state child protection law, and negligent treatment. Counselors should be knowledgeable of state and other mandates regarding the report of child abuse.

It is important to remember that the counselor is obligated to report suspicion of child abuse. Counselors who suspect child abuse and do not report it could lose their license or certification, face disciplinary action, and/or have their employment terminated. It is also significant to remember that an individual who reports reasonable suspicion of child abuse is not required to prove the abuse, but rather just to report suspicion. The law protects the individual who reasonably suspects child abuse. Also notable is that parents and guardians are not granted rights to information during this process, and should not be informed regarding the report. The department of social services and/or law enforcement agencies will contact the parents as appropriate, and will conduct the investigation. Counselors should be knowledgeable about laws regarding child abuse, as well as school, district and other applicable procedures.

Practice Test

Practice Questions

1. What developmental theory describes an adolescent's ability to think abstractly?
   a. Cognitive Development
   b. Erickson's Theory of Development
   c. Social Cognitive Theory
   d. Dynamic Systems Theory

2. According to the Social Cognitive Theory, to what does the term "perspective taking" refer?
   a. Internalizing another person's situation
   b. Thinking cognitively about another person's situation
   c. Role playing
   d. Thinking cognitively about your own situation

Questions 3 and 4 pertain to the following vignette:

A 5-year-old boy continues to attempt to play with children who openly ridicule him and leave him out of games. His persistence with this group of children has recently resulted in a number of fights on the playground. After being referred to your office, you learn that he has an unsupportive home life. His parents were divorced last year. He lives with his mother who works at night, and he does not see his father. He is often left at home alone; however, a neighbor watches him from time to time.

3. According to the Cognitive Behavior Theory, what developmental skills is this child lacking?
   a. Interpersonal skills
   b. Abstract thinking skills
   c. Concrete thinking skills
   d. Self-Identity

4. According to Pavlov's theory of development, what would you expect to occur in terms of this child's learning and behavior?
   a. Nothing, he would naturally continue to try to fit in.
   b. The child would become conditioned to the negative response and avoid the situation.
   c. The child would take cues from his social environment and act accordingly.
   d. The child would grow out of this stage and soon make friends.

5. Which of the following would be a barrier to a child's mental development?
   a. Malnutrition
   b. An abusive home
   c. A lack of family support
   d. All of the above

6. When dealing with middle school students, it is important for a counselor to understand the developmental relationship between Industry and Inferiority. This is an example of a theory of development based on the work of what psychologist?
   a. Freud
   b. Piaget
   c. Erickson

d. Bandura

7. According to Piaget, what is a schema?
   a. Information that has been taught
   b. A universal view of the world
   c. An individual's representation of something
   d. The visualization of a concept

8. Beginning around the age of 11, children can think in logical, abstract terms. According to Piaget's theory of development, what stage does this represent?
   a. Formal operational
   b. Pre-operational
   c. Concrete operational
   d. Sensory-motor

9. What is Bandura's main argument concerning behavior development?
   a. Behavior and environment affect each other.
   b. The ego is affected by the id and superego.
   c. Genetics is the sole cause of behavior.
   d. Behavior has no effect on the environment.

10. According to Kohlberg's theory of moral development, a student will follow school rules in order to avoid receiving detention. This is an example of what stage of moral development?
    a. Personal Reward
    b. Law and Order
    c. Good Boy-Nice Girl
    d. Punishment-Obedience

11. When a diagnostic assessment for learning needs is conducted, what factors are not considered?
    a. Prior knowledge
    b. Interests
    c. Learning style preferences
    d. Sociability

12. When would a formative assessment be conducted?
    a. Prior to an intervention
    b. During an intervention
    c. After an intervention
    d. Only if the student refuses an intervention

13. What is one explanation if a student continues to perform poorly on Summative Assessments?
    a. Formative assessments were not properly conducted.
    b. The intervention was successful.
    c. The student is bored and is not trying.
    d. The assessment is too difficult.

14. According to Bloom's Taxonomy of Learning, what is the highest level of learning?
    a. Evaluation
    b. Comprehension

c. Application

d. Knowledge

Questions 15 to 17 pertain to the following information:

In survey type assessments, a Lykert-type scale is often used. These scales use either an even or an odd number of responses. For scales using an even number of responses, there is no neutral answer, and the individual must choose either a negative or a positive response. For scales using an odd number of responses, the individual has the opportunity to choose a neutral or undecided response.

15. As a counselor, you decide to use a 5-point Lykert scale student survey to determine your students' knowledge and use of drugs and alcohol. What is one flaw of this method that you must be aware of?

a. Students might not understand the scale.

b. Students might choose the neutral selection to avoid committing to a positive or negative answer.

c. The method can produce unrealistic results due to social desirability factors.

d. None of the above

16. What is one downside to using a 4-point Lykert-type scale?

a. It does not provide enough choices.

b. It forces a student to choose either positive or negatively.

c. Responses cannot be validated.

d. There are is no downside.

17. A student is given a 5-point Lykert Type scale and selects all Neutral responses. What would a counselor determine from these results?

a. The student is laid back and easy going.

b. The student did not want to share his own thoughts and wanted to get the assessment does as quickly as possible.

c. The student did not understand the task.

d. The student is in need of intervention for indecisiveness.

18. What is the benefit of continued assessments?

a. Student progress is monitored.

b. Areas of weakness are identified.

c. Learning styles and goals can be modified.

d. All of the above

19. What is the purpose of demographic information on survey assessments?

a. No real purpose

b. This information should not be included.

c. Identify differences

d. Identify similarities

20. Pre–post tests are important tools for assessments. What is the main thing to consider when developing a pre-post test?

a. Who will take the test

b. Key ideas and concepts

c. Number of questions

d. When to give the test

21. Elementary school counselors must have a strong understanding of what?
    a. Child development
    b. Continued education options
    c. Relationship building
    d. Adjustment and coping mechanisms

22. What issues might a primary prevention group address for adolescent girls?
    a. Grief and loss
    b. Aggressive behaviors
    c. Self esteem
    d. Abuse

23. Communication and conflict resolution can be taught most effectively in what type of setting?
    a. Primary prevention group
    b. Structured intervention group
    c. Individual counseling
    d. Group detentions

24. Rather than requiring students who disobey the rules on fighting to serve a silent detention, you suggest conducting a problem-centered, structured intervention group. What issues should you focus on during this group?
    a. Self-actualization
    b. Aggressive behaviors
    c. Safety
    d. Physiological issues

25. Teachers need basic safety training in school violence to learn how to keep themselves and students safe. In addition to this basic safety training, what other issues should be discussed to assist teachers in understanding problems in their schools?
    a. Student dynamics
    b. Basic psychology of the student involved in violence
    c. Nonviolent reactions to student behavior
    d. All of the above

26. In group interventions, there are typically three stages involved in the group dynamics: group formation, group awareness, and group action. What is the focus of the Group Formation stage?
    a. To facilitate cooperation
    b. To introduce all participates
    c. To find out why everyone is in the group
    d. To ask what group members hope to gain from the group

27. What is the main premise behind Solution-Focused Brief Counseling?
    a. Serious underlying psychological problems must be addressed before counseling can take place.
    b. Individuals have the ability to solve their own problems with the assistance of a counselor.
    c. Individuals cannot understand their own issues and need a counselor to help them.
    d. This counseling technique is effective after only three sessions.

28. Solution-Focused Brief Counseling consists of what six steps?
   a. Define problem, determine goals, develop intervention, assign strategic tasks, emphasize positive behavior, terminate counseling
   b. Define problem, determine goals, develop intervention, revisit goals, develop a second intervention, terminate counseling
   c. Conduct psychoanalysis, determine underlying problem, develop group intervention plan, reinforce behavior, assign strategic task, terminate counseling
   d. Identify prevention steps, define problem, determine goals, develop intervention, assign strategic task, terminate counseling

29. When developing an intervention, a counselor should state the problem in a positive way. What is this known as?
   a. Positive problem statements
   b. Utilization
   c. Reframing
   d. Rephrasing

30. Some counselors give students assignments related to the problems and goals that have been identified in counseling sessions to complete in between sessions. What is this kind of an assignment called?
   a. Homework
   b. Counselor Tasking
   c. Strategic Task
   d. Goal-oriented Task

31. A student comes into your office with a referral from her English teacher. This is typically a straight A student; however, her grades have been slipping lately. She states that she has been "stressed out" but that nothing serious is going on. What issues might you want to ask about in order to determine the reason for her lower grades?
   a. Self-esteem issues
   b. Problems with a friend or boyfriend
   c. Difficulty level of her classes
   d. Mental health history

32. There are a number of risk factors affecting children and adolescents. Which is not considered a risk factor?
   a. Poverty
   b. Uneducated parents
   c. Single-parent family
   d. One parent with a high school diploma and one with a bachelor's degree

33. A known bully in the school is referred to your office. In addition to providing intervention for his violent behavior, what common issue or risk factor should you take into consideration?
   a. Pathology
   b. Potential to drop out of school
   c. Future self-esteem issues
   d. Poor conflict management skills

34. Young girls who experience abuse in the home or in a relationship have increased risk factors including:
   a. Drug abuse
   b. Teen pregnancy
   c. Poor grades
   d. All of the above

35. As a high school counselor, you observe that the numbers of pregnant teens on campus have been increasing over the past few years. What steps can you put into place to address this issue?
   a. Continue to focus on student academics
   b. Allow pregnant students to have a lighter course load in order to focus on their health and the pregnancy
   c. Develop prevention and intervention programs to address this issue
   d. Counsel students on the difficulties of having a child at this age and assist with federal aid paperwork

36. A recent transfer student came from an inner city school to your rural school. She is having difficulty adjusting to the area and the school. As the counselor, what steps can you take to ease this student's transition?
   a. Announce that there is a new student and ask volunteers to show her around the school
   b. Create a support team with the help of other students, teachers, and the new student's parents
   c. Provide Solution-Focused Brief Counseling to the student to find out the underlying problem
   d. Provide information about making friends and offer this information to the student and her parents

37. A local plant recently closed down, causing hundreds of adults in your community to lose their jobs. How might this affect the school district's community?
   a. Schools may experience a drop in attendance and achievement.
   b. Students will be able to spend more time with their parents and, as a result, do better in school.
   c. The number of students in schools will decrease as families move to find work.
   d. There may be an increase in participation in the school's on-the-job training program, as students need to work to help the family financially.

38. The school you work in has a high rate of parent participation. You would like to use this information to further increase the success of your students. What can a counselor do to make sure parents have the opportunity to continue supporting the school?
   a. Send notes home thanking them for their continued support
   b. Develop programs that encourage parent participation
   c. Offer parent education programs addressing the needs of their children in terms of success in the future
   d. Provide students with mentoring programs so that they can gain the support of adults in the business community

39. One major risk factor for students is having parents with little or no education or parents who do not speak English as a first language. As a counselor, how could you address this issue?
   a. Offer educational opportunities for parents, such as reading and writing classes
   b. Suggest to parents that they enroll in college and earn degrees
   c. Develop educational programs that teach students to be independent of their families
   d. Provide counseling services to all students who have uneducated parents

40. Studies have suggested that training in social skills benefits gifted and special needs students. What specific factor does such training address?
   a. Self-esteem
   b. Sociability
   c. Attendance rates
   d. Family risk factors

41. Collaboration with other teachers is a good way to incorporate positive behaviors and communication throughout the school. How can a teacher advisor program assist in this collaboration?
   a. Provides all-around support to the students
   b. Makes the teacher feel important and more willing to work with the counselor
   c. Provides more watchful eyes for bad behavior
   d. Gives students more opportunities to get help with their school work

42. The DIRECT technique is a consulting method used in many school districts. What does DIRECT stand for?
   a. District Initiative Regarding Educational Counseling Techniques
   b. Dynamic Introspective Reasoning for Educational Counseling Theory
   c. Direct Individual Response Educational Consulting Technique
   d. Direct Individual Reaction to Educational Counseling Theories

Questions 43 to 46 pertain to the following vignette:

You work in an inner city school where students are subject to a number of risk factors. The rate of violent incidences is above average, as are the numbers of drug offensives and teen pregnancies. The school currently has various in-house prevention and intervention programs offered on a volunteer or referral basis to all students. However, even the most successful of these programs yield few positive results. As the counselor, you decide to restructure the programs in an attempt to increase their effectiveness by collaborating with the community.

43. Collaborations with the community will help provide students with more effective programs in what main way?
   a. The number of support systems for students both during school and outside of school will increase.
   b. Opportunities to keep a close eye on students when outside of school will be offered.
   c. School programs will receive increased funding.
   d. Volunteer opportunities for community members will grow.

44. You would like to enhance your school's drug prevention programs. Which community agency will you most likely collaborate with?
   a. Local police department
   b. Local courthouse
   c. Local jail
   d. Local AA group

45. It comes to your attention that some of the teachers in this school are treating students in drug intervention programs differently. As the school counselor, what should you do to stop this behavior?
   a. Conduct training for the teachers on discrimination and diversity in the schools
   b. Report these teachers to the proper superiors
   c. Nothing, your job is to deal only with the students

d. Speak to each teacher individually about the effects of their negativity

46. Even after the restructuring of prevention and intervention programs, you feel the results could be better. What further action could you take to increase program effectiveness?
    a. Change participation in the prevention programs from voluntary to mandatory
    b. Increase the number of programs available
    c. Bring in a consultant to review programs and brainstorm new ideas
    d. Ask administration to increase funding for programs

47. What is the best strategy for choosing teacher advisors for students?
    a. Divide the students alphabetically by last name
    b. Obtain a list of students each teacher would like to advise
    c. Obtain a list of preferred teacher advisors from the students
    d. Obtain a list of preferred teacher advisors from the parents

48. You have implemented a new teacher-advising program for students in the school. What do the teachers need to know about their new role?
    a. They should both provide support and serve as advocates for their students.
    b. They need to meet with students only once a year.
    c. They should provide tutoring services to the students when necessary.
    d. They will be required to report all interactions with the students on a monthly basis.

49. Why are collaborations between teachers and the community important for a counselor?
    a. Collaborations provide insight and information that might not otherwise be readily available.
    b. Collaborations provide additional financial support for students.
    c. Collaborations could be an additional funding source for programs.
    d. With the community's assistance, a counselor's work load will be reduced.

50. What is one strategy a counselor can use to increase job experience and skills that would require community collaboration?
    a. Creating an on-the-job training program
    b. Finding part time jobs for students
    c. Offering more career-based or skill-improvement courses, such as auto shop and computer applications
    d. Offering programs that focus on resume writing and interviewing skills

51. Counselors are often responsible for initiating a parent conference by making a phone call or sending a letter home. What should a counselor do in order to avoid an automatic negative reaction from parents?
    a. State all the problems their child is having
    b. Speak with a level of equality and openness
    c. State that things at home must change
    d. Suggest that their child seeks additional help

52. Conferences with parents and the school can come in many forms. What is one type of conference that will promote communication between parents and students, as well as the school?
    a. Parent-teacher
    b. Student led
    c. Teacher-student
    d. Counselor-student

53. A counselor initiates a home visiting program to be conducted when a student is at a transition point in school, such as moving from elementary to middle school. What would the goal of a home visit be?
    a. To check up on the home environment and the parents
    b. To provide supportive services and education to the parents
    c. To make sure the home is suitable for studying
    d. To inform the parents of their child's new teacher and classroom location

54. A counselor finds that many of the parents of the students she works with do not speak English, and the counselor is not bilingual. What should the counselor do with regard to communication between the school and parents?
    a. Send letters home and have the students translate them
    b. Do not communicate with the families
    c. Provide a translator for meetings
    d. Require the parents take English courses

55. What is one strategy that a high school counselor can implement to increase parent participation in their children's academics?
    a. Provide training sessions that teach parents to be tutors for their children
    b. Require parents to sign a form confirming that students have completed outside reading assignments
    c. Suggest that parents help students with home work every night
    d. Offer regular reports and information on student performance, as well as school events and programs

56. Parents can be involved in the school in a number of ways. You would like to increase parent participation in the career resource room at the school. In addition to contacting the PTA, how else might a counselor recruit parents to volunteer?
    a. Distribute annual surveys for parents to identify their volunteer interests and abilities
    b. The PTA is the only place to find volunteers.
    c. Place an ad in the newspaper
    d. Recruit teachers because they are easier to contact

57. There is little parent involvement in many schools due to large numbers of working parents. What is one strategy to use to increase participation?
    a. Offer incentives for participation
    b. Focus on the unemployed parents to work with
    c. Suggest holding meetings and events on the weekends
    d. Offer opportunities at various times during the week

58. How are School Advisory Boards connected with parent collaboration?
    a. They include the participation of parents and community in the decision-making process, which results in a feeling of ownership from these groups.
    b. They are a way to get parents to volunteer and increase a school's parent participation rate.
    c. Meetings are held at night so that working parents can attend.
    d. They allow parents to see what is really going on with the school

59. How might training workshops be misperceived by parents?
    a. Parents are uneducated.

b. Parents do not welcome additional training.

c. They see such programs as trying to change their core values and methods of raising their children.

d. They have problem children.

60. There are generally six levels of parent participation. Which of the following is not considered a level of parent participation?

a. Parenting

b. Communication

c. Continued Education

d. Volunteering

61. Children learn their cultural identity by the time they are three years old. What implication does this have on a school counselor?

a. Counselors of a different culture should meet with parents to discuss their cultural beliefs before counseling a student.

b. This will not be an issue since cultural identity is already established by time the child begins school.

c. This established identity must be respected and taken into consideration when addressing students' issues.

d. Cultural identity can be discounted in young children but must be addressed in older children.

62. A counselor who assesses a student according to his or her microsystem, macrosystem, and exosystem will have a complete picture of the student's cultural and racial identity. What is this model called?

a. Systems model

b. Ecological model

c. Cultural assessment model

d. Full overview model

63. Why should cultural identity be integrated into early interventions for developmental issues?

a. Culture will affect how children and parents view the learning environment and respond to various programs or interventions.

b. Interventions should focus on a student's culture, as the child may not understand concepts that are otherwise unrelated.

c. Students within the same area should learn the same information, and culture should not be taken into consideration.

d. Each group deals with issues differently; therefore, there may be confusion between the student and the counselor if these issues are considered when developing the intervention

64. A school counselor begins at a new school and notices that there are few cultural diversity programs available. What might she do to increase cultural expression in the school?

a. Ask teachers to provide information on the ethnic demographics of their classes

b. Encourage families to discuss cultural diversity at home

c. Coordinate a field trip to a more diverse school

d. Develop programs and events that celebrate and educate students about cultural diversity

65. A counselor from a small town begins working at urban school. What action should the counselor take to ensure that she is aware of the difference in cultures between herself and her students?

a. Refer those students of differing cultures to another counselor. Since their cultures are different, she will not be able to help them.
b. Educate herself on the diversity of the school and the community.
c. Counsel the students with the confidence that she can help them no matter what.
d. Offer cultural diversity programs so that students can learn about each other.

66. What is one of the primary reasons why counselors have a difficult time getting support from immigrant parents?
    a. Immigrant parents do not challenge school authority.
    b. Immigrant parents are oftentimes unfamiliar with American school systems.
    c. Immigrant parents do not have time to talk with school counselors.
    d. Immigrant parents have to work during the day.

67. A counselor initiating a school-family curriculum program will probably structure the program in what way?
    a. Take-home activities for students and their parents
    b. Group discussions
    c. Surveys for parents
    d. Counseling sessions for those in need of cultural diversity education

Question 68 pertains to the following vignette :
    A teacher approaches a school counselor complaining that her students tend to get into fights because of racial tensions. These fights typically begin with students yelling racial slurs at each other and often end up with one or more of the students being sent to the office because of violence or the threat of violence.

68. How might the implementation of human relations training be beneficial in this class?
    a. This type of training teaches anger management techniques.
    b. This type of training teaches students how to be friends.
    c. This type of training promotes conflict resolution.
    d. This type of training promotes an understanding of cultural differences.

69. A counselor begins seeing a student who has issues with low self-esteem. This student is of Chinese descent but was adopted by an African American family as a baby. What responsibility does the counselor have toward the student regarding culture?
    a. Provide the student with information on her Chinese heritage and encourage her to embrace it
    b. Suggest she join the Chinese American Club at school
    c. Question her feelings of being of Chinese descent but being raised in an African American home
    d. Respect the student's cultural identity as it is and assist her instead with the problems she brought to the attention of the counselor

70. A counselor in a predominately-white school does not feel that cultural diversity programs are important in the school. What is wrong with this belief?
    a. Non-white students may feel left out of school activities.
    b. White students might feel left out of school activities.
    c. Cultural diversity involves more than just the color of one's skin.
    d. A student may want to attend a college that is very diverse.

71. When beginning a program evaluation, what documentation will be necessary?

a. Satisfaction surveys from previous program sessions
b. A list of programs offered
c. The number of participants in last year's programs
d. Guidance curriculum guides

72. When developing a school's counseling programs, a counselor should consider what students would like to gain from the programs. Which of the following are factors important to students in regard to school counseling?
    a. Academic counseling
    b. Available resources and personnel
    c. College-preparation assistance
    d. All of the above

73. When developing counseling programs, what type of outcomes are associated with success?
    a. Counselor-activity outcomes
    b. Community involvement outcomes
    c. Parent involvement outcomes
    d. Student outcomes

74. Unrealistic demands on time and job duties refer to what?
    a. Role ambiguity
    b. Role conflict
    c. Role mutations
    d. Role confusion

75. A counselor develops a peer-mentoring program. What is the main responsibility of the counselor during the implementation of this program?
    a. Overseeing all actions of the peer mentors
    b. Training peer mentors in various counseling aspects
    c. Meeting with mentees to make sure the mentors are doing their jobs
    d. Monitoring progress and supporting the peer mentors

76. How might a counselor serve a School Advisory Committee?
    a. Provide general information about the state of the students
    b. Lead the committee to make sure his or her recommendations are followed
    c. Email reminders to members about upcoming meetings
    d. Make sure the committee is following all bylaws when voting on student issues

77. A student goes into a counseling office at the end of the day wanting to speak to the counselor. What would be the best approach to this situation?
    a. The counselor should stay late to speak to the student immediately.
    b. The counselor should give the student her home phone and ask her to call when she gets home.
    c. The secretary should state that the counselor is going home in 10 minutes and schedule an appointment during school hours.
    d. The counselor should briefly speak to the student and schedule a meeting for the next day if possible.

78. When conducting a program evaluation, what outcomes measure the intended effects of the program or intervention?

a. Immediate outcomes
b. Proximal outcomes
c. Distal outcomes
d. Intervention outcomes

79. Why are evidence-based evaluations important in program management?
a. Evaluations contribute to training and an increase in professional knowledge.
b. Evaluations prove that counselors are conducting programs.
c. Evaluations that show positive change will receive state funding.
d. Evaluations provide a paper trail of the counselor's work.

80. A counselor has developed a comprehensive developmental counseling program in a large school. This program consists of daily meetings and programs to address the various needs of students. In order to avoid burnout, how might the counselor effectively manage so many meetings and programs?
a. Schedule meetings a few hours after school ends so she or he can take a break
b. Recruit the help of teachers and peer mentors to assist with the programs
c. Try to combine groups so that there are not so many
d. Rely on consultants to run the programs that are scheduled for after school

81. What is the main premise behind a developmental guidance program?
a. All students develop at different rates, so various programs must be designed.
b. Guidance programs are developmental in nature, beginning with simple concepts and progressing to more abstract concepts.
c. Developmental guidance programs are used for students with developmental disabilities to help them achieve their full potential.
d. Developmental guidance programs focus on human development and positive self-concepts.

82. What type of students are developmental guidance programs designed for?
a. Those with developmental delays
b. Those with learning disabilities
c. All students
d. Those with emotional issues

83. Which of the following is not considered a major developmental task of children and adolescents?
a. Sense of identity
b. Autonomy
c. Self-esteem
d. Knowledge acquisition

84. Kohlberg proposes a developmental theory in which developmental domain?
a. Psychosexual
b. Vocational
c. Moral
d. Life-style systems

85. Ego, esteem needs, confidence, sense of mastery, positive self-regard, self-respect, and self-extension refers to what developmental theory?
a. Erikson's Theory of Psychosocial Development
b. Maslow's Hierarchy of Human Needs

c. Sullivan's Interpersonal Theory
d. Havighurst's Stages of Childhood Development

Questions 86 and 87 pertain to the following vignette:
A counselor currently works in a school with a traditional counseling program that offers crisis counseling in times of need. Additionally, due to a lack of support programs, students who get into fights are often sent to the crisis-counseling program. After witnessing a number of students repeatedly getting into fights, a counselor sees that many fights are due to communication problems and simple misunderstandings, and the school's traditional counseling program is having little effect on students involved in fights. As a result, the counselor decides to change the current counseling model to a developmental counseling program.

86. In developing the new programs, the counselor decides to address essential skills with the students. What specific skills does he want to address?
    a. Developmental skills
    b. Social literacy skills
    c. Cognitive skills
    d. Emotional literacy skills

87. In terms of the crisis program, what can he do to adapt this program to fit a developmental counseling model?
    a. Implement prevention and intervention programs
    b. Discuss developmental issues during the crisis counseling sessions
    c. Include family members in the counseling
    d. Offer crisis counseling to younger students

88. A counselor wishing to increase students' ability to control feelings and understand their own feelings would develop what type of program?
    a. Social literacy program
    b. Cognitive literacy program
    c. Emotional literacy program
    d. Conflict resolution program

89. What are three essential developmental skills?
    a. Self-concept, self-esteem, self-respect
    b. Ego, Id, Super-ego
    c. Operational thinking, concrete thinking, abstract thinking
    d. Thinking, feeling, relating

90. What type of skills will a counselor focus on if he wants to increase students' ability to think out problems and find positive solutions to such problems?
    a. Basic academic skills
    b. Relating skills
    c. Conflict resolution skills
    d. Cognitive literacy skills

Question 91 to 93 pertain to the following vignette:
At the beginning of a counseling relationship, the counselor informs the student of confidentiality, stating that he cannot revel anything that is discussed during the sessions no matter what. After a

- 149 -

few sessions, the counselor feels that the student would benefit from extra sessions and offers to meet the student outside of school to talk over coffee. During these after school sessions, the student informs the counselor that she is considering suicide. Since the counselor does not think this student will follow through, he disregards the statement.

91. What exception relating to confidentiality did the counselor neglect to discuss with the student?
    a. Pregnancy
    b. Harm to self or others
    c. Sexual relationships
    d. Problems with self-esteem

92. What ethical consideration did this counselor violate with the sessions outside of school?
    a. Professional Competence
    b. Dual Relationship
    c. Appropriate Referrals
    d. Confidentiality

93. What ethical consideration did the counselor violate by disregarding the threat of suicide?
    a. Appropriate referral
    b. Danger to self
    c. Danger to others
    d. Dual relationships

94. If a school counselor has a private practice, why would she refer a student in need of intensive counseling to someone else rather than seeing the client at her private practice?
    a. She cannot see a client more than once a week.
    b. She does not offer the counseling that this student needs.
    c. She must have a full case load with her private practice.
    d. She cannot use her position within the school to benefit her private practice.

95. Professional counselors are expected to contribute to the profession of counseling. What is one way for counselors to participate and contribute?
    a. Maintain an active case load
    b. Hold group sessions for students
    c. Participate in professional associations
    d. Maintain their licensure regardless of whether they are currently providing counseling services

96. A new counselor feels that it is necessary to help all students solve their problems as quickly as possible. Because of this she, routinely brings paperwork home. Why would this practice be frowned upon in the field of counseling?
    a. Counselors are not paid to work at home.
    b. Counselors should establish boundaries between their professional and personal lives.
    c. Colleagues may become jealous because the counselor is more efficient then they are.
    d. This practice could lead to dual relationships.

97. Counselors have a professional responsibility to provide parents with what type of information?
    a. The details of sessions with their children
    b. Objective reports with respect to ethical guidelines
    c. Subjective reports on their child's progress

d. Positive parenting information

98. If a counselor witnesses unethical behavior from a colleague, what actions should she take?
    a. Do nothing so that the colleague does not get in trouble
    b. Let the colleague know she is aware of his or her behavior and inform the colleague that they must stop immediately or face the consequences
    c. Inform the colleague of intentions to alert the proper authorities and follow school policy on such matters
    d. Inform parents of the students who may be victims of the unethical behavior

99. It is important that school counselors manage their stress on a regular basis to avoid career burnout. What is one way to do this?
    a. Take a vacation
    b. Have daily "down time"
    c. Schedule the most difficult students in the morning
    d. Volunteer for school activities to spend non-counseling time with students

100. What forms can professional development take?
    a. Continued education
    b. Evaluating and reporting on program outcomes
    c. Presenting research at professional conferences
    d. All of the above

Answer Key and Explanations

1. **A:** The Cognitive Behavior Theory suggests that as children grow into adolescents, they begin to form abstract thought. This is the ability to think about things that cannot be seen. This is an important part of youth development because as abstract thought develops, moral thought increases. For example, a young child may not understand consequences, because thought at this point is concrete. In order to fully understand consequences, one must be able to understand right from wrong, as well as be able to visualize what future consequences will come about by present actions. In most cases, an adolescent will understand these consequences because of their ability to think abstractly.

2. **B:** Perspective taking is similar to empathy; however, it involves different mental processes. While a person can be empathic toward another, this function involves only an attempt to understand another person's feelings based on previous experience. Perspective taking involves more complex cognition. The individual involved in perspective taking will attempt to understand another's situation, analyze this situation, and gain an understanding of and respect for different points of view. Perspective taking is a useful activity for children requiring conflict resolution. By asking children to look at a situation from another person's point of view, they can begin to understand why there was conflict and possibly begin to formulate their own ideas for a resolution.

3. **A:** Interpersonal skills are the skills necessary to relate to and understand peer interactions. These skills begin developing at an early age and are reinforced by responses from others. Typically, a child with adequate interpersonal skills has the ability to understand if he is not liked or welcomed by his peers. This situation would result in the child's becoming withdrawn and possibly depressed. However, in this case, the child does not seem to possess this ability. While his interpersonal skills are so stunted that he does not recognize when he is not liked, there may be a deeper physiological explanation for his problems. It will be important for the counselor to gain as much information as possible from the family and others in contact with this child, and a referral to a specialist may be necessary.

4. **B:** Pavlov's theory of conditioning responses states that when an action is repeatedly followed by a response, the one performing the action will either continue or stop doing so depending on the response. In this case, the child continually receives a negative response from his peers. Theoretically, the child would begin to relate his actions to this negative response and cease the action. However, this is not occurring and may be an indication of developmental delays. As seen in the vignette, the child has little social support at home, and there is a clear indication of other interpersonal issues with his parents. To help this child, a counselor could explore social development delays he has and propose some type of intervention

5. **D:** All of the above problems can affect a child's mental development. Without proper nutrition, children will not receive the vitamins and minerals necessary for both physical and mental development. Abuse can also cause many mental issues that will oftentimes manifest in the form of poor grades and poor social skills. Finally, all children need support and encouragement to develop into healthy adults. Without this support, counselors may see developmental problems in the form of delays. As a counselor, one should always be mindful of the family dynamics of students. With proper interventions and family education, issues related to these factors may be corrected or avoided altogether.

6. **C:** Erickson suggests that children begin to associate with either industry or inferiority in early adolescence. Industry refers to a person's ability to succeed and feel worthy. Typically, healthy children who receive the appropriate support and encouragement at home and at school will feel a sense of industry. This identification is important, as it can be the basis of future educational, social, and coping

skills. For example, a child who has a strong sense of industry will be more likely to cope with a low grade on a test. He will understand that he may need to study harder for the next test or seek assistance. On the other hand, a child with a poor school, family, or peer support system may experience feelings of inferiority. In this case, he is likely to have insufficient coping mechanisms and not perform well in school.

7. C: As information is learned, individuals develop their own thoughts, beliefs, and representations about that information. These schemas are abstract and unique and assist the individual in understanding the world around them. Individuals also use schema to determine how they will act and respond to the world around them. For example, a common schema is how individuals perceive different cultures. Often in the form of stereotypes, these schemas are difficult to reverse once in place. Because of this, an individual with a negative schema about a certain type of ethnic group will react negatively to all individuals in that group.

8. A: Children begin in the sensory-motor stage. During this time, a child acts and learns based on senses and reflexes. An infant who receives a laugh from his mother when he makes a face will continue to make the face. The reflex of making a face slowly becomes a voluntary learned expression. In the pre-operational stage, children can use representative language. For example, they begin to understand that a round toy is a ball. This is also the time when the concept of conversation is understood. During the concrete operational stage, children begin to think logically. For example, children in this stage begin to understand mathematical concepts. The formal operational stage refers to the time when children master abstract thinking. Concepts such as death become easier to understand during this time.

9. A: Bandura proposed a social behavioral theory of development. This theory combines behaviorism and social psychology and suggests that each one affects the other. More specifically, a child's environment may dictate what behaviors he displays, but the behaviors displayed will also affect his environment. The environment that an individual lives in may present certain opportunities that elicit certain behaviors. A child with two parents who are highly supportive of education may be more inclined to study more. At the same time, the behaviors presented will determine the environments. The child who studies and gets good grades has a greater likelihood of being accepted into a good college and getting a good job. In this scenario, we can see that the supportive environment affected the behavior (studying) and that this behavior affected the environment (good college and job).

10. D: Personal reward is a high level of development. For this level, individuals behave accordingly and reward themselves for it. For example, an individual wanting to quit a bad habit may decide to treat herself to a nice diner if she is successful for one month. Law and Order are determined by the society and state that if one disobeys the set laws, punishment will be in the form of fines or jail time. This is in order to ensure that there is a peace and order in a society. Good Boy-Nice Girl is often applied to children. This is the impression that good and nice are synonymous. In other words, if you are good, then you are also nice; if you are bad, then you are mean. Finally, punishment-obedience is used with children to enforce obedience. If you misbehave in school, you will be sent to detention.

11. D: A diagnostic assessment for learning needs focuses on four main factors: prior knowledge, misconceptions, interests, and learning style preferences. The purpose of this type of assessment is to determine the student's strengths and weaknesses in order to develop an effective intervention strategy. Diagnostic assessments can be done in either formal or informal settings and in either individual or group settings. In the case of a formal setting, counselors can conduct a student survey or skills test. For informal settings, the counselor can simply ask a student or groups of students various questions pertaining to each factor. For example, a counselor may ask, "Do you like to learn by reading a book or seeing material presented in picture form?"

12. B: Formative assessments are used to determine the effectiveness of an intervention and can be used to modify the treatment. This is an important step in the intervention process, as a student's rate of learning is not always apparent. This type of assessment can be in the form of informal questions to determine if the student understands the topic. The goal of a formative assessment is to provide the best possible setting for the student in order to increase learning and understanding. When done at regular intervals, the counselor can determine if the goals of the intervention are being met in a timely manner. A formative assessment will also provide an indication of an ineffective intervention strategy.

13. A: Summative assessments are designed to determine the effectiveness of an intervention. These outcome measures should show at least some improvement if the intervention was properly done, and formative assessments were conducted throughout the intervention time. When improvement is not found, it is an indication that the intervention was not meeting the needs of the student. It is the responsibility of the counselor to monitor progress during this time carefully in order to modify interventions to meet the student's needs. Failure to do so will result in no improvement and may cause frustration in the student, counselor, and parents.

14. A: Bloom's Taxonomy of Knowledge describes six levels of knowledge. At the lowest level, *Knowledge* is the ability to name and identify things. *Comprehension* occurs when a student can explain a topic or concept. *Application* refers to a student's ability to use information in the real world. *Analysis* is the ability to analyze and make comparisons. *Synthesis* is the ability to develop hypotheses and produce results. Finally, the highest level in Bloom's Taxonomy is *Evaluation*, which refers to the ability to assess and critique an idea or concept. Assessments should touch on all six levels of learning. By making sure all levels in Bloom's Taxonomy are covered, the counselor will have an indication of areas that need improvement and what level of understanding to focus on. For example, a student may be able to identify parts of a sentence but not understand how to analyze that sentence. The intervention would then focus more on sentence analysis and less on defining parts of the sentence.

15. C: When taking an assessment relating to topics that may be socially undesirable, individuals have a tendency to report answers that conform to mainstream society. In this case, students may be afraid of getting in trouble if they answer positively in response to questions about drug or alcohol use. Conversely, if this assessment is given in a group setting, students may want to "show off" to their peers by giving a greater number of positive answers. While this type of assessment may provide the counselor with preliminary results, the results may be skewed. This type of assessment should always include a variety of questions in different forms in order to validate findings and to control for false answers.

16. B: This type of scaling can be beneficial for a preliminary view of a student's thoughts on a topic. However, providing only four choices means that the student must choose in a positive or negative direction. This can produce skewed results and lead the counselor to believe that a majority of students are for or against a topic. What may be the case is that students are neutral on some topics but are required to make a decision. For example, consider the following statement: "Morning announcements are a waste of time." This statement may elicit a natural response for students; however, they are forced to agree or disagree. If students choose a negative answer, does this necessarily indicate that they would like more announcements in the morning? Conversely, if students respond positively, does this indicate that they want no morning announcements?

17. B: Although using this type of assessment may result in more neutral responses, most individuals will provide their true thoughts. Receiving an assessment with all neutral responses should be considered as an outlier. Depending on the purpose of the assessment, the counselor may consider disregarding it in the

results and providing an explanation in any required report. Depending on the nature of the assessment, the counselor can conduct additional assessments with the student to determine any difficulties this student may be having. Regardless, when giving students surveys, it must be indicated that all responses are confidential, and the students should respond as honestly as possible.

18. D: Continued monitoring and assessment of the learning environment can be beneficial in many ways. This process provides the counselor, teacher, student, and parents an ongoing progress report. Additionally, regular assessments allow problems to be identified sooner rather than later. This will ensure that the student is not falling behind his classmates or his intervention goals. Ongoing monitoring and assessment also allow the counselor to update and to modify goals and target dates. When considered a fluid process, assessments, goal monitoring, intervention modification, and encouragement will ensure that students are progressing at a comfortable and successful rate.

19. C: Typically, a counselor will conduct a student survey in order to gain an overall view of the student body. By collecting demographic information, the counselor can determine important differences in the student body. This information will assist in developing additional programs, activities, or interventions. When conducted as a formative assessment, demographic information can provide an indication of whether different groups of students are finding more benefit in a particular program or intervention. Again, this information will allow the counselor to modify a program or add programs to better fit the needs of all students involved.

20. B: Naturally, all of the answer choices are important to consider when administering pre-post tests. A counselor would not want to give a posttest designed for a first grader to kindergarten students. Also, an assessment for first graders is not likely to have 100 questions. However, during the development of this type of test, key ideas and concepts are important to consider. These key ideas and concepts will be the basis for all questions on the pre-post tests. This information must be related to the content being learned and be linked to state curriculum standards. These key ideas also must be grade appropriate. Pre-post tests will fail when this information is not appropriately presented.

21. A: Elementary School is the time when children are learning the most and developing important motor skills and mental functions. Counselors must be able to recognize developmental delays, as well as advanced learners. School counselors will be major advocates for students who may experience developmental delays. While the other options may be important, these issues are more likely seen at the junior high and high school levels. Knowledge in continued education will be important for high school students who wish to pursue a college education; counselors with students in these age groups will need to educate students and offer assistance in applying to colleges and obtaining financial aid and scholarships. Additionally, relationship building, adjustment, and coping mechanisms are issues most often seen in junior high school, as these years are a time of many changes physically, emotionally, and educationally.

22. C: Primary prevention groups aim at providing education and preventative counseling for a variety of problems. This type of group is beneficial for students who may have risk factors for future issues. These groups should focus on developing healthy lifestyles and center on the student's social, emotional, and cognitive abilities. Typically, a primary prevention group will discuss issues such as self-esteem, self-concept, listening skills, academic achievement, and methods of effective communication. Issues such as grief and loss, aggressive behaviors, and abuse are more often the focus of a problem-centered, structured intervention-counseling group. School counselors may conduct this type of group with students who have recently experienced a loss, have repeatedly violated school rules for fighting, or are known to have an abusive relationship.

23. A: Primary prevention groups are most beneficial for dealing with potential issues. School counselors should be cognizant of the school environment. This awareness will allow the counselor to determine main areas in which students are struggling. A counselor who notices a lot of bickering and fighting in the hallways in between classes may decide that school-wide prevention groups are necessary. A school-wide prevention program in communication and conflict intervention will serve to educate the students about these basic skills. On the other hand, if the counselor provides only individual counseling or problem-centered counseling, the focus is likely to be on a specific problem rather than on education on how to avoid or resolve a conflict.

24. B: Problem-centered, structured counseling groups allow students to share their experiences and hear similar experiences from their peers in a safe environment. This type of group setting also allows students to gain the support of their peers as well as receive feedback. Counselors conducting these groups should focus on changing deviant behaviors and encouraging participants to try out new behaviors during the week. These exercises can be discussed during sessions, and students can learn how to brainstorm appropriate behaviors together by sharing their experiences. While it is possible to conduct a problem-centered group for a number of different issues, topics such as self-actualization, safety, and physiological issues are typically the focus of primary prevention groups.

25. D: Teachers need to understand some of the basic psychology of their students and their students' behaviors. Counselors can help provide teachers with such information in a number of a ways, including offering discussion and training sessions throughout the school year. These sessions should provide teachers with a basic understanding of student dynamics and the psychology of student violence. When teachers are aware of these aspects of their students, they will be more aware of what is going on and may be able to respond to issues before a situation escalates to violence. Additionally, teachers need to be aware of their own emotions when dealing with angry or upset students. In order to control a situation that is or may become violent, teachers will need to remain calm and react in non-violent ways: for example, trying to separate fighting students and talking calmly to them vs. pushing a student out of the way and yelling at him.

26. A: A group setting in counseling can be very effective when a counselor takes time to develop positive group dynamics. During the group formation phase, participants are getting to know one another. Because of personal reasons, participants may be resistant to the group, be uncomfortable sharing, or not trust others in the group. It is important to focus the first session or sessions on developing guidelines for cooperation within the group. This process includes encouraging the participation of all group members and agreeing on group rules, goals, and objectives. A common technique during this stage is to allow group members themselves to develop their own rules, goals, and objectives. This activity encourages participation and gives the participants a sense of ownership and belonging within the group.

27. B: Solution-Focused Brief Counseling has recently become a popular counseling method due to time and budget constraints on schools and students. This method is based on the premise that individuals can solve their own problems with assistance and prompting from a counselor. Students play an active role in deciding the goals of their counseling with focused attention on a specific problem. Additionally, the counselor will assist the student in identifying the appropriate behavioral changes that are needed in order to reach the state's educational goals. With Solution-Focused Brief Counseling, the counselor plays a supportive role as the student identifies his strengths and determines alternative solutions to the problem.

28. A: Beginning a Solution-Focused Brief Counseling session involves having the student define the problem and determine his desired goals of the counseling. With the assistance of the counselor, the intervention or behavior change is both determined and initiated by the student. Strategic tasks are assigned by the counselor and involve a direct behavior change. For example, if a student is having difficulty with academics and has a goal to raise his grades, then a strategic task would be for him to study for one hour every night. In subsequent counseling sessions, the counselor would offer support and positive feedback in order to encourage the student to reach his academic goals. Once the goals for that particular problem have been reached, the sessions are no longer required and counseling is terminated.

29. C: Reframing is the restatement of a problem or issue in a positive light. This is the first step when developing an intervention for Solution-Focused Brief Counseling. Utilization is the second step in this process. Utilization involves taking a student's values and belief system into consideration. Also at this stage, the counselor must consider the student's motivations in applying the intervention. This information will be gathered from the student during initial discussions. By reframing the question and determining the student's beliefs and motivations, the counselor can assign the appropriate strategic tasks. This process is important to the success of the counseling.

30. C: The strategic task is the intervention treatment. This can be an actual task, such as completing one hour of homework a night, or a behavior change, such as taking a deep breath when angry. It is the student's responsibility to act according to the intervention plan in situations related to the problem and the goals of the counseling. These tasks will be discussed during the counseling sessions. Depending on the success or failure of the tasks, the counselor may decide to introduce different tasks throughout the counseling period. Doing so would be beneficial in a case in which the student is having difficulty controlling his anger. One week, for example, the counselor's task for the student may involve counting to ten. If this strategy is successful, the counselor may assign a breathing exercise as a task. This method would provide the student with a number of strategies for dealing with anger.

31. B: There are a number of factors that can affect students, especially during middle and high school. In this case, it would be wise to discuss problems with friends or a boyfriend with this student. Social problems are often a cause of problems in school, including a marked drop in grades. If this student is having problems with a boyfriend, it may be important to determine the seriousness of the problems, as abusive relationships in schools do occur. Since this student typically does well in school, the difficulty level of the classes would not be the major concern, unless she recently began new advanced courses. Additionally, there is nothing in this student's history to indicate that she may have problems with self-esteem or mental health issues.

32. D: Having only one educated parent is typically not considered a risk factor for students. Often, parents with some education can provide their children with academic support that uneducated parents cannot. However, if a student is from a single-parent family, then that child may be at risk. Additionally, students with parents with no education and those who live in poverty are also at risk for problems in school. These risk factors can be addressed by the counselor in a number of ways. These include providing support for both the family and the student, referrals to community social service agencies, and offering free educational programs to parents.

33. B: Bullies are at risk for a number of negative outcomes, including the increased potential to drop out of school. Counselors can implement a many intervention strategies for bullying. School wide interventions can include posted rules, announcements, and programs. Classroom interventions can involve the same intervention strategies as those implemented school wide, except on a smaller level. Individual interventions will address the student bully specifically. This type of intervention should be

tailored to the individual and aim to define the root problem while providing education and intervention to change the negative behaviors. Referrals can also be made to anger management, communication, and conflict resolution programs.

34. D: Regardless of the type of abuse a girl may experience, there will be deep psychological effects that may last much longer than the actual abuse. Oftentimes, these girls will have low self-esteem and look for ways to make themselves feel better. Additionally, those children who are abused may turn to drugs and alcohol to numb the effects of the abuse. Teenage girls who experience abuse are also more likely to become pregnant than those girls who do not experience abuse. Finally, those experiencing abuse will often lose interest in school and their futures, and counselors will see a decline in their grades. Since the idea of abuse if often thought of taboo and embarrassing, counselors should be aware of these risk factors and outcomes when assessing students.

35. C: Programs addressing teen pregnancy are designed to offer students education and support for various issues. As a counselor, regardless of your personal beliefs, you must be sensitive to the needs and views of your students. Prevention programs can provide education about safe sex, as well as information about the reality of being pregnant and a teenage parent. These prevention programs should be geared toward those who are not pregnant but may currently be or thinking about being sexually active. Intervention programs should be geared toward those who are currently pregnant or recently had a child. These programs should provide supportive services along with education about being a teenage parent. Whenever possible, involving the student's parents in the programs will help increase the student's support system.

36. B: Making a broad announcement about the student's arrival is likely to embarrass the student and possibly create more alienation from the general student body. As this student does not necessarily have a problem, direct counseling and education may not beneficial. School counselors who offer the student, as well as her family, supportive services will be the most beneficial in easing the transition from one school to the next. Counselors can enlist the support and assistance from other students by providing the new student a peer guide for the first couple of days. The guide will show them around the school and make sure the student knows where her classes are. This guide can also provide information about the school, such as the various clubs and sports available and upcoming events. Additional support from the school and the community will provide the student and her family with important information about the school and the new area.

37. A: Poverty is one of the main risk factors for students. Often, those children who live in poverty do not eat properly or get enough sleep. Some students may be homeless or living with multiple families. Additionally, the strain of a sudden loss of income can cause fighting or tension in the household. As a result, students may not be prepared for school, as they may be too tired or hungry to participate. As a counselor, keen attention to the dynamics of a community will be beneficial in assisting students. In this case, the counselor can encourage families to participate in free or reduced-price breakfast or lunch plans at school. Additionally, the counselor can provide families with community resources to assist with financial emergencies

38. B: Parent participation is the key to developing physically, emotionally, and academically healthy children. When a school already has a high parent interest, it is important to foster that interest. By developing programs for parents to participate in, a school can keep these parents excited and motivated. Parent programs such as the PTA or school advisory councils are good ways for parents to take an active role in their children's schools. Additionally, offering one-time volunteer activities will allow working

parents to participate in some school functions. Counselors should also encourage regular meetings with parents and teachers to keep all parties informed about the students both in and out of school.

39. A: As communities become more diverse, counselors are seeing an increase in the number of parents who do not speak English as a first language. Because this dynamic often creates a barrier between these parents and their children's schools, a lack of participation from these parents is common. In these cases, counselors can provide information or opportunities for parents to increase their English skills through free or low cost programs. Additionally, adult education programs in basic reading, writing, and GED preparation can be offered to parents who wish to increase their skills or earn their GED. Educated parents are able to offer more academic assistance to their children.

40. B: Researchers have studied the effects of providing social skills training to gifted and special needs students. These trainings often take a cognitive-behavioral approach to learning new behaviors. The results of these studies show that these students demonstrate a significant increase in their sociability. This includes their willingness to participate in social situations, such as on the playground. Social skills trainings often focus on listening skills, empathy, building rapport, self-disclosure, and appropriate eye contact. This training typically does not affect a student's self-esteem or other school related issues, such as attendance or grades.

41. A: Teacher advisors cooperate with school counselors to provide students all-around support. These advisors help students adjust to a new school by offering orientation and support. Additionally, teacher advisors provide students with a sounding board when resolving disputes or misunderstandings with faculty members or other students. Oftentimes, advisors will initiate student work groups for various issues students may experience. These groups may focus on communication, conflict resolution, or general adjustment strategies. Overall, teacher advisors serve as advocates for students in order to make school and the educational experience both pleasant and rewarding.

42. C: This training method is intended to increase consulting and interview skills for the counselor. This model is comprised of seven steps. *Establishing a Consulting Relationship* involves relationship building and goal setting with the client. *Identifying and Clarifying the Problem Situation* requires a counselor to hear beyond what is being said in order to uncover any underlying problems. *Determine Desired Outcome* is a simple restatement of the problem and goals. *Develop Ideas and Strategies* requires the client and counselor to set objectives for achieving the goals. *Developing a Plan* requires the counselor and client to determine the best course of action for implementing objectives and achieving goals. *Specify the Plan* serves to further determine the specific steps for success. Finally, *Confirming the Consulting Relationship* will be complete when the student understands the problem-solving process and is comfortable with the plan of action developed with the counselor.

43. A: Community support provides schools, staff, and students with a sense of connectedness, which in turn enhances the learning environment. This support works to provide individuals with clear expectations. These factors serve to provide staff and students with a healthy learning environment with reduced stressors and less burn out. Additionally, when students have numerous avenues of support, they typically perform better academically, and schools experience a lower dropout rate. Having the community as a support system for a school also helps reduce some risk factors that students often experience. For example, links to financial aid resources and parenting education classes can serve to reduce child abuse and poverty.

44. A: Students may benefit from speaking to representatives from all of these organizations. However, a representative from the local police department would be the best option. These individuals are usually

trained in drug education for school-aged children. Additionally, most police departments have drug prevention programs in place that have been proven to have positive outcomes. By bringing in individuals from the community, students get a different perspective of the issue at hand. Students will be able to ask questions and receive life experience answers from the presenter. This helps to show students the reality of the problem, as well as its consequences.

45. A: Students in drug intervention programs may be experience a number of feelings and barriers as they attempt to stop using drugs. Teachers must be aware of these issues, along with the recovery process. It will be important for those students in intervention programs to receive support from all staff members to ensure success. As a counselor, you may offer training for teachers and other staff members. This training can include information about the specific intervention programs offered at your school, the recovery process, and sensitivity training specific to this population of students.

46. C: Consultation is one way to improve school programs and involve the community. Consultants provide assessments and evaluations of programs, as well as suggestions for improvements. When schools and the community work together, there will be certain expectations that reduce stressors caused by unclear roles and responsibilities. Also, having an unbiased professionals evaluate school programs is the accepted way to report on school programs. Using a consultant on a regular basis for programs and services also serves as a system of checks and balances. These measures allow both the school and the community to view school programs on an outcomes-based perspective with little to no underlying agendas being intermingled.

47. C: Teacher advisors serve as advocates for students. They are respected adults whom students can turn to for support when problems arise. Therefore, it is important for students to be comfortable with their teacher advisors. While it is not practical to allow students to make a final decision on the advisor, schools should include students in the decision making process. It is suggested that students be able to choose three to five teachers they would like to work with. Based on this information, counselors and teachers can then assign teacher advisors while keeping the student's wishes in mind.

48. A: The primary role of the teacher advisor is to provide support and serve as advocates for their students. In addition to this, advisors can assist the student when he is experiencing academic or personal problems. This added support system provides students with the opportunity to seek help before problems escalate. While regular meetings are encouraged, each school can determine specific meeting requirements based on the school environment and the needs of the student body. Aside from the primary role of the advisors, specific tasks will depend on the needs of the student and the number of students a teacher has.

49. A: School counselors may oftentimes feel overworked and can easily become burned out. This is typically due to a high client load and few resources. If a school counselor can enlist the help of teachers and community members, his or her burden is lightened. These outside individuals can offer the counselor new ideas and information about students or community programs that might not otherwise be available to the counselor. This additional support will result in more services for students and their families. Additionally, when communities and schools are strong and able to offer a supportive environment, students' academic performance tends to increase.

50. A: Counselors can be responsible for more than just the mental and emotional well-being of students. When a school offers various career development programs, students who participate gain valuable skills for the future. On-the-job training programs are an excellent way to increase job skills. Additionally, these programs often help students decide what career path to follow. These programs allow students to go to

school and work while earning school credits and gaining practical business experience. Counselors must understand that cooperation and communication with the community and leaders in the business community can be the key to success for these types of programs.

51. B: Almost all parents believe that they have well-behaved, intelligent children; therefore, some parents are quick to become defensive and be unwilling to listen when schools call regarding problems with their children. As a counselor, it often falls on you to set up parent conferences. It is important to keep in mind the feelings and beliefs of the parents as well as the policies of the school. By speaking to parents with openness and allowing them to be a part of decision-making processes, a partnership can develop. By creating this sense of partnership and cooperation, the student's best interest will remain the focus.

52. B: A student-led conference is one in which the student participates in the preparation and presentation of the conference. This is a good strategy to encourage student-parent communication. This is also a good strategy to use to show parents the capabilities of their children. Student-led conferences offer students a number of advantages. By preparing a presentation for the conference, the student develops a sense of ownership. Additionally, this strategy holds the student accountable for school work that is presented during the meeting. Finally, this type of conference gives the student the opportunity to improve on oral and visual presentation skills in a nonthreatening environment.

53. B: This is a good strategy to use in lower income school districts. In these areas, transportation is often an issue, and parents are typically less able to participate in school activities because traveling to the school is difficult. In these situations, counselors must find alternative options for including parents in the academic lives of their children, especially during times of transition. Home visits can be used for regular parent-teacher conferences if a counselor feels participation would increase with this additional option. Prior to initiating any home visiting program, a counselor must ensure that all individuals conducting these visits have received the proper safety training.

54. C: A counselor must always take into consideration the cultural barriers and needs of students and their families. In situations where language barriers are present, a counselor should offer a translator during any meeting. This will ensure that the parents receive the correct information. This will also show the parents that they are welcome and accepted into the school. By offering translation services, parents may become more comfortable, which means that their participation with the school and their children's education will increase. Another effective strategy is to offer free or low cost English courses. While a counselor cannot require anyone to take these courses, making them available to those who are interested will be beneficial to families.

55. D: Keeping parents informed about their students' academic progress is one important factor in the success of a student. These reports are useful in tracking a student's progress and identifying when intervention is necessary. By including the parents in these reports, counselors can take a step in gaining the parents' participation and cooperation if problems do arise. These reports also allow parents to send comments to the teachers, as well as request conferences. Additionally, providing parents' with information about school events and activities will allow parents opportunities to volunteer with the school and stay up-to-date on the extracurricular programs offered at a school.

56. A: Annual surveys are an easy and effective way to learn about the level of participation, interests, and abilities of parents. These surveys can be sent to parents at the beginning of the year and offer parents the opportunity to volunteer for long or short-term projects. Surveys should include information about the parents' willingness to participate, their availability, and any special skills they may have. A

preliminary list of volunteer events or projects should also be included in these surveys so that parents can select opportunities that correspond with their schedules and interests. By reaching beyond the PTA for support and assistance, schools will develop lasting partnerships with parents and improve the learning environment for the students.

57. D: Oftentimes, schools get into the habit of holding meetings at the same times year after year. In the case of parent-teacher conferences, which are often held during the day, working parents may have to take off work to attend. Additionally, many school council and PTA meetings are held in the evening. While this may be more convenient for working parents, busy families often find it difficult to participate in these events. By offering various times and days of these meeting and events, a school can maximize the participation of the parents.

58. A: School Advisory Boards consist of teachers, administrators, parents, and members of the business community. The makeup of this type of council is often directly related to the makeup of the school and the community at large. These boards discuss issues related to the general management of the school, along with district wide policies and procedures. School Advisory Boards are also responsible for developing school improvement and safety plans. These types of advisory boards are also responsible for delegating financial resources to various school programs. Parent involvement is necessary, as parents provide a voice for the parent community as a whole with students' best interests in mind.

59. C: Counselors must be careful when conducting training programs involving parents. Parents may be sensitive and misinterpret these trainings as the school's trying to change their core values and methods in raising their children. Schools can offer other types of support to increase parent involvement. Some suggestions include providing parents with information on effective study skills, recommending time limits for homework, or babysitting during PTA meetings and parent-teacher conferences. The goal of offering parents these various services is to increase participation and develop strong parent support for the school. Counselors should also keep in mind that parents do not necessarily have to be at the school to be active with the school. When parents help their children with homework or participate in a phone tree, they are offering much needed support.

60. C: While students with educated parents are not a risk factor, this is not considered a type of parent involvement. Involvement begins at the parenting level. Schools cannot tell individuals how to parent; however, they can provide information for parents about encouraging good academic practices while at home. For example, informing parents about the appropriate amount of time their child should spend on homework is one strategy. Communication is the next level of participation. Sending home progress reports and holding conferences both increase communication between schools and parents. The third level involves volunteering, which can include one-time projects or long-term participation. The last three levels include learning at home. Examples of this are providing information on the skills their children will learn throughout the school year, decision-making by encouraging participating on a school advisory board, and collaboration with the community.

61. C: One crucial role of the school counselor is to assist students when they face problems. Counselors must be sensitive to students' needs, beliefs, and values, including their established cultural identity. A student's cultural identity will affect the way he learns and responds to counseling. Understanding cultural diversity and identity will also be important for counselors when developing working relationships with the student's parents. Those who are insensitive to culture identity will find it difficult to gain student and parent trust and cooperation. In order to do this, school counselors must fully educate themselves on cultural diversity in general, as well as learning the specific demographics of the school they work in.

62. B: The ecological model consists of the microsystem, macrosystem, and excosystem. The microsystem encompasses the students' immediate family and support systems. This will include parents, siblings, extended family, and friends. The macrosystem is defined by the students' culture. This will vary from student to student and often may include various subcultures. The exosystem refers to students' social support systems, such as their community. Understanding these three aspects of students' support systems will assist in developing appropriate programs and interventions, as the counselor will be able to incorporate the students' beliefs, morals, and values into counseling programs.

63. A: Developing a comprehensive intervention program will offer students support from a number of sources and increase their chances of success. By understanding a student's culture, the counselor can optimize participation from the student, parents, and the community. Every culture views child development in a slightly different way; therefore, it is important to understand that what is classified as a developmental delay in one culture may not be considered so in another. This discrepancy can lean to resistance from students and parents, and the counselor must handle these situations with care in order to provide effective services to the student. It is not the counselor's responsibility to change the parents' and students' views; rather, the counselor must work with these cultural outlooks in order to offer the student the best environment for success.

64. D: Education is the key to increasing tolerance and understanding between various cultures. Developing educational programs for students as well as teachers can offer a venue for these individuals to ask questions and gain a clear understanding of cultural diversity. It is also an opportunity to eliminate negative stereotypes. Additionally, offering programs or opportunities for students to celebrate their cultures will serve to provide education about other cultures to students from all backgrounds. These opportunities can be as simple as announcing various holidays celebrated by the different cultures in the school or allowing students to display pictures or information about their cultures in the halls of the school.

65. B: While there may be times when a counselor will refer a student to a different counselor, this is not an effective alternative to a lack of cultural diversity education. Additionally, a counselor cannot effectively treat students based on the counselor's belief system. When offering programs for cultural diversity education within the school, the counselor must have education in this area in order to create effective programs. Therefore, counselor education is the best way to ensure that students' needs are met. Most counselor training programs today offer multicultural training and education. Additionally, there are many opportunities for continued education in this area.

66. B: Immigrant parents have many challenges when sending their children to school in America. Oftentimes, the parents do not speak English and are unfamiliar with the American school system. While language barriers often result in parents not participating in their children's education, a counselor can easily offer translators and other educational opportunities to overcome these barriers. However, if parents continue to be unclear about the needs and expectations of the school system, immigrant parents will continue to be inactive. This can be overcome by providing a supportive environment for both the parents and the students. Counselors in school systems with a high immigrant population will need to serve as "school-home-community liaisons" in order to promote the needs of the students and their families.

67. B: Discussion groups are effective ways to get parents and students involved in learning about cultural diversity. These discussion groups can offer participants the opportunity to talk about their particular cultures. Additionally, these groups offer a nonthreatening venue for others to ask questions

and work out misunderstandings about various cultures that have been perpetuated by stereotypes. These groups also offer parents and students the chance to celebrate different cultures though activities. In addition to group discussions about participants' cultures, discussions about various types of families and lifestyles are beneficial. For example, biracial families, families with adopted or foster children, and families with stepparents are increasingly common in American society, and education about these various types of families is just as important as learning about other cultures.

68. D: Human relations training offers students the opportunity to see each other as individuals. This type of training serves to increase students' understanding of one another. In the given situation, there appears to be a lot of racial tension, which is leading to regular fighting. When a school offers students human relations training, they will learn to view each other as human beings rather than racial stereotypes. This training should serve to increase cultural understanding and decrease the current level of fighting in the classroom. This situation may prompt a counselor to study the school overall to see if this behavior is occurring elsewhere. If so, a school-wide human relations training program may be appropriate.

69. D: Counselors must respect the cultural identity of their students. Since the student is not seeing the counselor because of cultural identity issues, it would be considered professionally unethical for the counselor to address her Chinese heritage. It is, however, the counselor's responsibility to understand this student's cultural identity in order to develop effective interventions for this student's presenting problem. The counselor must also have a clear understanding of her own beliefs and stereotypes in this situation that may cause bias when treating this student. Counselors who are unaware of these issues may inadvertently treat a student of another culture with negativity or less support than she would a student of her own culture.

70. C: Cultural diversity education is important in all schools, regardless of demographics. In this situation, it could be argued that the counselor is acting in an unprofessional and possibly unethical manner. What this counselor is failing to understand is that culture expands beyond the color of someone's skin. Culture includes various lifestyles, family types, religious beliefs, and ethnicities. Even in a predominantly white school, many cultures may be observable. If the counselor in this situation were aware of her own culture as well as that of others, she may realize the importance of offering these programs to all students.

71. D: Program evaluations are essential for guidance counseling programs. These evaluations will provide information on the effectiveness of a program and allow the counselor to make adjustments and improvements to these programs as necessary. When beginning an evaluation, the counselor should compile various forms of documentation about the program. This will include curriculum guides, unit lesson plans, and the school's master schedule for the counseling programs. This information will help give the counselor a picture of the school's current programs, which will allow the counselor to determine if the guidance curriculum is meeting the students' academic, emotional, and social needs.

72. D: When developing a counseling program, the counselor should take a number of factors into consideration, including what the students would like to gain from the programs. One factor that students often consider is academic counseling. This type of counseling provides students with additional support as they progress through their courses, as well as support during transitional periods such as moving from high school to college. In addition to this, students are often interested in counseling programs pertaining to career and self-awareness. Many students would also like to know the availability of counselors and the frequency of planning sessions they have with the counselor. Finally, visibility of

counselors and their ability and availability to answer questions and assist with problems is often listed as a student concern for counseling programs.

73. D: Ultimately, counseling programs are designed for students. Accordingly, student outcomes will determine the success of a program. As a counselor, it is important to conduct regular evaluation measures on each program offered. These measures will show the success of a program by including information about student improvement and students' ratings of satisfaction with the programs. For example, if a program is intended to improve a student's grades in a math course, outcome measures will include the student's final grades compared to her grades when she began the program. Additionally, conducting student surveys to find out how the students enjoyed the program is beneficial in creating future programs that both engage students and increase their performance.

74. B: Role conflict refers to unrealistic demands on the counselor. This often occurs when counselors does not establish appropriate boundaries between themselves and the students. In addition, not establishing boundaries with teachers can lead to unrealistic expectations of the counselor. Role conflict often leads to counselor burnout because the counselor tries to help everyone. On the other hand, role ambiguity occurs when an individual is unclear about his role within a particular occupation. Role mutations occur when counselors serve in roles not intended for those in the counseling profession, which often leads to inconsistent counseling practices and programs. Schools and counselors must be clear on the expectations and responsibilities of the school counselor in order to provide effective programs for the students.

75. D: Peer mentoring programs are beneficial for many students and can address a number of issues. These programs give students the opportunity to guide and lead other students. Counselors spearheading peer mentoring programs are responsible for overseeing these programs and being available when questions or problems arise. Since the focus of these programs is students helping students, micromanagement of peer mentors by a counselor would result in an ineffective and potentially unfulfilling experience for the students. Also, it is not necessary that peer mentors know all aspects of counseling, as their responsibilities in the program will not deal directly with counseling another students. Peer mentors should receive training in leadership and sensitivity to other student's needs.

76. A: School Advisory Committees are run by parents, members of the community, and teachers. Oftentimes, the school counselor, principal, or vice principal may attend these meetings in order to serve as a resource for information and assistance. The role of the school counselor is to provide the committee with objective information about the state of the school and its students. This information will often be in the form of reports from program evaluations. The advisory board will use this information to make decisions about such matters as the school's education improvement plan and allocation of funds.

77. D: It is important that the counselor set appropriate boundaries for herself and the students. In this situation, the counselor will want to speak briefly to the student to make sure that there is no immediate threat of danger. After a quick assessment, the counselor may want to schedule an appointment with the student to discuss the problem in more detail the next day. By addressing this situation in this manner, the counselor has shown concern for the student's needs and safety and addressed her own need for boundaries. It would be inappropriate to give a student the counselor's home phone number, and staying late would eventually cause the counselor to experience burnout in her job. Finally, not addressing the student at all does not show concern for the student and does not assess any potential danger the student may be in.

78. B: Immediate outcomes will occur during the program or intervention. These outcomes could include members of an anger management group being nicer to each other or students in a study skills group utilizing different study strategies. Proximal outcomes are specific to an intervention and are often observed after the intervention. For example, a member of an anger management group has a confrontation with teacher. The reaction of the student will be the proximal outcome of the group. Finally, distal outcomes are long-term effects of the intervention which the intervention was not necessarily designed to address. For example, the student in the anger management group reacted positivity to the teacher confrontation because he applied a calming strategy learned during the group. A few months later, he witnesses a friend yelling at another student for bumping into him. The group participant teaches his friend a calming strategy to better deal with confrontations.

79. A: All counselors have a professional responsibility to contribute to the counseling profession. One way of doing this is to report on the success or failure of various school counseling programs. In doing so, the reporting counselor can make visible various strategies for addressing student needs. This also allows other counseling and educational professionals to learn from their successes and failures alike. Opportunities to present program outcomes can range from school advisory meetings, PTA meetings, professional conferences, publication in professional journals, and attending professional association meetings.

80. B: Proper delegation of responsibilities will lead to more effective counseling programs. There are many opportunities for teachers and students to participate in leading programs. For example, developing a teacher advisor program increases participation from teachers and offers students a larger support system. Peer mentoring programs allow mentors the ability to increase their leadership skills and allow mentees the opportunity to widen their network of support systems. Counselors who encourage the assistance of teachers and students with various programs will foster a cohesive school that works together toward a common goal. This cohesiveness will provide all students with the best possible learning environment.

81. D: Developmental guidance programs offer schools a full service guidance program. These programs take all factors of a student's life into consideration: academics, developmental growth, social skills, and emotional maturity. By focusing on developmental stages as well as positive self-esteem, counselors can assist students in reaching their full potential as human beings rather than succeeding only academically. When creating this type of guidance program, counselors are aware of human development in various aspects including, social, emotional, and cognitive growth and development. Developmental guidance programs often rely on the support and participation of the school, families, and communities in order to offer students support and opportunities for learning and personal growth.

82. C: Developmental guidance programs are geared toward all students. These programs focus on understanding and assisting the students with their academic needs by offering services such as tutoring or peer mentoring. In order to meet the social needs of students, developmental programs embrace the cultural identities of students and aim to provide programs, increase student support systems, and offer opportunities for students to express their individuality. This type of program will also enhance students' cognitive development and provide opportunities to increase their understanding of themselves and the world around them. Because programs developed as part of a comprehensive developmental guidance program offer positive opportunities for growth and development, they are appropriate for all students.

83. D: Knowledge acquisition will occur throughout a person's life through formal education and life experiences; however this is not considered a developmental task or milestone. A child's sense of identity is a developmental task that is developed in the early stages of life. Self-identity tells the child who they

are and what that means to others. Delays or deficiencies in this process can lead to insecurities or confusion for a child. Autonomy, or the sense of independence, is typically developed during adolescence. This developmental milestone provides youth with a sense of purpose and self-ability. Finally, self-esteem is continuously developed throughout life. These developmental tasks are essential for a healthy emotional mind set.

84. C: Kohlberg's Theory of Moral Development involves the development of an individual's ethics, values, and principles. This theory consists of three stages: pre-conventional, conventional, and post conventional. In the pre-conventional stage, children learn morals and values though obedience and punishment. For instance, children learn that it is not acceptable to hit others when they are punished for hitting a sibling. In the conventional stage, youth learn through conformity and social order. Individuals learn by observing the world around them and understanding social norms. Finally, in the post-conventional stage, individuals learn through universally accepted ethical considerations.

85. B: Maslow's Hierarchy of Human Needs suggests that human needs can be divided into five levels. The most basic level is the physiological level, which includes the necessities of life: food, breathing, water, etc. At the next level is safety, which includes an individual's sense of security, availability of resources, employment, etc. Love and belonging comprise the next level, which also includes a person's support systems. Esteem is the next level and includes a person's self-concept and respect of self and others. Finally, the top level is self-actualization, which includes one's morality and acceptance. Maslow indicates that the lower levels of human needs must be met in order for an individual to meet the needs of the higher levels.

86. B: Social literacy skills are also known as interpersonal skills. These skills refer to how individuals relate to one another. The level of these skills also determines an individual's self-esteem, peer acceptance, and self-efficacy. In this situation, it appears that these students are having a difficult time relating to and communicating with each other. A group on crisis intervention will not offer these students the appropriate social skills, as a crisis group is typically geared toward students who are affected by issues such as a death in the family, a natural disaster, or another large crisis. A group that focuses on social literacy skills can help students understand themselves as well as others. This type of group teaches students appropriate social behaviors, communication skills, and techniques for dealing with conflict.

87. A: Traditional counseling programs tend to focus on issues after something has occurred. In the given situation, this crisis intervention program is probably reserved for students who have recently experienced some type of personal crisis. In a developmental counseling model, the counselor will develop programs to meet the needs of students by using a full-service approach. This counselor may implement crisis prevention as well as intervention programs. By including a crisis prevention program, the counselor is meeting the needs of at-risk students. This program will assist these students in avoiding potential crisis situations by offering various emotional and cognitive skills that these students may not already possess.

88. C: Emotional literacy is also referred to as intrapersonal skills. Individuals with good intrapersonal skills are aware of their own feelings and have an understanding of how these emotions affect their actions. This understanding helps individuals cope with emotional personal situations as well as display empathy for others. Additionally, understanding emotions also helps students manage and control their emotions. This type of program also helps students understand the importance and value of teamwork and cooperation with others. Developing a program that addresses intrapersonal skills serves to increase students' self-awareness and self-esteem.

89. D: Thinking, feeling, and relating are considered a modern model of human development. Thinking begins at home and consists of the values, thoughts, and beliefs imposed by parents. These thoughts are further supported by social interactions. Cognitive skills training assists students in further developing these abilities. Feelings can also be associated with the development of self-concept and self-esteem. Emotional literacy skills training and programs help students become more aware of their own feelings. Finally, relating involves an individual's interpersonal skills. Social literacy skills programs will assist students in relating to other students and adults.

90. D: Cognitive literacy skills teach students how to problem solve and make decisions. Programs designed to address cognitive skills focus on critical thinking, analysis, evaluation, classification, and conceptualization. According to Bloom's Taxonomy of Learning, these skills are essential in the education process. Schools can use organizational planners for homework and schools events in order to teach some of these skills. As students develop their cognitive skills, their study skills will also improve. Finally, cognitive skills development can also focus on self-regulation and self-monitoring. These abilities allow the student to think about their actions and the consequences of those actions.

91. B: Although counselors have a responsibility to their clients, they are also ethically accountable for the safety of others; this must be disclosed at the beginning of a counseling relationship. If a client ever threatens to harm himself or someone or something else, the rules of confidentiality do not apply. It is up to the counselor to make a professional judgment about any threatening statements a client might make to determine if alerting authorities and breaking confidentiality is necessary. Many counselors will consult with another professional if a situation is ambiguous. After determining the validity of a threat to do harm, counselors must inform their clients of their intent to notify the proper authorities.

92. B: Dual relationships occur when a counselor and client know each other prior to beginning a counseling relationship. In the school setting, this may occur if the counselor has family members in the same school. In these cases, the counselor should refer their family members to another counselor if possible. In the situation described above, inviting a student to talk outside of school creates a dual relationship and violates professional guidelines against using a school to promote or benefit any private practice or nonschool counseling activities. This situation also illustrates that the counselor is crossing professional boundaries by suggesting that they meet over coffee.

93. B: The third leading cause of death among 15-24 year olds is suicide. Actions should be taken to include individual therapy, group therapy, and appropriate referral for students displaying risk factors of suicide. Counselors can develop prevention and intervention programs for this issue. Gaining the support of the school and the community is one way to help prevent this tragedy. However, any threat of danger to self should be fully investigated. When a student threatens suicide, the counselor has a responsibility to alert the proper authorities and refer the client to appropriate help.

94. D: It is considered an unethical professional practice for a counselor to use the school as a place to gain private practice clients. While many issues can be resolved within the capacity of a school counseling program, there may be times when a counselor feels a student needs additional therapy or support. In these cases, the counselor should discuss these options with the student and the parents while keeping in mind rules of confidentiality. Additionally, after a referral is made, the school counselor does not have a right to information that the new counselor and student share. In certain circumstances, the school counselor may be asked to consult on various issues. If this occurs, the school counselor and the private practice professional must discuss the case only in factual, objective ways.

95. C: There are a number of professional associations available for counselors to participate in at the local, state, and national levels. For example, the American School Counselor Association is a national organization made up of professionals from various backgrounds, from child development to clinical training. These associations provide professionals with current information on counseling practices, opportunities to attend conferences, and continued education. Additionally, professional associations offer a network of other professionals who are available to discuss counseling strategies and other issues a counselor may face. Counselors must keep in mind the ethical practices of sharing confidential information with colleagues.

96. B: Counselors must establish boundaries between their professional and personal lives. It is a very common characteristic in this field for a counselor to want to help or fix all students in need. However, this is not practical and will eventually cause counselors to experience burnout. Counselors can avoid this by managing their work time properly and not taking work home. Additionally, counselors should schedule short breaks throughout the day where they can focus on something not related to counseling. These professionals should have down time every day and try to spend quality time with their friends and family when not at work.

97. B: Students have the right to seek confidential counseling. Counselors should inform parents of this confidentiality, as well as the roles, responsibilities, and expectations of the counselor and the student being counseled. Counselors should also work to provide parents with objective information regarding their children within the scope of confidentiality. At times, it may be necessary to inform the parents of certain issues pertaining to safety. This information will be provided only after the counselor has made a professional judgment that the client is in danger or intends to inflict harm on another and after telling the client of their intention to inform their parents. Finally, the counselor also has a responsibility to keep conversations he has with the parents confidential.

98. C: Any unethical behaviors should not be tolerated in this profession. When these situations occur, the integrity of the profession is threatened. When one professional witnesses unethical behaviors or practices from another, he should make his intention to report the action clear. All schools have policies on unethical behaviors and reporting guidelines for staff and administrators. In order to ensure proper protocol when reporting unethical behaviors, a thorough review and consultation with another professional, most likely the principal of the school, should be conducted.

99. B: Daily down time is one way to manage stress in the counseling profession. By giving herself 5-10 minutes during the day or 30-40 minutes after work, a counselor is able to calm down and refocus. While taking a vacation is a way to manage stress, this is not a long-term solution to the daily stressors faced in the counseling profession. Additionally, volunteering for additional school activities could increase a counselor's workload and cause unnecessary stress. Managing stress must be an essential part of someone's daily routine in order for that person to maintain mental, emotional, and physical health.

100. D: Continued education is required for professional licenses. Depending on the state board of education, a counselor will have a specific number of hours in continued education to complete. This education is intended to provide the counselor with the latest counseling information and practices. Additionally, by evaluating and reporting on programs, counselors are able to learn about the success of specific programs as well as areas of improvement. By reporting on the outcomes, counselors are educating the community about the school and its counseling programs. Giving presentations at professional conferences allows the counselor the opportunity to share different counseling practices and strategies with other professionals. The sharing of information promotes professional development and is highly recommended in the counseling profession.

Secret Key #1 – Time is Your Greatest Enemy

To succeed on the TExES, you must use your time wisely.

Pace Yourself

Wear a watch. At the beginning of the test, check the time (or start a chronometer on your watch to count the minutes), and check the time after every few questions to make sure you are "on schedule."

If you are forced to speed up, do it efficiently. Usually one or more answer choices can be eliminated without too much difficulty. Above all, don't panic. Don't speed up and just begin guessing at random choices. By pacing yourself, and continually monitoring your progress against your watch, you will always know exactly how far ahead or behind you are with your available time. If you find that you are one minute behind on the test, don't skip one question without spending any time on it, just to catch back up. Take 15 fewer seconds on the next four questions, and after four questions you'll have caught back up. Once you catch back up, you can continue working each problem at your normal pace.

Furthermore, don't dwell on the problems that you were rushed on. If a problem was taking up too much time and you made a hurried guess, it must be difficult. The difficult questions are the ones you are most likely to miss anyway, so it isn't a big loss. It is better to end with more time than you need than to run out of time.

Lastly, sometimes it is beneficial to slow down if you are constantly getting ahead of time. You are always more likely to catch a careless mistake by working more slowly than quickly, and among very high-scoring test takers (those who are likely to have lots of time left over), careless errors affect the score more than mastery of material.

Secret Key #2 - Guessing is not Guesswork

You probably know that guessing is a good idea - unlike other standardized tests, there is no penalty for getting a wrong answer. Even if you have no idea about a question, you still have a 20-25% chance of getting it right.

Most test takers do not understand the impact that proper guessing can have on their score. Unless you score extremely high, guessing will significantly contribute to your final score.

Monkeys Take the Test

What most test takers don't realize is that to insure that 20-25% chance, you have to guess randomly. If you put 20 monkeys in a room to take this test, assuming they answered once per question and behaved themselves, on average they would get 20-25% of the questions correct. Put 20 test takers in the room, and the average will be much lower among guessed questions. Why?

1. The test writers intentionally writes deceptive answer choices that "look" right. A test taker has no idea about a question, so picks the "best looking" answer, which is often wrong. The monkey has no idea what looks good and what doesn't, so will consistently be lucky about 20-25% of the time.
2. Test takers will eliminate answer choices from the guessing pool based on a hunch or intuition. Simple but correct answers often get excluded, leaving a 0% chance of being correct. The monkey has no clue, and often gets lucky with the best choice.

This is why the process of elimination endorsed by most test courses is flawed and detrimental to your performance- test takers don't guess, they make an ignorant stab in the dark that is usually worse than random.

$5 Challenge

Let me introduce one of the most valuable ideas of this course- the $5 challenge:

You only mark your "best guess" if you are willing to bet $5 on it.
You only eliminate choices from guessing if you are willing to bet $5 on it.

Why $5? Five dollars is an amount of money that is small yet not insignificant, and can really add up fast (20 questions could cost you $100). Likewise, each answer choice on one question of the test will have a small impact on your overall score, but it can really add up to a lot of points in the end.

The process of elimination IS valuable. The following shows your chance of guessing it right:

If you eliminate wrong answer choices until only this many remain:	1	2	3
Chance of getting it correct:	100%	50%	33%

However, if you accidentally eliminate the right answer or go on a hunch for an incorrect answer, your chances drop dramatically: to 0%. By guessing among all the answer choices, you are GUARANTEED to have a shot at the right answer.

That's why the $5 test is so valuable- if you give up the advantage and safety of a pure guess, it had better be worth the risk.

What we still haven't covered is how to be sure that whatever guess you make is truly random. Here's the easiest way:

Always pick the first answer choice among those remaining.

Such a technique means that you have decided, **before you see a single test question**, exactly how you are going to guess- and since the order of choices tells you nothing about which one is correct, this guessing technique is perfectly random.

This section is not meant to scare you away from making educated guesses or eliminating choices- you just need to define when a choice is worth eliminating. The $5 test, along with a pre-defined random guessing strategy, is the best way to make sure you reap all of the benefits of guessing.

Secret Key #3 - Practice Smarter, Not Harder

Many test takers delay the test preparation process because they dread the awful amounts of practice time they think necessary to succeed on the test. We have refined an effective method that will take you only a fraction of the time.

There are a number of "obstacles" in your way to succeed. Among these are answering questions, finishing in time, and mastering test-taking strategies. All must be executed on the day of the test at peak performance, or your score will suffer. The test is a mental marathon that has a large impact on your future.

Just like a marathon runner, it is important to work your way up to the full challenge. So first you just worry about questions, and then time, and finally strategy:

Success Strategy

1. Find a good source for practice tests.
2. If you are willing to make a larger time investment, consider using more than one study guide- often the different approaches of multiple authors will help you "get" difficult concepts.
3. Take a practice test with no time constraints, with all study helps "open book." Take your time with questions and focus on applying strategies.
4. Take a practice test with time constraints, with all guides "open book."
5. Take a final practice test with no open material and time limits

If you have time to take more practice tests, just repeat step 5. By gradually exposing yourself to the full rigors of the test environment, you will condition your mind to the stress of test day and maximize your success.

Secret Key #4 - Prepare, Don't Procrastinate

Let me state an obvious fact: if you take the test three times, you will get three different scores. This is due to the way you feel on test day, the level of preparedness you have, and, despite the test writers' claims to the contrary, some tests WILL be easier for you than others.

Since your future depends so much on your score, you should maximize your chances of success. In order to maximize the likelihood of success, you've got to prepare in advance. This means taking practice tests and spending time learning the information and test taking strategies you will need to succeed.

Never take the test as a "practice" test, expecting that you can just take it again if you need to. Feel free to take sample tests on your own, but when you go to take the official test, be prepared, be focused, and do your best the first time!

Secret Key #5 - Test Yourself

Everyone knows that time is money. There is no need to spend too much of your time or too little of your time preparing for the test. You should only spend as much of your precious time preparing as is necessary for you to get the score you need.

Once you have taken a practice test under real conditions of time constraints, then you will know if you are ready for the test or not.

If you have scored extremely high the first time that you take the practice test, then there is not much point in spending countless hours studying. You are already there.

Benchmark your abilities by retaking practice tests and seeing how much you have improved. Once you score high enough to guarantee success, then you are ready.

If you have scored well below where you need, then knuckle down and begin studying in earnest. Check your improvement regularly through the use of practice tests under real conditions. Above all, don't worry, panic, or give up. The key is perseverance!

Then, when you go to take the test, remain confident and remember how well you did on the practice tests. If you can score high enough on a practice test, then you can do the same on the real thing.

General Strategies

The most important thing you can do is to ignore your fears and jump into the test immediately-do not be overwhelmed by any strange-sounding terms. You have to jump into the test like jumping into a pool- all at once is the easiest way.

Make Predictions

As you read and understand the question, try to guess what the answer will be. Remember that several of the answer choices are wrong, and once you begin reading them, your mind will immediately become cluttered with answer choices designed to throw you off. Your mind is typically the most focused immediately after you have read the question and digested its contents. If you can, try to predict what the correct answer will be. You may be surprised at what you can predict.

Quickly scan the choices and see if your prediction is in the listed answer choices. If it is, then you can be quite confident that you have the right answer. It still won't hurt to check the other answer choices, but most of the time, you've got it!

Answer the Question

It may seem obvious to only pick answer choices that answer the question, but the test writers can create some excellent answer choices that are wrong. Don't pick an answer just because it sounds right, or you believe it to be true. It MUST answer the question. Once you've made your selection, always go back and check it against the question and make sure that you didn't misread the question, and the answer choice does answer the question posed.

Benchmark

After you read the first answer choice, decide if you think it sounds correct or not. If it doesn't, move on to the next answer choice. If it does, mentally mark that answer choice. This doesn't mean that you've definitely selected it as your answer choice, it just means that it's the best you've seen thus far. Go ahead and read the next choice. If the next choice is worse than the one you've already selected, keep going to the next answer choice. If the next choice is better than the choice you've already selected, mentally mark the new answer choice as your best guess.

The first answer choice that you select becomes your standard. Every other answer choice must be benchmarked against that standard. That choice is correct until proven otherwise by another answer choice beating it out. Once you've decided that no other answer choice seems as good, do one final check to ensure that your answer choice answers the question posed.

Valid Information

Don't discount any of the information provided in the question. Every piece of information may be necessary to determine the correct answer. None of the information in the question is there to throw you off (while the answer choices will certainly have information to throw you off). If two seemingly unrelated topics are discussed, don't ignore either. You can be confident there is a relationship, or it wouldn't be included in the question, and you are probably going to have to determine what is that relationship to find the answer.

Avoid "Fact Traps"

Don't get distracted by a choice that is factually true. Your search is for the answer that answers the question. Stay focused and don't fall for an answer that is true but incorrect. Always go back to the question and make sure you're choosing an answer that actually answers the question and is not just a true statement. An answer can be factually correct, but it MUST answer the question asked. Additionally, two answers can both be seemingly correct, so be sure to read all of the answer choices, and make sure that you get the one that BEST answers the question.

Milk the Question

Some of the questions may throw you completely off. They might deal with a subject you have not been exposed to, or one that you haven't reviewed in years. While your lack of knowledge about the subject will be a hindrance, the question itself can give you many clues that will help you find the correct answer. Read the question carefully and look for clues. Watch particularly for adjectives and nouns describing difficult terms or words that you don't recognize. Regardless of if you completely understand a word or not, replacing it with a synonym either provided or one you more familiar with may help you to understand what the questions are asking. Rather than wracking your mind about specific detailed information concerning a difficult term or word, try to use mental substitutes that are easier to understand.

The Trap of Familiarity

Don't just choose a word because you recognize it. On difficult questions, you may not recognize a number of words in the answer choices. The test writers don't put "make-believe" words on the test; so don't think that just because you only recognize all the words in one answer choice means that answer choice must be correct. If you only recognize words in one answer choice, then focus on that one. Is it correct? Try your best to determine if it is correct. If it is, that is great, but if it doesn't, eliminate it. Each word and answer choice you eliminate increases your chances of getting the question correct, even if you then have to guess among the unfamiliar choices.

Eliminate Answers

Eliminate choices as soon as you realize they are wrong. But be careful! Make sure you consider all of the possible answer choices. Just because one appears right, doesn't mean that the next one won't be even better! The test writers will usually put more than one good answer choice for every question, so read all of them. Don't worry if you are stuck between two that seem right. By getting down to just two remaining possible choices, your odds are now 50/50. Rather than wasting too much time, play the odds. You are guessing, but guessing wisely, because you've been able to knock out some of the answer choices that you know are wrong. If you are eliminating choices and realize that the last answer choice you are left with is also obviously wrong, don't panic. Start over and consider each choice again. There may easily be something that you missed the first time and will realize on the second pass.

Tough Questions

If you are stumped on a problem or it appears too hard or too difficult, don't waste time. Move on! Remember though, if you can quickly check for obviously incorrect answer choices, your chances of guessing correctly are greatly improved. Before you completely give up, at least try to knock out a couple of possible answers. Eliminate what you can and then guess at the remaining answer choices before moving on.

Brainstorm

If you get stuck on a difficult question, spend a few seconds quickly brainstorming. Run through the complete list of possible answer choices. Look at each choice and ask yourself, "Could this answer the question satisfactorily?" Go through each answer choice and consider it independently of the other. By systematically going through all possibilities, you may find something that you would otherwise overlook. Remember that when you get stuck, it's important to try to keep moving.

Read Carefully

Understand the problem. Read the question and answer choices carefully. Don't miss the question because you misread the terms. You have plenty of time to read each question thoroughly and make sure you understand what is being asked. Yet a happy medium must be attained, so don't waste too much time. You must read carefully, but efficiently.

Face Value

When in doubt, use common sense. Always accept the situation in the problem at face value. Don't read too much into it. These problems will not require you to make huge leaps of logic. The test writers aren't trying to throw you off with a cheap trick. If you have to go beyond creativity and make a leap of logic in order to have an answer choice answer the question, then you should look at the other answer choices. Don't overcomplicate the problem by creating theoretical relationships or explanations that will warp time or space. These are normal problems rooted in reality. It's just that the applicable relationship or explanation may not be readily apparent and you have to figure things out. Use your common sense to interpret anything that isn't clear.

Prefixes

If you're having trouble with a word in the question or answer choices, try dissecting it. Take advantage of every clue that the word might include. Prefixes and suffixes can be a huge help. Usually they allow you to determine a basic meaning. Pre- means before, post- means after, pro - is positive, de- is negative. From these prefixes and suffixes, you can get an idea of the general meaning of the word and try to put it into context. Beware though of any traps. Just because con is the opposite of pro, doesn't necessarily mean congress is the opposite of progress!

Hedge Phrases

Watch out for critical "hedge" phrases, such as likely, may, can, will often, sometimes, often, almost, mostly, usually, generally, rarely, sometimes. Question writers insert these hedge phrases to cover every possibility. Often an answer choice will be wrong simply because it leaves no room for exception. Avoid answer choices that have definitive words like "exactly," and "always".

Switchback Words

Stay alert for "switchbacks". These are the words and phrases frequently used to alert you to shifts in thought. The most common switchback word is "but". Others include although, however, nevertheless, on the other hand, even though, while, in spite of, despite, regardless of.

New Information

Correct answer choices will rarely have completely new information included. Answer choices typically are straightforward reflections of the material asked about and will directly relate to the question. If a new piece of information is included in an answer choice that doesn't even seem to relate to the topic being asked about, then that answer choice is likely incorrect. All of the information needed to answer the question is usually provided for you, and so you should not have to make guesses that are unsupported or choose answer choices that require unknown information that cannot be reasoned on its own.

Copyright © Mometrix Media. You have been licensed one copy of this document for personal use only. Any other reproduction or redistribution is strictly prohibited. All rights reserved.

Time Management

On technical questions, don't get lost on the technical terms. Don't spend too much time on any one question. If you don't know what a term means, then since you don't have a dictionary, odds are you aren't going to get much further. You should immediately recognize terms as whether or not you know them. If you don't, work with the other clues that you have, the other answer choices and terms provided, but don't waste too much time trying to figure out a difficult term.

Contextual Clues

Look for contextual clues. An answer can be right but not correct. The contextual clues will help you find the answer that is most right and is correct. Understand the context in which a phrase or statement is made. This will help you make important distinctions.

Don't Panic

Panicking will not answer any questions for you. Therefore, it isn't helpful. When you first see the question, if your mind goes blank, take a deep breath. Force yourself to mechanically go through the steps of solving the problem and using the strategies you've learned.

Pace Yourself

Don't get clock fever. It's easy to be overwhelmed when you're looking at a page full of questions, your mind is full of random thoughts and feeling confused, and the clock is ticking down faster than you would like. Calm down and maintain the pace that you have set for yourself. As long as you are on track by monitoring your pace, you are guaranteed to have enough time for yourself. When you get to the last few minutes of the test, it may seem like you won't have enough time left, but if you only have as many questions as you should have left at that point, then you're right on track!

Answer Selection

The best way to pick an answer choice is to eliminate all of those that are wrong, until only one is left and confirm that is the correct answer. Sometimes though, an answer choice may immediately look right. Be careful! Take a second to make sure that the other choices are not equally obvious. Don't make a hasty mistake. There are only two times that you should stop before checking other answers. First is when you are positive that the answer choice you have selected is correct. Second is when time is almost out and you have to make a quick guess!

Check Your Work

Since you will probably not know every term listed and the answer to every question, it is important that you get credit for the ones that you do know. Don't miss any questions through careless mistakes. If at all possible, try to take a second to look back over your answer selection and make sure you've selected the correct answer choice and haven't made a costly careless mistake (such as marking an answer choice that you didn't mean to mark). This quick double check should more than pay for itself in caught mistakes for the time it costs.

Beware of Directly Quoted Answers

Sometimes an answer choice will repeat word for word a portion of the question or reference section. However, beware of such exact duplication – it may be a trap! More than likely, the correct choice will paraphrase or summarize a point, rather than being exactly the same wording.

Slang

Scientific sounding answers are better than slang ones. An answer choice that begins "To compare the outcomes..." is much more likely to be correct than one that begins "Because some people insisted..."

Extreme Statements

Avoid wild answers that throw out highly controversial ideas that are proclaimed as established fact. An answer choice that states the "process should be used in certain situations, if..." is much more likely to be correct than one that states the "process should be discontinued completely." The first is a calm rational statement and doesn't even make a definitive, uncompromising stance, using a hedge word "if" to provide wiggle room, whereas the second choice is a radical idea and far more extreme.

Answer Choice Families

When you have two or more answer choices that are direct opposites or parallels, one of them is usually the correct answer. For instance, if one answer choice states "x increases" and another answer choice states "x decreases" or "y increases," then those two or three answer choices are very similar in construction and fall into the same family of answer choices. A family of answer choices is when two or three answer choices are very similar in construction, and yet often have a directly opposite meaning. Usually the correct answer choice will be in that family of answer choices. The "odd man out" or answer choice that doesn't seem to fit the parallel construction of the other answer choices is more likely to be incorrect.